Research Methods for Criminology and Criminal Justice: A Primer

Research Methods for Criminology and Criminal Justice: A Primer

M.L. DANTZKER, Ph.D.
and
RONALD D. HUNTER, Ph.D.

Boston • Oxford • Auckland • Johannesburg • Melbourne • New Delhi

Butterworth-Heinemann supports the efforts of American Forests and the Global ReLeaf program in its campaign to the betterment of trees, forests, and our environment.

Library of Congress Cataloging-in-Publication Data
Dantzker, Mark L., 1958–
   Research methods for criminology and criminal justice: a primer/by M.L. Dantzker and Ronald D. Hunter.
      p. cm.
   Includes bibliographical referaences and index.
   ISBN 0–7506–9951–5 (hardcover:acid-free paper)
   1. Criminology—Research—Methodology. 2. Criminal justice, Administration of—Research—Methodology. I. Hunter, Ronald D. II Title
   HV6024.5.D36 2000
   36'.07'2—dc21   99-053865
                                                                                        CIP

British Library Cataloguing-in-Publication Data

A catalogue record for this book is available for the British Library.

The publisher offers special discounts on bulk orders of this book.
For information, please contact:
Manager of Special Sales
Butterworth-Heinemann
225 Wildwood Avenue
Woburn, MA 01801-2041
Tel: 781-904-2500
Fax: 781-904-2620

For information on all Butterworth-Heinemann publications available, contact our World Wide Web home page at http://www.bh.com

10 9 8 7 6 5 4 3 2 1

Printed in the United States of America

Contents

Preface   vii

Acknowledgments   xi

PART I   **Purpose of Research**   1

CHAPTER 1   Research: What, Why, and How   3

CHAPTER 2   Research Ethics   23

PART II   **Problem Formulation**   39

CHAPTER 3   Getting Started   41

CHAPTER 4   The Language of Research   57

PART III   **Research Design**   71

CHAPTER 5   Qualitative Research   73

CHAPTER 6   Quantitative Research   87

CHAPTER 7   Research Designs   103

PART IV   **Data Collection**   115

CHAPTER 8   Questionnaire Construction   117

CHAPTER 9   Sampling   135

CHAPTER 10   Data Collection   151

PART V   **Data Analysis**   169

CHAPTER 11   Data Processing and Analysis   171

CHAPTER 12   Inferential Statistics   193

CHAPTER 13   Writing the Research   209

PART VI   **Closure**   235

CHAPTER 14   Summing Up   237

Index   263

Preface

Whether research is done by a college student completing a project for his or her degree (or just trying to understand an assigned reading) or by a professor meeting requirements or expectations associated with his or her position, it should be enjoyable, not a chore. The first step is to learn the basics for conducting research. There are a number of textbooks available that can assist in this task, but many make learning about research, let alone conducting it, appear daunting. This text has made every attempt to ease the task of learning how to conduct research less daunting and perhaps even to put the prospect of conducting research in a favorable light, thus it is called a *primer*. To accomplish this task, several pedagogical tools are used.

Each chapter begins with a vignette that describes a situation students might find themselves in, which relates to the particular chapter's topic. By the end of the chapter, students should be able to identify how to address the confusion or problem presented in the vignette. Within the text, realistic examples are given to enhance the way the specific aspect of research is applicable to criminal justice and criminology. Another enhancement tool is the Methodological Link. These are excerpts from actual criminal justice and criminological research, the full text of which is available in a companion text, *Readings for Criminological and Criminal Justice Research*. These excerpts reinforce the discussion of the concept. Interspersed throughout the text are Internet Links, web page addresses relevant to the given topic. Finally, each chapter ends with Methodological Queries, questions and exercises requiring students to apply what has been learned from the chapter.

The text begins by discussing what research is, why it is conducted, and how. It addresses such questions as: What are criminal justice and criminological research? Why conduct this research? And how can this research be completed? In general, it lays the foundation for conducting research.

Because criminal justice research often deals with human behavior, the ethics associated with such research is important. Chapter 2, Research Ethics, discusses the ethics relevant to conducting research.

Deciding what to conduct research on can often be frustrating. However, there are numerous sources available to assist in making a decision on what to research. Chapter 3, Getting Started, explores what sources to use and the issue of developing the research question, which often is the driving force behind social science research.

In Chapter 4, The Language of Research, students are introduced to the researchese or terminology associated with conducting research, such as theory, hypothesis, population, sample, and variables. Furthermore, it briefly explores the processes required for conducting research through a researchese perspective.

Because of its long-standing image of being an applied social science, and because of its lack of statistical sophistication, some of the research conducted and published has had its detractors. As a result, a debate continues as to what is more "academic," qualitative or quantitative research. Chapter 5, Qualitative Research, does not enter the debate but simply explains how this type of research fits into both criminology and into criminal justice.

To help balance the debate over qualitative versus quantitative research, Chapter 6, Quantitative Research, takes over where Chapter 5 ends by exploring the other important type of research conducted in both criminology and criminal justice.

To successfully complete any type of research, it is important to establish a feasible plan or blueprint, the research design. Chapter 7, Research Designs, discusses the various research designs available for criminal justice and criminological research. They include historical, descriptive, inferential, developmental, case and field, correlational, and causal-comparative. A brief mention is made of true and quasi-experimental, and action designs.

One of the most popular means of collecting data is the questionnaire. While a rule of thumb is to use an established questionnaire, many individuals choose to design their own. Chapter 8, Questionnaire Construction, discusses the intricacies of designing a questionnaire, including issues of measurement, reliability, and validity.

It would be great if information could be gathered from a complete population, but this is almost impossible for criminal justice and criminological research. Therefore, sampling is an important aspect of research. In Chapter 9, Sampling, this concept and its related issues are examined.

In establishing the research design, a key component is how the data is to be collected. The four primary means for collecting data, survey, observation, archival, and unobtrusive means, are identified and explored within Chapter 10, Data Collection.

Once the data is collected the question is, what to do with it? There are a number of statistical techniques from which to choose. This is not a statistics book. However, to assist the student in better understanding the role of statistics in the research process, we offer Chapters 11, Data Processing and Analysis, and 12, Inferential Statistics.

Now that the data is collected and analyzed, all there is left to do is write up the findings. For many this is a daunting task. To help ease the fear and frustration, Chapter 13, Writing the Research, takes the student through a step-by-step introduction to writing the research.

Finally, to bring all the information offered throughout this text into a handy reference guide, we offer Chapter 14, Summing Up, an extensive, yet simple review of all the main concepts.

A final note concerns what this text is not. *Research Methods for Criminology and Criminal Justice: A Primer* is not a statistics book. However, it could be used in conjunction with a text, such as *Criminal Justice Statistics: A Practical Approach*, for a course that offers both methods and statistics in the same course. The fact is, separate books are often required to provide students the fullest extent of the knowledge required to conduct research and to analyze the data. This text allows students to learn how to conduct the research, leaving the statistics for another course and text.

We hope you will find the text as useful as it is intended to be. If nothing else, upon its completion we hope you will at least feel more comfortable about reading or conducting criminal justice and criminological research.

M.L. Dantzker, Ph.D.
University of Texas Pan American

Ronald D. Hunter, Ph.D.
State University of West Georgia

Acknowledgments

As with each book, there are several people who deserve recognition and our gratitude. It all begins with the person who takes the chance of signing someone to write a book. In this case it is Laurel DeWolf, Acquisitions Editor. Our thanks for her support and confidence. Laurel could not have done her job as well without the capable assistance of Rita Lombard. Who knows what kind of shape this book would have been in were it not for Rita's editorial skills. Making this book a final publishable product is due to the efforts of Cecile Kaufman, Project Manager. Finally, we'd like to thank our wives, Dr. Gail Dantzker and Mrs. Vi Hunter, for the constant love and support, especially during "crunch time." Thank you one and all.

PART I

Purpose of Research

Research: What, Why, and How

■ Vignette 1-1
The Research Paper

Research Methods: It is a required course, so you had no choice but to take it. But, you wondered, how hard could it be? The big project is just preparing to write a research paper. No big deal! You have written several "research papers" in college, so how hard could it be to simply go through the stages to prepare to write such a paper? The first class session is about to begin; you settle into your desk and wait to hear what, exactly, is expected in this course.

As the professor begins the introduction to the class, you recall that other students have said this professor is fair but extremely tough. He has very high expectations of students and does not give too many breaks. Again, no problem, you are not afraid of a little work or a challenge. Besides, you feel that you can write pretty well and have had fairly good grades on previous criminal justice and criminology papers, so you should do all right. Suddenly, your attention is caught when the professor advises the class that anyone who thinks they have written a research paper in their other major courses, actually has not, but has written what he calls a "literature review" paper. He explains that what is most often required in most college courses are papers where students choose a topic, find a certain amount of resources or "references," and then write a descriptive or explanatory paper. Yes, it might have had an introduction, thesis statement, evidence, and a conclusion, but it was not a research paper, at least not in the same sense as what you will be doing in this class. The instructor continues by noting that in answering the following questions, you will soon see that there is a difference in what you had believed to be a research paper and what a research paper really is. The questions include: What is criminal justice research? Why conduct the research? How is this research done? He finishes by advising the class that by the end of the first week, you will have been introduced to the foundations for conducting research on criminological and criminal justice related topics. So, let the learning begin!

■ CHAPTER 1
Learning Objectives

After studying this chapter the student should be able to:

1. Discuss tradition and authority as sources of human learning. Contrast their strengths and weaknesses.
2. Present and discuss the errors that plage casual observation.
3. Define what is meant by the scientific method. Explain how it seeks to remedy the errors of casual observation.
4. Compare and contrast the relationship between theory and research within the inductive and deductive logic processes.
5. Define research and explain its purpose.
6. Compare and contrast basic, applied, and multipurpose research.
7. Present and discuss the various types of research.
8. Present and discuss the reasons for criminological research.
9. Present and discuss the various factors that influence research decisions.
10. Describe the primary steps in conducting research.

The purpose of this text is to assist criminal justice and criminology students in developing an understanding (and hopefully an appreciation) of the basic principles of social research. We do not seek to turn you into a research scientist in one short course of study. However, we do hope to give you a rudimentary foundation that can be built upon, should you be interested in doing criminological research in the future. This primer will enable you to grasp the importance of scientific research, to read and comprehend all but the more complex research methodologies of others, as well as provide you with the basic tools to conduct your own social research.

The Nature of Scientific Inquiry

It was not that long ago, at least in our minds, that we were criminal justice students taking a first course in research methods. Our thoughts were, we want to be police officers, why do we have to take this course? This is even worse than criminal theory, another useless course. What does it have to do with the real world that we want to work in? Later police experience in that "real world" taught us the value of both theory and research in the field of criminal justice. When we subsequently returned to school for graduate studies, the importance of theory and research was more readily apparent to us. We had learned that scientific investigation is very similar to criminal investigation: the use of a logical order and established procedures to solve real-world problems.

Social Science Research and the "Real World"

As police officers we (the authors) sought to determine whether a crime had been committed (what occurred and when it occurred), who had done it, how they had done it, and why they had done it. We then sought to use that investigatory knowledge to develop a successful prosecution of the offender. Our endeavors in the field taught us that the theory course that we had grudgingly endured had provided the rationale for human behavior that the strategies of policing, courts, and corrections were based upon. We also discovered that those theories were not developed in some esoteric vacuum. They were in fact the products of trial-and-error experiments conducted in policing, the courts, and corrections that had been refined and reapplied to their appropriate subject area. Today's police-deployment strategies, legal processes, and correctional techniques are all solidly based upon prior theory and research.

The above statements can also be applied to social science research in general. Typical "real world" conclusions are often flawed due to a number of issues that cause our observations as well as our reasoning to be inaccurate. The scientific method seeks to provide a means of investigation to correct (or a least limit) the inaccuracies of ordinary human inquiry. Babbie (1999, pp. 7-8) argues that we learn from direct observation and what we are taught by others. How we interpret our own observations as well as what we learn from others is based upon tradition and authority. Tradition is the cultural teaching about the real world. "Poisonous snakes are dangerous. Beware of them!" You don't have to be bitten by a rattlesnake to appreciate its hazard. You have been taught by other members of your culture to respect the threat to you. This is an example of positive learning from tradition. It is based upon the experiences of others in your society who passed their knowledge on to you. Unfortunately, knowledge based on tradition is often erroneous.

"Women are not suited to be police officers. They are too weak and too emotional." A multitude of highly competent and professional police officers have proven this sexist stereotype to be a fallacy.

The other source of secondhand knowledge cited by Babbie (1999, p. 8) is authority. Authority refers to new knowledge that is provided from the observations of others whom we respect. The cool aunt or uncle (or older cousin) who explained the "facts of life" to you was an authority figure. How accurate their explanations were, we leave to you to decide. As you got older you learned that much free advice was worth what you paid for it and that a great deal of "bought advice" had little value as well. The importance of knowledge gained from authority figures depends upon their qualifications relative to the subject being discussed. Therefore, you go to a physician for help with your health problems and hire a plumber to fix a broken water pipe. These individuals are expected to have the expertise to provide solutions that laypersons do not have. Like tradition, the knowledge gained from dealings with authority figures can be extremely accurate or highly erroneous.

Science versus Casual Inquiry

Casual inquiry is influenced by the sources of knowledge discussed in the previous section. In addition there are other pitfalls that create errors in our own observations. According to Babbie (1999, pp. 8-9) casual inquiry may be flawed due to inaccurate observation, over-generalization, selective observation, and illogical reasoning.

Inaccurate observation occurs when we make conclusions based upon hasty or incomplete observations. As an example, a young police officer once walked by a break room where a young records clerk was in tears. Sitting on each side of her were the Captain in charge of Internal Affairs and an IA Investigator. The Captain was telling her to stop crying in a harsh tone of voice. The officer immediately thought, "Those jerks. They could have at least taken her into their office before interrogating her." Several years later, the officer, then a Sergeant for whom the woman in question now worked, learned that she had been extremely distraught over the break-up of her marriage and that the Captain was a father figure to her who had actually been consoling her.

Over-generalization occurs when we make conclusions about individuals or groups based upon our knowledge of similar individuals or groups. "All lawyers are liars!" would be an example. Despite the preponderance of lawyer jokes and any bad experiences that you or a friend may have had with an attorney, you cannot accurately make that conclusion about all attorneys. There are simply too many attorneys (men and women of honesty and integrity as well as those of questionable ethics) to make such a conclusion without an individual knowledge of the person.

Selective observation is when you see only those things that you want to see. Racial and ethnic stereotyping would be an example of negative selective observation. The attitude that "All whites are racists who seek to oppress minorities" may cause the observer to see what he or she believes in the behaviors of all European Americans with whom they come into contact. Selective observation may also be positively biased. "My darling wonderful child has never done anything like that." Such selective observation can lead to major disappointment such as when "He's a wonderful man who caters to my every whim" becomes "He's a selfish jerk who doesn't ever consider my feelings.'

Finally, illogical reasoning happens when we decide that despite our past observations, the future will be different. Babbie (1999, p. 9) uses the gambler's fallacy that bad luck has to change as an example of illogical reasoning. If the odds of success are unlikely, it is illogical to assume that by sheer willpower you can make it occur.

Science seeks to reduce the possibility of the above errors occurring by imposing order and rigor on our observations. The means of doing so is the application of the scientific method.

The Scientific Method

The scientific method seeks to prevent the errors of casual inquiry by utilizing procedures that specify objectivity, logic, theoretical understanding, and knowledge of prior research in the development and use of a precise measurement instrument designed to accurately record observations. The result is a systematic search for the most accurate and complete description or explanation of the events or behaviors that are being studied. Just as a criminal investigation is a search for "the facts" and a criminal trial is a search for "the truth," the scientific method is a search for knowledge. The criminological researcher seeks to use the principles of empiricism, skepticism, relativism, objectivity, ethical neutrality, parsimony, accuracy, and precision to assess a particular theoretical explanation.

In the above formula, empiricism is defined as seeking answers to questions through direct observation. Skepticism is the search for disconfirming evidence and the process of continuing to question the conclusions and the evidence that are found. Objectivity mandates that conclusions are based upon careful observation that sees the world as it really is, free from personal feelings or prejudices. Criminological researchers often acknowledge that total objectivity is unattainable but every reasonable effort is made to overcome any subjective interests that might influence the research outcomes. This is known as intersubjectivity. Ethical neutrality builds upon objectivity by stressing that the researcher's beliefs or preferences will not be allowed to influence the research process or its outcomes. Parsimony is the attempt to reduce the sum of possible explanations for an event or phenomenon to the smallest possible number. Accuracy requires that observations be recorded in a correct manner exactly as they occurred. Precision is specifying the number of subcategories of a concept that are available. (Definitions adapted from: Adler and Clark, 1999; Fitzgerald and Cox, 1998; and, Senese, 1997.)

The Relationship Between Theory and Research

As was discussed in a prior section, the practice of criminal justice is based upon theories about the causes of crime and how to respond to them. Criminology is an academic discipline that studies the nature of crime, its causes, its consequences, and society's response to it. Criminal Justice as an academic discipline tends to focus more upon the creation, application, and enforcement of criminal laws to maintain social order. (For a detailed analysis of the complex interrelationships between criminology and criminal justice, Dantzker, 1998, is recommended reading.) There is so much of an overlap between the two disciplines that within this text we shall deal with the two as one discipline (as indeed many criminologists and justicians consider them to be). Regardless of the reader's orientation, theory is integral in the development of research. Likewise, theory that has been validated by research is the basis for practice in the criminal justice system.

Theory

Theory deals with "what is," not "what should be" (Babbie, 1999, p. 13). Personal ideologies are of no value in criminological theory unless they can be evaluated scientifically. We shall define theory as "an attempt to explain why a particular social activity or event occurs." A theory is a generalization about the phenomenon that is being studied. From this broad theory, more precise statements (concepts) are developed. Specific measurable statements are hypotheses. It is through observation and measurement that the validity (correctness or ability to actually predict what it seeks to examine) of a hypothesis is examined. If the hypothesis cannot be rejected, then support for the theory is shown. The method by which the hypothesis is observed and measured is research. The relationship between theory and research may be either inductive or deductive in nature.

Inductive Logic

In the stories by Sir Arthur Conan Doyle his detective hero, Sherlock Holmes, continuously assails Dr. Watson, a man of science, about the merits of "deductive logic." It is through deductive logic that Holmes is said to solve his cases. In actuality, the process that Holmes describes is inductive logic. In this process the researcher observes an event, makes empirical generalizations about the activity, and constructs a theory based upon them. Only rarely does Holmes engage in the deduction that he speaks so highly of. Another example of inductive logic would be Sir Isaac Newton's alleged formulation of the Theory of Gravity after observing an apple fall from a tree.

Deductive Logic

Deductive logic begins with a theoretical orientation. The researcher then develops research hypotheses that are tested by observations. These observations lead to empirical generalizations that either support or challenge the theory in question. Had our hero Holmes followed up his theory construction with such observation, then he would have engaged in deduction. The scientific method is based upon deductive theory construction and testing. In criminological research, the distinctions between inductive and deductive logic are often obscured because the two processes are actually complementary. Although described in a circular model (Babbie, 1999; Wallace, 1971) (see Figure 1-1), the elements of both inductive and deductive logic may also be viewed as part of a never-ending continuum that begins with theory, which encourages creation of hypotheses, which in turn calls for observations. The result of observations is generalizations, and the conclusions of the generalizations assist in modification of the theory.

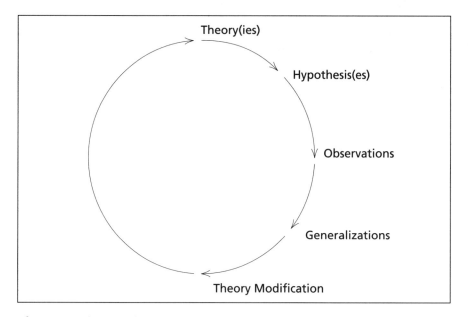

Figure 1-1 The Continuum of Logic: Inductive and Deductive

The Purpose of Research

The average college student truly believes he or she knows what it means to conduct research. Many have written a "research paper" either in high school or for a college course. Realistically, few have ever had the opportunity to truly write a research paper because even fewer have ever conducted scientific research.

What Research Is

Research is the conscientious study of an issue, problem, or subject. It is a useful form of inquiry designed to assist in discovering answers. It can also lead to the creation of new questions. For example, a judge wants to know how much effect her sentencing has had on individuals convicted of drug possession, particularly as it compares to another judge's sentencing patterns. She asks that research be conducted that focuses on recidivism of these individuals. The results indicate that 30 percent of drug offenders sentenced in her court are rearrested, compared to only 20 percent from the other judge's court. Between the two courts, the judge has discovered that her sentencing does not appear to be as effective. This answered the primary question of the research but it has also created new questions, such as, why are her methods not working as well as the other judge's?

Research creates questions, but ultimately, regardless of the subject or topic under study, it is the goal of research to provide answers. One of the more common uses of the term *research* is a description of what a student might be asked to accomplish for a college class. Many times you hear instructors and students refer to the choosing of a topic, using several sources, and writing a descriptive paper on the topic as research. If done thoroughly and objectively, this may actually constitute qualitative research (discussed in detail in Chapter 6). Unfortunately, these "research papers" are too often essays based more upon the individual's ideologies rather than upon scientific discovery. For the purpose of this text, the emphasis shall be upon *empirical research* that yields scholarly results.

There are many formal definitions for the term *research*. We use the following: *Research is the scientific investigation into or of a specifically identified phenomenon* (Dantzker, 1998, p. 128) and is applicable to recognizable and undiscovered phenomena. Therefore, in terms of criminal justice and criminology, related research can be viewed as *the investigation into or of any phenomenon linked to any or all aspects of the criminal justice system.* Using this definition, criminal justice and criminological research is not limited to any one area. List 1-1 offers just a few of the related topics someone might research.

Along with the plethora of research topics, there are several methods for conducting the research. They include surveys, observation, conducting case studies, and reviewing official records. These methods will be discussed in further detail, but prior to that it is important to understand all the underlying characteristics of research. To begin with, criminal justice and criminological research is often divided into two forms: applied and basic.

Applied Research

Perhaps the most immediately useful type of research in criminal justice is applied research, which is primarily *an inquiry of a scientific nature designed and conducted with practical application as its goal.* In other words, it is the collection of data and its analyses with respect to a specific issue or problem so that the applications of the results can influence change (see List 1-1).

List 1-1

Applied Research Topics: Some Examples

> *Policing:*
> stress, patrol effectiveness, use of force,
> job satisfaction, and response times;
>
> *Courts:*
> types of sentencing, plea bargaining, race and
> sentencing, and jury versus judge verdicts;
>
> *Corrections:*
> rehabilitation versus punishment,
> effectiveness of programs, boot camps, prisonization, and the death penalty
>
> *Other:*
> criminal behavior, victims, drugs, gangs,
> juvenile criminality

A major form of applied research is evaluative research, which focuses on answering questions (Eck and La Vigne, 1994, p. 6) such as:

1. Is the program, policy, or procedure doing what it was meant to do?
2. If not, how is the program, policy, or procedure deficient?
3. How can it be improved?
4. Should it be continued as is, changed, or discontinued?

In essence, applied research provides answers that can be used to improve, change, or help decide to eliminate the focus of study.

Methodological Link

To evaluate the effectiveness of Florida's mandatory human diversity course for police and correctional officers, Ford and Williams (1999) conducted a survey among justice personnel who
had completed the course. Their findings indicated that the course was seen as important, but
did little to change on-the-job conduct. These findings were considered very timely because of
how they would relate to community policing initiatives in Florida.

Applied research can be quite useful to criminal justice practitioners.
Despite its usefulness, it is not conducted as frequently in criminology
or criminal justice research as is basic research.

Basic Research

Basic research, sometimes referred to as "pure" research, is the conducting of scientific inquiries that may offer little "promise or expectation of
immediate, direct relevance" (Talarico, 1980, p. 3). Instead, it is concerned with the acquisition of new information for the purpose of helping develop the scholarly discipline or field of study in which the
research is being conducted. This type of research is more often consistent with criminological inquiries. The more common nature of this
research is descriptive and tries to respond to such questions as:

1. How big is the issue or problem?
2. Whom or what does the issue or problem affect?
3. What causes the issue or problem? (Eck and La Vigne, 1994, p. 5)

The findings from basic research often have little or any applicable
usage in the field of criminal justice. However, such research may
become the foundation upon which subsequent applied research and
criminal justice policy is based. It is such research that leads to the development of the criminological theories that guide the actions of lawmak-
ers, police, courts, and corrections.

Methodological Link

To understand whether a college course changed the perceptions of students about policing,
Dantzker and Waters (1999) surveyed several different sections of criminal justice and American government courses. Their findings indicated that the perceptions of the students in the
criminal justice classes became more positive after completing the course while the perceptions of the students in the American government classes had little or a negative change. While
this research offered some interesting findings, it had little to no applicable use. Yet, it could
serve as the foundation for future research in the recruitment into policing of individuals from
diverse backgrounds.

Multipurpose Research

Both basic and applied research are vital in the study of crime and justice. Yet, a good portion of the research conducted by criminal justice and criminological academicians tends to come under a third area of research best labeled as *multipurpose research*. Multipurpose research is the scientific inquiry into an issue or problem that could be both descriptive and evaluative. That is, it is between the basic and applied realms. This type of research generally begins as exploratory but is of such a nature that its results could ultimately be applicable. For example, a police chief is interested in the level of job satisfaction among his sworn employees. A job satisfaction survey is conducted that offers a variety of findings related to officers' satisfaction. From a basic perspective, the data may simply describe how officers perceive their jobs, thus becoming descriptive in nature. However, these same findings could be used to evaluate the police agency by examining those areas where satisfaction is the lowest and leading to efforts to determine how to improve them. This is the applied nature of the research. The result is research that is multipurpose.

Whether applied, basic, or multipurpose, research can provide interesting findings about a plethora of problems, events, issues, or activities. Regardless of the strategies utilized, criminological and criminal justice research is necessary for both understanding crime and criminality as well as developing suitable responses.

Types of Research

Prior to conducting research, one must understand something about research; that is, one must first study how research is correctly conducted. At some point in one's college career or during one's employment, a person may be asked to "look into something" or "research this topic." Often, the individual has no clue where to look, how to begin, or what to look for. Then, once the information is obtained, the person may not understand how the information was found and what it actually means.

The primary reason for studying research is to be able to attain a better understanding of why it was done and how it may be used. Ultimately, if we do not understand what research is and how it works, we cannot understand the products of research. Therefore, the answer to why we study research is the same reason as why we conduct research, to gain knowledge. This knowledge may occur in one of four formats or types: descriptive, explanatory, predictive, and intervening knowledge (Philliber, Schwab, and Sloss, 1980).

Descriptive Research

Knowledge that is descriptive allows us to understand what something is. Research of this nature helps us to gain a better grasp about an issue or problem we know little about. For example, women have played some role in criminality in this country for years. Yet, very little is known about women and criminality, especially with respect to certain types of crime (e.g., organized crime). To better understand what role women have played, a descriptive study might be conducted.

Methodological Link

As noted above, women have taken part in many forms of crime in this country. One area we know little about is women in organized crime. To provide some insight into this arena of thought, Liddick (1999) examined the role of women in the numbers gambling industry in New York City. The study's findings about women in this extremely lucrative form of criminality provided knowledge that was previously unknown.

Descriptive knowledge is a very common result of criminal justice and criminological research. While the results might be very informative, what can be done with this knowledge is often limited.

Explanatory Research

Explanatory research tries to tell us why something occurs, the causes behind it. This research can be very important when trying to understand why certain types of individuals become serial murderers, or what factors contribute to criminality. Knowing the causes behind something can assist in finding ways to counteract the behavior or the problem. For example, research focusing on gang membership may help to explain why some individuals join gangs and others do not. This information could assist in deterring potential future gang members. Ultimately, this type of research may provide answers to questions of how and why.

Methodological Link

A relatively new form of punishment is asset forfeiture. Because of its newness, little is really known about how it actually works and whether it has been successful. Topics of this nature often require explanatory research. Warchol and Johnson (1999) went beyond description by defining and explaining the application of this punishment in their study of federal asset forfeiture usage. Their explanations of what forfeiture is, its related concepts, its appropriate application and its impacts, provide insights that have not been readily available.

Predictive Research

Knowledge that is predictive in nature helps to establish future actions. This type of research can be useful to all criminal justice practitioners. For example, if research indicates that a large percentage of juveniles placed in boot-camp environments are less likely to become adult offenders, these results could be used in the future sentencing of juvenile offenders. Conversely, if boot camps are shown to have little or no effect, other alternatives may then be explored. Predictive knowledge gives some foresight into what may happen if something is implemented or tried. Because one of the concerns of criminal justice is to lower criminality, predictive knowledge could be quite useful in attaining this end.

Intervening Research

Finally, intervening knowledge allows one to intercede before a problem or issue gets too difficult to address. This type of research can be quite significant when a problem arises that currently available means are not addressing properly. Research on the effectiveness of certain community policing programs is a good example of intervening research. It can demonstrate whether a specific type of action taken before a given point will provide the desired results. For example, current research has shown that community policing initiatives from "foot patrol to limiting pay phones to outgoing calls," has helped meet desired outcomes of lowering drug-related crimes. (See Brodeur, 1998; Rosenbaum, 1994).

Whether the research is descriptive, explanatory, predictive, or intervening, it is important to understand what research is and how it is valuable. If one fails to study research in and of itself, then all research is of little value. This becomes especially true for the criminal justice and criminological academic or practitioner who wants to make use of previously conducted research or to conduct his or her own. It is important to have a grasp of what research is and why it is conducted, before one can actually conduct research.

Why Research Is Necessary

There are a number of specific reasons for conducting criminal justice or criminological research. Three primary reasons include curiosity, addressing social problems, and the development and testing of theories.

Curiosity

Wanting to know about an existing problem, issue, policy, or outcome is being curious. For example, in an earlier methodological link it was noted that two researchers were interested in what effect a course might have on students' perceptions of policing. A primary reason for this research was the curiosity of one of the researchers who taught police courses and wanted to see whether there were any differences between perceptions at the beginning of the course and at the end of the course.

Social Problems

The most salient social problem related to criminal justice is crime. Who commits it? Why do they act as they do? How do they do it? These are questions of interest for many criminal justice and criminological practitioners and academics. Concern over the effects of crime on society only adds further reason to conduct related research. This research can help identify who is more likely to commit certain crimes and why, how to better deal with the offenders and the victims, and what specific parts of the system can do to help limit or even alleviate crime. As a major social problem, crime provides many reasons for research as well as avenues for exploration.

Theory Testing

Linked more closely with pure criminological research, theories provide good cause to conduct research. The relationship between theory and research was discussed earlier in this chapter. Theory construction will be discussed in detail in Chapter 4.

Factors That Influence Research Decisions

Regardless of why the research is conducted, one must be cognizant of factors that can influence why the research is conducted and how it is conducted. There are three main influential factors: social and political, practicality, and ethical considerations (Philliber et al., 1980).

The social and political influences are often specific to the given research. Criminology and criminal justice as social sciences are greatly influenced by social and political events that are taking place in society. For example, race and ethnicity, economics, and gender might be influential on research about prison environments. Research on whether a particular law is working might have political ramifications. The inability of the criminal justice system to address problems identified by research may not be due to the lack of system resources but to the lack of social desire or political will for it to do so.

When it comes to conducting research, practicality can play an extremely important role. Economics and logistics are two elements of practicality. How much will the research cost? Can it be conducted in an efficient and effective manner? Would the benefits that are anticipated justify the social, political and economic costs? Would limited resources be taken from other areas? These are just some of the questions of practicality that could influence the conducting of research and the subsequent uses of that research.

Because ethics plays an important role in conducting research, a more in-depth discussion is offered in the next chapter. It is briefly noted here that there are three ethical considerations of importance: invasion of privacy, deception, and potential harm. Within a free society citizens jealously protect their rights to privacy. These rights are not just expected by citizens but protected by law. Deception can have adverse effects not only upon the research findings but also upon the individuals who were deceived by the researcher. Harm to others, especially to those who did not willingly accept such risks, must be avoided. Each will be explored in greater detail later.

Whatever the reason, researchers must be aware of the influences that have led to the research and those that might affect the research outcomes. Each could be detrimental to the outcome of the research.

How Research Is Done

Whether the research is applied or basic, qualitative or quantitative (to be discussed in later chapters), certain basic steps are applicable to each. There are five primary steps in conducting research:

1. Identifying the Research Problem
2. Research Design
3. Data Collection
4. Data Analyses
5. Reporting of Results

Each of these will be given greater attention later in the text, but a brief introduction here is appropriate.

Identifying the Problem

Prior to starting a research project, one of the most important steps is recognizing and defining what is going to be studied. Identifying or determining the problem, issue, or policy to be studied sets the groundwork for the rest of the research. For example, embarking on the study of crime can be too great an undertaking without focusing on a specific aspect of crime, such as types, causes, or punishments. Therefore, it is important to specify the target of the research first. Doing this makes completing the remaining stages easier.

Research Design

The research design is the "blueprint," which outlines how the research is to be conducted. Although the design will depend on the nature of the research, there are several common designs used in criminal justice and criminology. Various designs will be presented in this section. They will be discussed in detail in later chapters.

Survey Research

One of the most often employed methods of research is the use of surveys. This approach obtains data directly from the targeted source(s) and is often conducted through self-administered or interview questionnaires.

Field Research

Field research is when researchers gather data through firsthand observations of their targets. For example, if a researcher wanted to learn more about gang membership and activities he or she might try "running" with a gang as a participant-observer.

Experimental Research

Experimental research is also observational research. Unlike field research, however, observational studies involve the administration of research stimuli to participants in a controlled environment. Due to ethical and economic concerns, this kind of experimental research is conducted less frequently in criminal justice than are other research strategies.

Life Histories or Case Studies

Probably one of the simplest methods of research in criminology and criminal justice is through the use of life histories or case studies. Often these studies require the review and analysis of documents. This type of research might focus on violent behavior where the researcher investigates the lives of serial murderers to try and comprehend why the persons acted as they did.

Record Studies

Another research design is where the researcher evaluates and analyzes official records for relevant data. For example, to determine patterns and influences of robbery, the research design might utilize data from Uniform Crime Reports.

Content Analysis

In this research design documents, publications, or presentations are reviewed and analyzed. A researcher might review old documents to determine how crime events were publicized in a prior century or may monitor current television broadcasts to assess how the entertainment media influences public perceptions of crime.

Despite the options these designs offer, other design methods are possible, but will be discussed later in the text. Ultimately, the design used will depend on the nature of the study.

Data Collection

Regardless of the research design, data collection is a key component. A variety of methods (which will receive greater attention later in the text) exist. They include surveys, interviews, observations, and previously existing data.

Data Analysis

How to analyze and interpret the data is more appropriately discussed in another course, perhaps one focusing on statistics. Still, it is an important part of the design and cannot be ignored. The most common means for data analysis today is through the use of a computer and specifically oriented software.

Reporting

The last phase of any research project is the reporting of the findings. This can be done through various means: reports, journals, books, or computer presentation. How the findings are reported will depend on the target audience. Regardless of the audience or the medium used, the findings must be coherent and understandable or they are of no use to anyone.

Before leaving this section, there is one last area worthy of a brief discussion. Information has been offered on why and how to conduct research, but when is it inappropriate to conduct it?

Often it appears that research is conducted with little concern as to the appropriateness of the research. Failing to consider this might render the findings useless. Therefore, it is necessary that the prospective researcher be able to answer all the following questions with a negative response (Eck and La Vigne, 1994: 39):

(1) Does the research problem involve question(s) of value rather than fact?
(2) Is the solution to the research question already predetermined, effectively annulling the findings?
(3) Is it impossible to conduct the research effectively and efficiently?
(4) Are the research issues vague and ill defined?

If the answer to any of these questions is yes, the research in question should be avoided.

Summary

Conducting criminological research goes beyond looking up material on a subject and writing a descriptive paper. Prior to conducting research, one must understand what it is, why it is, and how it might be conducted.

For the purposes of this text criminal justice and criminological research is defined as *the investigation into or of any phenomenon linked to any or all aspects of the criminal justice system.* The type of research conducted can be applied, basic, or multipurpose. A primary reason for conducting research is to gain knowledge, which can be descriptive, explanatory, predictive, or intervening in nature. Studying research is required to better understand the results offered.

All research tends to follow five basic steps: recognizing and defining a problem, issue, or policy for study; designing the research; collecting data through survey, interviews, observation, or examining previously collected data; analyzing the data; and reporting the findings. Finally, it is important to determine whether it is prudent to conduct the research in question.

Research plays a very important role in criminal justice and criminology. It brings questions and answers, debates, and issues. Knowing what it is, why it is done, and how it can be accomplished is necessary if one is to study crime and criminal behavior.

Methodological Queries:

(1) Your roommate has just returned from the first day of classes and says that he has to write two research papers. What questions will you ask in reference to these papers?

(2) What is the first thing you need to do to prepare to start your first criminal justice research paper? What will affect or influence this decision?

(3) You have chosen a topic that fits the "multipurpose" research mode. What is that topic? Explain how it fits the applied and basic categories.

(4) Identify and discuss what items might make researching your topic inappropriate.

References

Adler, E. S. and Clark, R. (1999) *How It's Done: An Invitation to Social Research.* Belmont, CA: Wadsworth Publishing.

Babbie, E. (1999) *The Basics of Social Research.* Belmont, CA: Wadsworth Publishing.

Brodeur, J. (Ed.) (1998). *How to Recognize Good Policing; Problems and Issues.* Thousand Oaks, CA: Sage Publications.

Dantzker, M. L. (1998) *Criminology and Criminal Justice: Comparing, Contrasting, and Intertwining Disciplines.* Woburn, MA: Butterworth-Heinemann

Dantzker, M. L. and Waters, J. E. (1999). Examining students' perceptions of policing: A pre- and post-comparison between students in criminal justice and non-criminal justice courses. In M. L. Dantzker (Ed.), *Readings for Research Methods in Criminology and Criminal Justice,* pp. 27-36). Woburn, MA: Butterworth-Heinemann.

Eck, J. E. and La Vigne, N. G. (1994). *Using Research: A Primer for Law Enforcement Managers.* Washington, D.C.: Police Executive Research Forum.

Ford, M. C. and Williams, L. (1999). Human/cultural diversity training for justice personnel. In M.L. Dantzker (Ed.), *Readings for Research Methods in Criminology and Criminal Justice,* pp. 37-60. Woburn, MA: Butterworth-Heinemann.

Fitzgerald, J. D. and Cox, S. M. (1998). *Research Methods in Criminal Justice: An Introduction, Second Edition.* Chicago: Nelson-Hall Publishers.

Liddick, Jr., D. R. (1999). Women as organized criminals: An examination of the numbers gambling industry in New York City. In M.L. Dantzker (Ed.), *Readings for Research Methods in Criminology and Criminal Justice,* pp. 123-138. Woburn, MA: Butterworth-Heinemann.

Rosenbaum, D.P. (Ed.) (1994). *The Challenge of Community Policing: Testing the Promises.* Thousand Oaks, CA: Sage Publications.

Senese, J. D. (1997). *Applied Research Methods in Criminal Justice.* Chicago: Nelson-Hall Publishers.

Warchol, G. L. and Johnson, B. R. (1999). A cross-sectional quantitative analysis of federal asset forfeiture. In M.L. Dantzker (Ed.), *Readings for Research Methods in Criminology and Criminal Justice,* pp. 139-156. Woburn, MA: Butterworth-Heinemann.

Wallace, W. (1971) *The Logic of Science in Sociology.* New York: Aldine deGrutyer.

Research Ethics

■ **Vignette 2-1**
A Question of Ethics?

While doing a literature search, you come across a study that is very similar to what you are considering for your senior project. Although the study is about 25 years old, much of what was written could be applicable today. The best thing about this study is that all the questions used to gather the data are listed. Knowing you are being encouraged to create your own survey questionnaire, you start to ponder using these questions. It is an old study, in a somewhat obscure journal. Who would know if you borrowed the questions and offered them as your own? Of course, that would not only be plagiarism, but extremely unethical. But, then again, is ethics that big a concern for you? Getting caught cheating might not go over well, but you think you would be able to get around that by pleading ignorance. The ethical dilemma is another story.

Later that evening you meet with some friends at the local hangout to celebrate one of your friend's successful masters' thesis defense. At one point during the evening's conversation, the topic of ethics in research arises. Informed consent, or more appropriately the lack of that consent, was an issue during your friend's defense. Apparently your friend did a survey among individuals booked into the county jail during a six-month period but never told them what the survey was for or that they did not have to complete it. They were simply advised to fill it out during the booking process. There was a good deal of debate as to whether this method was right or wrong. Was it ethical? Obviously, the decision was in your friend's favor, but in the past twelve hours you have been confronted with two ethical questions regarding research. How many others can there be?

■ CHAPTER 2
Learning Objectives

After studying this chapter the student should be able to:

1. Define what is meant by ethics and explain its importance to criminological research.
2. Present and discuss the various characteristics of ethical problems in criminological research.
3. Explain how the researcher's role influences and is influenced by ethical concerns.
4. Discuss the various ethical considerations that were presented.
5. Describe the relationship that exists between ethics and professionalism. Include "code of ethics" within this discussion.
6. List and describe the four ethical criteria.
7. Present and discuss the five reasons why confidentiality and privacy are important research concerns.
8. Describe the impacts of institutional review boards and research guidelines (such as those mandated by the National Institute of Justice) upon criminological research.

Learning how to conduct research is important. The previous chapter set the foundation for understanding what it means to conduct research in criminology and criminal justice. However, before we actually start to show how to do the research, it is important that the prospective researcher be aware of the ethical aspects.

Criminology and criminal justice are virtual playgrounds of ethical confrontations. There is no aspect of them in which ethical questions or dilemmas do not exist, including research. This is particularly true when the research is of an applied nature.

The ethical issues encountered in applied social research are subtle and complex, raising difficult moral dilemmas that, at least on a superficial level, appear unresolvable. These dilemmas often require the researcher to strike a delicate balance between the scientific requirements of methodology and the human rights and values potentially threatened by the research (Kimmel, 1988, p. 9).

Ethics as discussed in this chapter is doing what is morally and legally right in the conducting of research. This requires the researcher to be knowledgeable about what is being done; to use reasoning when making decisions; to be both intellectual and truthful in approach and reporting; and to consider the consequences, in particular, to be sure that the outcome of the research outweighs any negatives that might occur. Using this approach, ethical decisions will be much easier.

Criminal justice and criminological research almost always involves dealings with humans and human behavior. It is prudent to be aware of the characteristics associated with ethical problems in social research. Although there does not appear to be a consensus as to what these characteristics are, nor is there a comprehensive list, the following have been identified as recognizable characteristics of ethical problems:

1. A single research problem can generate numerous questions regarding appropriate behavior on the part of the researcher.
2. Ethical sensitivity is a necessity but is not necessarily sufficient to solve problems that might arise.
3. Ethical dilemmas result from conflicting values as to what should receive priority on the part of the researcher.
4. Ethical concerns can relate to both the research topic and how the research is conducted.
5. Ethical concerns involve both personal and professional elements in the research. (Berg, 1998; Golden, 1976; Kimmel, 1988)

Basically, when dealing with humans, ethics plays an important role. It all begins with the researcher's role.

The Researcher's Role

Contrary to popular belief, the justician or criminologist who conducts research is considered a scientist. Ignoring the distinctions made between a natural scientist and a social scientist, both are scientists who are governed by the laws of inquiry (Kaplan, 1963). Both require an ethically neutral, objective approach to research. As you may recall from Chapter 1, ethical neutrality requires that the researcher's moral, or ethical beliefs are not allowed to influence the gathering of data or the conclusions that are made from analyzing the data. Objectivity is striving to prevent personal ideology or prejudices from influencing the process. As you can see, the two have a similar concern: maintaining the integrity of the research. In addition to these concerns, the researcher, whether a nuclear physicist or a criminologist, must also ensure that the research concerns do not negatively impact upon the safety of others.

The researcher's role will often coexist and, at times, even conflict with other important roles, such as practitioner, teacher, academic, scholar, and citizen. This meshing of roles can often cause the researcher to lose objectivity in his or her approach to the collection, analysis, and reporting of the data. In particular there are the concerns over the individual's morals, values, attitude, and beliefs interfering with completing an objective study.

We are each raised with certain ideals, identified as morals and values. What those are will commonly be reflected in our attitudes and behaviors. Weak or strong morals and values can affect how we conduct research. For example, individuals raised to believe that success is very important, regardless of the costs, might regard the "borrowing" of someone else's research efforts and passing them off as their own as acceptable; or they might accept the manipulation of data to gain more desirable results. An even more repugnant scenario would be one in which the researcher continues with his/her research despite knowing that to do so will cause physical harm or emotional anguish for others. In each of these cases, ethically the decisions are wrong.

Because the researcher's role is intertwined with other roles, ethics becomes even more difficult to manage. Ultimately, it is up to the individual to decide the importance of personal ethics. However, this is just one aspect of ethics in research.

Ethical Considerations

Sometimes conducting research, in and of itself, can be problematic. Accessibility, funding, timing, and other factors may all impose problems. "Ethical concerns can enter at every stage of the research process, from the selection of a research problem to the use of research results" (Golden, 1976, p. 28). With this in mind, the considerations about to be discussed should not be viewed as more important at any one particular time in the process, but apply throughout the research.

Ethical Ramifications

One of the first things to consider is whether the topic to be studied has innate ethical ramifications. Some topics are controversial by their very nature. For instance, the individual interested in gangs might decide that the best way to gain data is to become a participant observer. As such, chances are that the researcher may have to witness or even be asked to participate in illegal activity. Ethically as well as legally, this information should be given to the police, but doing so might jeopardize the research. While it is apparent what decision should be made (the research should be adjusted to avoid such a dilemma or possibly even abandoned outright), the right one is not always made simply because of how important the research is perceived to be to the individual. Therefore, before embarking on a research topic, the ethical implications of the research itself must be addressed.

Harm to Others

Another consideration is what effects the research might have on the research targets. When the research involves direct human contact, ethics plays an important role. Whether the targets are victims, accused offenders, convicted offenders, practitioners, or the general public, a major consideration is whether the research might cause them any harm. Harm can be physical, psychological, or social.

Physical harm most often can occur during experimental or applied types of research, such as testing new drugs or weapons. Psychological harm might result through the type of information being gathered. For example, in a study of victims of sexual assault, the research might delve into the events prior to, during, and after the assault. This line of questioning may inflict more psychological harm in addition to that which already exists as a result of the assault. Finally, social harm may be inflicted if certain information is released that should not have been. Consider a survey of sexual orientation among correctional officers where it becomes public knowledge who is gay or lesbian. This information may cause those individuals to be treated differently, perhaps discriminated against, causing a sociological harm. Obviously, it is important that the researcher consider what type of harm may befall respondents or participants prior to starting the research (Babbie, 1999).

Privacy Concerns

The right to privacy is another ethical consideration. Individuals in America have a basic right to privacy. In many cases, research efforts may violate that right. How far should individuals be allowed to pry into the private or public lives of others in the name of research? Ethically speaking, if a person does not want his or her life examined, then that right should be granted. We all have a right to anonymity (Fitzgerald and Cox, 1998). However, there are a variety of documents accessible to the public in which information can be gathered that individuals would prefer to be unavailable, such as arrest records, court dockets, and tax and property files. The ethical question that arises here is whether a person should have the right to consent to access to certain types of information in the name of research. Giving consent in general is a major ethical consideration (Berg, 1998; Fitzgerald and Cox, 1998; Senese, 1997).

Methodological Link

As part of the university's requirements for conducting research, Dantzker and Waters (1999) had to establish "informed consent." To meet this requirement, the following statement was read to all students prior to the distribution of the survey.

You are being asked to participate in a "Students' Perceptions of Policing" study being directed by Dr. M. L. Dantzker, Department of Political Science, Justice Studies Programs, Georgia Southern University. There are two major purposes to this research: to examine college students' perceptions of policing, both Criminal Justice majors and non-majors and to measure changes in perceptions of same students, particularly those who may be taking a police course or attending a police academy. Participation is VOLUNTARY and CONFIDENTIAL. The only personal identifier you are being asked to provide is the last four digits of your social security number, or a four-digit identifier you can make up and recall for later use. *(Note to reader: If not absolutely necessary, do not require an identifier. This will make your subjects feel more secure in their anonymity.)* Participation or lack thereof will be used neither for nor against you. The data being collected will be used SOLELY FOR RESEARCH PURPOSES with the possibility of publishing of the results. Should you choose to participate, please follow the questionnaire's instructions for completion. Thank you for your assistance.

Informed Consent

Particularly in survey research it is common for the researcher to either ask for specific consent from the respondents or at least acknowledge that by completing the survey, the respondent has conferred consent. Normally, this only requires having the individual sign an "informed consent" form or for the instructions to indicate that the survey is completely anonymous, voluntary, and that the information is only being used for the purpose of research.

Voluntary Participation

As you probably noted in the Methodological Link, not only did the researchers seek to obtain consent, they also informed students that their participation was voluntary. Too frequently criminological researchers require their subjects to sign consent forms but (particularly within institutional settings such as military organizations, schools, and prisons) neglect to inform them that their participation is voluntary. In fact, in these environments, participation is often coerced. We are not stating that all research must use voluntary participation but we do wish to stress that there must be valid reasons that can be given showing that the knowledge could not otherwise be reasonably obtained and that no harm will come to the participants from their compulsory involvement.

Regardless of the fact that the research was not intrusive and could cause no harm to the respondents, informed consent was required. The rule of thumb in these situations is if you have any doubt as to whether your research could be in any way construed to be intrusive, get consent from your subjects. It is also best to assure them that their participation is voluntary and they may choose not to take part in the study.

Within the academic setting, informed consent and voluntary participation do not appear to be an unusual requirement. To ensure that informed consent is provided, and to judge the value and ethical nature of the research, many universities have an Institutional Review Board (IRB). The IRBs exist as a result of the Code of Federal Regulations, in particular, Title 28 Judicial Administration, part 46, which specifies all aspects of the IRB including membership, functions and operations, reviewing the research, and criteria for IRB approval (INTERNET Link: http://www.access.gpo.gov/nara/cfr/cfr-table-search.html).

Established primarily for the review of research, usually experimental or applied, dealing directly with human subjects, university IRBs often extend their review over any type of research involving human respondents (survey or otherwise). While having to attain IRB approval can be somewhat frustrating, it is a useful process because it helps to reaffirm the researcher's perceptions and beliefs about the research and can help identify prospective ethical problems. Also, reviewers may see problems overlooked by the researcher. It is better to err on the side of caution.

The process generally is not that difficult. It usually requires the researcher to submit basic information about the proposed research, often in a format designed by the university. At the end of this chapter is an example of a request submitted to an IRB for approval. While not all IRBs make use of the same format, the information required will be similar across institutions.

Informed consent is valuable because it is important that research targets are allowed the right to refuse to be part of the research. While in survey research consent may not be a major problem (because permission can be written into the documents), it does raise an interesting dilemma for observational research (when the researcher may not want the subjects to know they are being observed). The ethical consideration here is that as long as the subjects are doing what they normally would be doing and the observations will not in any way directly influence their behavior or harm them, it is ethically acceptable.

Deception

Some types of research (particularly field research that requires the researcher to in essence "go undercover") cannot be conducted if the subjects are aware that they are being studied. Such research is controversial and must be carefully thought out before it is undertaken (Babbie, 1999). All too often the deception is based more upon the researcher's laziness or bias rather than a real need to do so. For example, a researcher is interested in studying juvenile behavior within the confines of a juvenile facility. Rather than explain to administrators and the subjects what he or she is doing, the research is conducted under the guise of an internship or volunteer work.

Depending on the type of research, there are always some type of ethical considerations. What is interesting is that the science of research, itself, is viewed as ethically neutral or amoral. The ethical dilemmas rise from the fact that researchers, themselves, are not neutral. This fosters the need for regulation in the conducting of research so that it does meet ethical standards (Fitzgerald and Cox, 1998; Adler and Clark, 1999).

The Professionalism of Research

According to Funk and Wagnalls' *New International Dictionary of the English Language* (1995), professionalism is defined as "the methods, manner, or spirit of a profession; also its practitioners" (p. 1006). Research in itself is a profession and when mixed with other professions, there is an even greater need to conduct business in a professional manner. It has been offered that: "Professional ethics activities reflect the willingness of a profession to self-regulate the behavior of its members on behalf of the public and the profession" (Kimmel, 1988, p. 56). This often means that the profession has established a code of ethics.

While other professions tend to support written codes of ethics for research (for example, The American Psychological Association), criminal justice and criminology have yet to establish any such code. (Fortunately the Academy of Criminal Justice Sciences is in the process of developing such a code of ethics.) Furthermore, there appears to be no universal code of ethics with respect to research. This is believed to result from the wide variety of research conducted and calls for individually applied standards.

Grant-funded research is more likely to have ethical constraints imposed. For example, a popular source of funding for criminal justice and criminological research is the National Institute of Justice (NIJ). NIJ has developed its own "code of ethics" to which all grant recipients must agree. The NIJ is very specific in its guidelines, especially with respect to data confidentiality and the protection of human subjects.

Ethical Research Criteria

Even though there is no universally recognized research code of ethics, there are some specifically identified criteria which, when applied or followed, will assist in producing ethical research.

1. Avoid harmful research.
2. Be objective in designing, conducting, and evaluating your research.
3. Use integrity in the performance and reporting of the research.
4. Protect confidentiality.

Avoiding Harmful Research

The goal of research is to discover knowledge not previously known or to verify existing data. In many instances this can be done without ever having to inflict any undue stress, strain, or pain on respondents (that is, historical or survey research). Unfortunately, there are times when the research can be physically or emotionally harmful. The ethical approach is to avoid any such research regardless of how important its findings might be unless it can be shown that good from the information will far outweigh the harm (an eventuality that is rare even in criminological research).

Being Objective

Biases can be detrimental to a research project. One such bias deals with objectivity. Assume you do not like drinkers, that you perceive them as weak willed and careless. Your research deals with individuals convicted of Driving While Intoxicated (DWI). You are interested in their reasons for doing so. The chances are good that if you allow your personal feelings against drinkers to guide you in your research, the results will be skewed, biased, and subjective. It is important, for good ethical research, to maintain objectivity. Of course, being objective is just one important characteristic of the ethical researcher.

Using Integrity

The last thing a researcher wants is for the results to not meet expectations. Sometimes because of how important the research is perceived to be, there may be a tendency to manipulate the data and report it in a manner that shows the research was successful; that is, put a positive spin on an otherwise negative result. This is especially possible when the research is evaluative and its results could influence additional funding for the program being evaluated. When faced with this dilemma, because of the desire not to jeopardize the program's future or to improve future chances for research, the researcher may not report the true findings. This is extremely unethical, but unfortunately, may be more commonplace than one would like to believe. The ethical researcher will accept the findings and report them as discovered.

Protecting Confidentiality

Undoubtedly one of the biggest concerns in conducting research is the issue of confidentiality and/or privacy. As it has been suggested,

> privacy and confidentiality are two ethical issues that are crucial to social researchers who, by the very nature of their research, frequently request individuals to share with them their thoughts, attitudes, and experiences. (Kimmel, 1988, p. 85)

Because a good portion of criminal justice and criminological research involves humans, chances are great that sensitive information may be obtained that other non-research efforts might be interested in. For example, conducting gang research where street names and legal names are collected perhaps along with identifying tattoos, scars, etc., and voluntary statements of criminal history. This information would be extremely valuable to a police agency. Ethically that information must remain confidential.

Reasons for Confidentiality and Privacy

Overall, five reasons have been identified as to why confidentiality and privacy are important in research:

1. Disclosure of particularly embarrassing or sensitive information may present the respondent with a risk of psychological, social, or economic harm.
2. Sensitive information, if obtained solely for research purposes is legally protected in situations where respondents' privacy rights are protected.
3. Long-term research may require data storage of information that can identify the participants.

4. The courts can subpoena data.

5. Respondents may be suspicious as to how the information is truly going to be used.

Privacy Protections

The bottom line is that confidentiality and privacy must be maintained. There are two methods of accomplishing this: physical protection and legal protection (Berg, 1998; Kimmel, 1988; Senese, 1997).

Physical protection relates to setting up the data so that links cannot be made between identifying information and the respondents. Reducing who has access can also aid in protecting the data. Legal protection attempts to avoid official misuse (Kimmel, 1988). Researchers are aided with this by an amendment to the 1973 Omnibus Crime Control and Safe Streets Act, better known as the "Shield Law," which protects research findings from any administrative or judicial processes. Furthermore, as noted earlier, federally funded research through such institutions as NIJ have established their own regulations (See Box 2-1). Unfortunately, these guidelines do not completely protect the data, leaving researchers responsible for gathering the data in a manner that will best protect the respondents.

By simply meeting the four suggested criteria, a researcher can avoid many ethical problems. However, perhaps the best way to avoid ethical problems is to conduct research using a method that will not compromise ethical standards. That is, research that is legal, relevant, and necessary.

Summary

The simple act of research, especially when it involves humans, creates a plethora of possible ethical dilemmas. Because ethics is important to professions, researchers need to be cognizant of several ethical considerations.

These include determining whether the topic itself is ethical, what harm or risk is involved to respondents, and confidentiality and privacy. There are federal guidelines for protecting individuals' privacy and for obtaining their consent, which in the University setting is often reinforced through an IRB. The key to ethical research is a professional approach. While some professions have created a code of ethics applicable to research, criminal justice and criminology are just now establishing such a code. However, there are four criteria that when followed, alleviate the need for such a code. The best way to do this is to: (1) avoid conducting harmful research; (2) be objective; (3) use integrity in conducting and reporting the research; and (4) protect confidentiality.

Methodological Queries:

(1) When conducting survey research, how important is informed consent? Confidentiality?

(2) Is an ethical code specifically geared toward criminological and criminal justice research necessary?

(3) You are asked to write a code of research ethics for criminology and criminal justice. What do you put in it? Explain.

(4) Write an informed consent for conducting a criminality study among college students.

Box 2-1
NIJ Guidelines: Data Confidentiality and Human
Subjects Protection*

Research that examines individual traits and experiences plays a vital part in expanding our knowledge about criminal behavior. It is essential, however, that researchers protect subjects from needless risk of harm or embarrassment and proceed with their willing and informed cooperation. NIJ requires that investigators protect information identifiable to research participants. When information is safeguarded, it is protected by statute from being used in legal proceedings.

Such information and copies thereof shall be immune from legal process, and shall not, without the consent of the person furnishing such information, be admitted as evidence or used for any purpose in any action, suit, or other judicial, legislative, or administrative proceedings (42 U.S.C. 3789g).

Applicants should file their plans to protect sensitive information as part of their proposal. Applicants who do not intend to use data on individual subjects in their research should submit a statement to that effect. Necessary safeguards are detailed in 28 Code of Federal Regulations (CFR) Part 22. "Privacy Certificate Guidelines" for developing a privacy and confidentiality plan are included with the application forms packet, as is a sample format for a Privacy Certificate.

In addition, the U.S. Department of Justice has adopted human subjects policies similar to those established by the U.S. Department of Health and Human Services. In general, these policies exempt most NIJ-supported research from Institutional Review Board review. These exceptions will be decided on an individual basis during application review. Researchers are encouraged to review 28 CFR 46.101 to determine their individual project requirements.

*This was excerpted from the On-Line NIJ Grant Application Guidelines accessible at: http://www.ncjrs.org/fedgrant.htm#nij

References

Adler, E. S. and Clark, R. (1999). *How It's Done: An Invitation to Social Research.* Belmont, CA: Wadsworth Publishing.

Babbie, E. (1999). *The Basics of Social Research.* Belmont, CA: Wadsworth Publishing.

Berg, B. L. (1998). *Qualitative Research Methods for the Social Sciences (3rd Ed.).* Boston: Allyn and Bacon.

Dantzker, M. L. and Waters, J. E. (1999). Examining students' perceptions of policing: A pre- and post-comparison between students in criminal justice and non-criminal justice courses." In M.L. Dantzker (Ed.), *Readings for Research Methods in Criminology and Criminal Justice,* pp. 27-36. Woburn, MA: Butterworth-Heinemann.

Fitzgerald, J. D. and Cox, S. M. (1998). *Research Methods in Criminal Justice: An Introduction, Second Edition.* Chicago: Nelson-Hall Publishers.

Golden, M.P. (Ed.) (1976). *The Research Experience.* Itasca, IL: F.E. Peacock Publishers, Inc.

Kaplan, A. (1963). *The Conduct of Inquiry.* New York: Harper & Row, Publishers Inc.

Kimmel, A.J. (1988). *Ethics and Values in Applied Social Research.* Thousand Oaks, CA: Sage Publications, Inc.

Senese, J. D. (1997). *Applied Research Methods in Criminal Justice.* Chicago: Nelson-Hall Publishers.

Example of an IRB Submission

Institutional Review Board
Georgia Southern University

To be submitted to the Institutional Review Board for the protection of Human Subjects in Research prior to the initiation of any investigation involving human subjects. A copy of the research proposal and approval form must be attached.

Approval Form

Date: 13 Sept 96

Research Title: (1) Students' perceptions of policing: the research continues (2) Perceptions of Policing and the New Recruit

Principal Investigator: M.L. Dantzker

Title: Assoc. Professor

Department: Department of Political Studies

Campus Address: P.O. Box 8101   **Phone:** 871-1397

Signature: **Principal Investigator** (If student research, major professor)

        Department Head

Determination of Institutional Review Board:

Human Subjects: _____ **At Risk**   _____ **Not at Risk**

Action: _____ **Approved**   _____ **Not Approved**

       _____ **Reapproved**   _____ **Returned for Revisions**

Signed: **Date:**

Chair, Institutional Review Board

Institutional Review Board

Proposal Format for Conducting Research Involving Human Subjects

The purpose of this information is to provide the IRB with sufficient data to understand the use of and safeguards for human subjects in your research proposal. The IRB is not concerned with evaluating the quality or focus of your research, but only the use of human subjects. Please be as concise and brief as possible in providing the requested information. Please refer to the attached explanations of the types of information needed to complete this form. Thank you.

Statement of the Problem to Be Studied:

The various perceptions of policing are well noted and observed any time more than one person talks about some police-related incident. The literature offers many studies that have examined the differing perceptions and possible reasons for such. Yet, despite the amount of literature, there appears to be little literature that examines how students, particularly criminal justice students, perceive policing. This research is the continuation of a project started a year ago that examines the perceptions of students about policing. The research is being expanded to include students in justice studies and criminal justice classes, non-criminal justice courses, and new recruits attending police academies.

Describe Your Research Design:

Measurement is accomplished through a fourteen-item perceptions questionnaire designed specifically for this research (see attached). This questionnaire will be distributed the first and last day of classes at several universities (including GSU). At GSU four courses will be targeted: two introductory justice studies and two American government courses. At the other cooperating institutions, only criminal justice courses or police academy classes will be targeted. The data is then coded and analyzed using SPSS.

DESCRIPTION OF POSSIBLE RISK TO HUMAN SUBJECTS: (If there is a possibility of subjects or researchers being exposed to body fluids (drawing blood, etc.) as part of the research, please explain how the Centers for Disease Control "universal precautions" will be followed.)

There is no known risk of any nature to human subjects.

DESCRIPTION OF POSSIBLE BENEFITS TO HUMAN SUBJECTS AND SOCIETY IN GENERAL:

The results will hopefully provide criminal justice/justice studies educators with a better idea of how students perceive policing. One outcome being examined is whether these perceptions change due to the course being taken. Ultimately, the results can help educators see what effect their courses may have on students' perception.

INFORMATION OF PARTICIPANTS TO BE UTILIZED IN THE RESEARCH STUDY:

Participants are all students enrolled in the selected courses at the various participating universities.

MATERIALS AND PROCEDURES TO BE USED: *(Please attach a copy of any questionnaire, interview questions, flyers and/or newsprint or other materials that may be used.)*

As noted earlier, the questionnaire is a 14-item survey that will be distributed the first and last day of class. The questionnaire is a revision of the 20-item survey used last year. (See attached article's appendix). The questionnaires will be distributed and collected by the instructors of the selected courses and then returned to the principal investigator either in person or through the mail.

PROCEDURES TO SECURE INFORMED CONSENT: *(Please attach a copy of the Informed Consent Form. When deception is necessary, attach a copy of the debriefing plan.)*

No special form has been or is considered necessary. Students are informed by the instructors prior to questionnaire distribution of the purpose of the survey. They are also advised that participation is voluntary and anonymous with the exception of a four-digit identifier that the student creates so that surveys can be matched after the second distribution.

PROCEDURES TO GAIN CONSENT AND UTILIZE MINORS IN THE RESEARCH:

Not Applicable

PLEASE PROVIDE AN EXPLANATION, IF ANY OF THE DATA COLLECTED WILL RELATE TO ILLEGAL ACTIVITIES.

Not Applicable

PART II

Problem Formulation

Getting Started

■ Vignette 3-1
Picking a Topic

It is only about a third of the way through the fall semester and you are already thinking about graduating in the spring. Next semester you must take the senior seminar—a capstone course—in which you will have to write a research paper based on your own original research. That is why you waited until this semester to take the methods course.

Older students have suggested that you start thinking about your topic before getting into that class because it will make things so much easier. The problem is, you have no idea what you would want to research. There are lots of areas that interest you, but which one intrigues you enough to research it in-depth is another question. Where do you start? You are aware of several possible sources of information. Yet, you are still a little confused and apprehensive.

Furthermore, you understand that the heart of your research revolves around something referred to as the research question, a statement explaining what it is you want to accomplish. Forming the research question then leads to the formation of hypotheses and the identification of variables. Obviously, there are several things yet to learn.

■ CHAPTER 3
Learning Objectives

After studying this chapter the student should be able to:

1. Discuss the issues that should be considered in selecting a research topic.
2. Present and describe the three purposes of research.

3. Describe what a literature review is and the sources that are available for such a review.
4. Compare and contrast the various writing styles utilized by criminologists.
5. Define what an article critique is and discuss its details.
6. Define what is meant by the research question. Give an example of a research question.
7. Define hypothesis and describe the types of hypotheses.
8. Define variable and describe the types of variables.

In the previous two chapters we have discussed why research is necessary and the importance of research ethics. These are important topics that warrant serious consideration. However, if you the reader are charged with writing an empirical research paper you may find that there is still a great deal that you need to know in order to satisfactorily complete such a project. In this chapter we shall present and discuss a number of issues that must be considered when starting a research project.

> One of the most difficult aspects of any endeavor is to begin, and research is no exception. By its very nature, the process by which a research problem is selected is a creative process. It involves thinking about various ideas and issues, asking questions about them, and considering whether possible answers to these questions even exist (Guy, Edgley, Arafat, and Allen, 1987, p. 34).

Picking a Topic

Prior to beginning the research project, one must first answer this: what should I study? Within the fields of criminology and criminal justice there are numerous research topics available. All one has to do is pick one. However, that is not as easy as it appears.

Obviously, the beginning of any research project must focus on what is to be studied. Defining the problem is the most important stage of the research (Eck and La Vigne, 1994). To start, it should be something of personal interest. If you are not interested in the topic before you begin, you will be sick of it before you are done. It must also comply with any topic restrictions imposed by the individuals and/or organization for whom you are conducting the research. For example, the authors frequently restrict the topics that their students may research in order to avoid emotional diatribes on controversial issues better left to experienced researchers. In addition, before the topic is chosen, one should consider:

1. what currently exists in the literature,

2. any gaps in theory or the current state of art,
3. the feasibility of conducting the research,
4. whether there are any policy implications, and
5. possible funding availability (Berg, 1998; Eck and La Vigne, 1994; Fitzgerald and Cox, 1998; Hagan, 1993; Senese, 1997)

There are a number of studies about community policing. Many of them suggest and support how effective community policing can be. What appears to be lacking are studies that explain why it may be successful in some places and a failure in other places. Thus, a gap in theory exists and needs filling. Finding such gaps in the literature can assist in choosing a topic.

Once an interesting and intriguing topic is found, you must consider the feasibility of conducting the research. Feasibility is primarily linked to logistics (for example, Is a sample accessible? Does a data collection instrument exist or must one be designed?). Sometimes the topic may be a very good choice for researching, but it is not feasible to attempt it. Prior to finalizing the research topic, the prospective researcher needs to be sure that the study can actually be accomplished.

Because of the popularity of some topics, such as job stress, capital punishment, sentencing disparity, and community policing, there is usually a wealth of information available to help build a research base. However, there may be times when the topic is legitimate, but there may be little information in the literature to support your research question. This should not stop one from going forward with the research. If the findings can be validated (shown to meet scientific rigor and supported by ensuing research), it may become a new and significant contribution to the literature, the discipline, and subsequently, the practice of criminal justice.

Choosing a research topic that could have policy implications can be very useful. For example, Dantzker's (1989) dissertation research dealt with job stress and educational level among police officers. In general, this topic might not have any policy implications, but he demonstrated how the findings could have policy implications for police agencies regarding educational requirements. This made gaining approval of the topic from his dissertation committee much easier.

Finally, while funding may not be applicable to many students' research efforts, it should be taken into consideration. One of the most popular means of funding research is through internal and external grants. Many universities offer both students and faculty opportunities to apply for internal grants that will at least allow the person to start the research project and may help offset personal costs. Ultimately, many researchers seek external grants. However, these are usually not sought by undergraduate students. Regardless of where the funding may come from, it is important to establish whether any monies will be needed and from where they may be sought.

The Purpose of the Research

Once consideration is given to the previous issues, the research can begin, but to address these issues, one must have an idea of what the research will cover. Perhaps the best place to start is to decide what the research should accomplish. As was discussed in Chapter 1, there are three possible expectations or accomplishments: (1) exploring, (2) describing, and (3) explaining (Singleton, Jr., Straits, Straits, and McAllister, 1988).

Exploring

The majority of us are explorers. Our curiosity about things begins at a very early age and should last until we die. What and how we explore something changes with age and time. Much of our exploration occurs either accidentally or intentionally. Intentional exploration may well be considered to be a form of research. Thus, when one wants to know more about something, the tendency is to explore the topic.

For example, prior to buying a new sports utility vehicle, you might read what various magazines say about them, check out prices through various dealers, and talk with current owners of such vehicles. When you are finished, you should have enough information to make an informed decision. You have conducted research. With respect to criminal justice and criminology, exploration of what interests us is often formal and intentional, and accomplished through some form of research.

Exploratory research provides information not previously known, or about which little is known. In other words, it seeks out information about something that is known to exist, but as to why or how, that must be discovered. Therefore, exploratory research offers additional insights about something for which there is an awareness but limited knowledge.

EXAMPLE

Several students in a rural high school known for not having any of the usual problems often found in the urban high school quite suddenly start participating in a variety of criminal activities. Furthermore, there appear to be signs associated with the formation and existence of a gang. School administrators are aware of the growing problems but do not understand why or how this could be happening in their school. The school board requests help from academics in the local university's criminal justice and criminology department to better understand the situation, and hopefully, find ways to eliminate the problems. Several professors suggest and eventually conduct an exploratory study in which they survey a sample of students about the criminal activities they may have participated in, focusing primarily on why they participated.

Describing

What is the phenomenon? How does it work? What does it do? These are just three of the types of questions answered when conducting research for the purpose of describing. The basic purpose is to be able to describe specific aspects or elements of the topic. Generally this type of research is informative in nature and is based on something we are already aware of, but know little about. For example, many people might know what a prison is. Yet, how many really know the details about a specific prison? A descriptive study could offer information about the inmates, correctional staff, programs, violent acts, and so forth, which would further enhance what is known about that prison. Descriptive studies are probably among the easier studies to do because the researcher simply needs to explain what he or she sees, hears, or reads with respect to the various elements of the topic. From a purely academic perspective, some literature reviews might serve as a descriptive study.

Explaining

Undoubtedly the most in-depth and difficult purpose for conducting research is to provide an explanation. Explanatory research attempts to analyze and fully understand the concept "why" as it applies to policies, procedures, objects, attitudes, opinions, etc. From a criminological perspective, to better understand why males commit sexual assaults, a study of several convicted rapists where questions are asked that answer "why" might be conducted. For criminal justice, examining acts of police corruption to determine "why" they occur would be an explanatory type study.

In our previous example, criminologists sought to find out what was going on in a rural high school. They conducted exploratory research to find out whether the criminal behaviors were the result of gang activities. Upon learning that it was gang related, they could rely on the literature to make recommendations as to how to deal with the problem. Or they might engage in further descriptive research to learn exactly how the gangs were made up and what they were doing. This could then lead to explanatory research as to why gangs were able to get a foothold in the high school, what the impacts of such activities will be, and how to combat them.

While all three reasons for conducting research are valid, it is most often the explanatory reason that many criminologists and justicians pursue. This type of study relies on strong, clear research question(s), hypothesis(es), and variables. Each of these will be discussed in greater length shortly. However, there is still the question of choosing a topic.

To demonstrate the myriad of possible topics for study, Box 3-1 offers a short list of potential research examples. Still, the question lingers on how to go about choosing a topic. This can be aided through personal observations, suggestions from academics and scholars, other students, and the existing literature in criminal justice and criminology. It is through this last means that a large number of research topics are chosen.

Reviewing the Literature

For many researchers, while the choice of an idea or concept to study may, at times, be frustrating, what becomes more frustrating is choosing a topic, and finding either too little or too much information available in the current literature. Neither of these situations should prevent the individual from conducting the research. However, they do make it more difficult to support the need to do so. There is usually a substantial amount of literature to support most topics one might wish to research in criminal justice and criminology. With the extensive number of journals currently available, data from government agencies, and Internet access to information, one can usually collect enough information to support a research effort.

Ultimately, the best way to begin a research effort is to focus on a particular issue, phenomenon, or problem that most interests the individual. In doing so, one must be sure to (1) determine what the problem, issue, or phenomenon is, and (2) organize what is known about it. This is where a literature search and review is valuable, and the best place to begin the search is the library.

Box 3-1
Possible Research Topics

---

1. Examine the role of criminal justice programs in a given state.
2. Survey education and job satisfaction among police, parole, or correctional officers.
3. Compare and contrast criminal justice educators: practitioner-academic vs. pure academic and their work products.
4. Evaluate the relationships between job stress and race/ethnicity.
5. Explore the causes and extent of criminality among high school students.
6. Conduct a cost-benefit analysis of private versus state prisons.
7. Research drug usage among adolescents.
8. Evaluate the success of electronic monitoring.
9. Evaluate the effectiveness of community policing.
10. Survey public attitudes toward corporal punishment.

Become Familiar with the Library

A first step in conducting a search of the literature is to familiarize oneself with your nearest library. As a criminal justice/criminology student, you should have access to a good library. If not, find out how far it is to a better library and make arrangements to go there. Too frequently students try to use the excuse that "it was not in our library" after a brief perusal of the texts and journals that are available. That is not an acceptable excuse. As an individual who is capable of thinking critically you are expected to solve problems regarding the availability of resources, not to just bemoan them. Familiarize yourself with the layout of your particular library, the search vehicles that are available, and get to know the librarians. You may find that there are many more resources available to you than you had imagined.

Text/Journal Abstracts

Literature or topical searches can start with the use of a source called an abstract. Two popular abstracts are the Sociological and Criminal Justice abstracts. With these sources the researcher can look for a particular term (a key word or words, such as job satisfaction), concept, or topic to see what has already been published about this subject.

Scholarly Journals

From the abstracts one can go directly to identified journals. Scholarly journals are refereed (meaning that to be published the article appearing in the journal had to pass review by other scholars who were asked by the journal to critique its contents). How critiques are conducted will be discussed in a following section. The findings from a perusal of journal articles may not only help you determine a topic but guide you in your research.

Textbooks

For research purposes introductory-level texts are generally not of sufficient depth to use as sources in your research. It is better to build from them by going to the sources that they cite within a subject area or to rely on texts devoted to the subject in question. However, they are often excellent starting sources for selecting a research topic. If you are assigned a research project for a certain class, review the contents of the text that is being used in that class to determine if something of personal interest may be revealed.

Social Science Indexes

Annual indexes for journals are another source of information. Today, journals are available on microfiche, as hard copy, or "on-line." Government documents and the Internet are additional sources for helping choose a topic or gathering information to support the research topic.

Internet Searches

A word of caution is appropriate regarding the use of the Internet. While it is useful for gaining preliminary information about a topic, it does not replace conducting a solid literature review of the subject area. For all its convenience, the Internet has a great deal of information that is unsubstantiated, if not outright erroneous. If the source is not clearly scholarly (such as a reputable on-line journal) be cautious about using it as a research reference. The Internet augments the library and social science indexes and/or abstracts as search vehicles; it does not replace them. Nor does it replace journals and textbooks. While the Internet may provide legitimate sources, a reference page filled with numerous web sites instead of text and journal citations is indicative of lazy scholarship on the part of the researcher.

Overall, there are a number of sources from which one can choose a topic or find support for a given topic. (Box 3-2 provides a sampling of refereed journals that publish articles in criminology and/or criminal justice. This is not intended to be viewed as an exhaustive listing). Once a literature search is completed, the research question(s) can be formulated.

Box 3-2
Literature Review: Examples of Sources

Journals
American Journal of Criminal Justice
American Journal of Sociology
British Journal of Criminology
Canadian Journal of Criminology
Crime and Delinquency
Criminal Justice Policy Review
Criminology
Justice Quarterly
Journal of Criminal Justice
Journal of Contemporary Criminal Justice
Police Quarterly
Prison Journal
Social Justice
Social Forces
Social Problems
Social Science Quarterly

Compendiums
Abstracts on Criminology and Penology
Criminal Justice Abstracts
Police Science Abstracts
Psychological Abstracts
Sociological Abstracts
Social Science Index

Government Agencies
Bureau of Justice Statistics
National Criminal Justice Reference Service (NCJRS)
www.ncjrs.org
National Institute of Justice
www.ojp.usdoj.gov/nij

Critiquing the Literature

In order to conduct a sound literature review (whether as a topical search or in developing the scholarly basis for the research that you are conducting) you must be able to properly interpret the research that you are reading. In this section we shall give you some guidance as to what to look for in evaluating other studies. These guidelines will also be helpful in preparing your own work for others to review. We shall provide more detail in a later chapter on preparing your work for submission.

Understanding Writing Styles

Scholarly journals and textbooks conform to specific writing styles. The various styles are precisely detailed in publication manuals. In criminal justice and criminology you will find that several styles are utilized. At some point in your research you may view Turabian (which uses numbers to indicate citations and footnotes at the bottom of each page); Chicago Style (also uses numbers after citations with endnotes instead of footnotes); American Psychological Association—APA (the most commonly used style in criminal justice/criminology; lists the author and year of publication within the text); and American Sociological Association—ASA (similar to APA but may use endnotes for specific details and varies in the format of the references). Occasionally you may also see MLA—Modern Languages Association style as well as styles unique to specific law or criminal justice journals (these are often variations of the above styles). It is important to know what style is utilized when critiquing an article or text and even more important to know what style is required when submitting a paper, article or text for review. For example, the authors require their students to submit all papers in APA format. The best way to become familiar with this format is through the APA stylebook.

Knowing What to Look For

In critiquing another's work there are a number of things that you should look for. The following guidelines are recommended (Babbie, 1998, p. 461-465 and Brown and Curtis, 1987, p. 14-17).

1. Synopsis of Article

This is nothing more than a brief overview of the article. What is the social issue that was studied? How was it investigated: exploration, description, explanation or a combination of strategies? Who conducted the research? Who financed it (and is there a conflict of interest)? Was it well written and well organized, and did it have clarity of purpose? Were the findings reasonable based upon the research design? What were the conclusions and recommendations?

2. Clarity of Problem Statement

What was the problem being investigated? Did the literature review support the need for this research? What was the theoretical orientation? What was/were the research hypothesis(es)? Were concepts properly defined? Were the dependent and independent variables identified?

3. The Literature Review

Did the literature review provide a thorough coverage of the prior research? Were previous studies adequately evaluated and discussed? Was the coverage complete (classic studies relevant to the research problem included as well as recent research)? Did the literature cited provide a justification for the current investigation?

4. Methodology Used

What was the research design? Was it clearly developed from the theoretical frame of reference alluded to in the problem statement? Who were the subjects and how were they included in the study? Did the study conform to ethical standards? What was the sampling method and was it adequate for this research? Was the measurement instrument/strategy satisfactory? How were the data analyzed? Were there any adverse effects or limitations due to the research design and the means of analysis being incompatible? Were measures of association and tests of significance clearly indicated and appropriately discussed? Were the measurement techniques valid and reliable?

5. Findings

Were the findings displayed in a concise and readily understandable manner? How were the data summarized? Were the tables logical and clear? Were the statistical techniques appropriate? Would other statistical techniques have been more appropriate? Did the findings relate to the problem, the method, and/or the theoretical framework? How did the findings relate to those of the prior research?

6. Discussion and Conclusions

Are the conclusions reached consistent with the findings that were presented? Are the conclusions compatible with the theoretical orientation presented in the problem statement? Based upon the problem statement, the prior research, the methodology, and the findings, do the conclusions and/or recommendations make sense? Based upon the problem statement and the literature are the conclusions and/or recommendations of this study a significant contribution to the field of study?

The Research Question

Once a topic has been chosen, the next step is to create the research question(s). The research question is a statement answered through the research process. Its focus, which must be clearly stated, should inform readers of the actual purpose of the research.

The research question may be synonymous with the research problem. Essentially what the researcher must do is decide what it is he or she is to study and why. It is the "Why" that helps form the research question.

Methodological Link

A 1995 study of students' perceptions of policing and the change of perceptions after completing a college course on policing was conducted. Those findings, while indicating that the course did make a difference, also led to several new research questions. In an attempt to answer these questions, Dantzker and Waters (1999) conducted a follow-up study that focused on the following research questions:

1. Was it the course that influenced the change or simply the passing of time?
2. Would students in non-police classes (other criminal justice topics or non-criminal justice) have a different perception of policing than those in police classes?
3. How would completion of these courses affect students' perceptions?

The research question(s) should allow others to gain a clear understanding of why the research was conducted. A well-worded research question should give some indication of the outcomes one might expect at the conclusion of the research.

After establishing the research question(s), the researcher must next explain what specifically is going to be studied and the expected results. This is usually accomplished through statements or propositions referred to as hypotheses.

Hypotheses

A hypothesis is *a specific statement describing the expected result or relationship between the independent and dependent variables.* The development of hypotheses and their linkages with theory and research will be discussed further in Chapter 4. The three most common types are:

1. the research hypothesis, which is a statement of the expected relationship between variables offered in a positive manner,
2. the null hypothesis, which is a statement that the relationship or difference being tested does not exist, and
3. the rival hypothesis, which is a statement offering an alternate explanation for the research findings.

The research hypothesis, which is the most common of the hypotheses, is generally a statement that fits the equation, If "X" then "Y." An example is "If there is an increase in the number of patrol units in a given area, the amount of reported crime increases." Note that the statement suggests a relationship between two variables, patrol units and reported crime, in a manner indicating the belief that more patrol cars will cause there to be more crime reported. Therefore, the research would focus on examining this relationship in an effort to disprove the null hypothesis.

The null hypothesis fits the equation, "X" has no relationship with "Y." For the previous research hypothesis, the null hypothesis would read "The increase in patrol units will not increase the amount of reported crime (no relationship exists)." A successful research effort will disprove this, which in essence supports the research effort.

What if the increase in patrol units decreases the amount of reported crime? This would lead to the rival hypothesis that fits an equation, in the above circumstance, of the more of "X" the less of "Y." Again, although the general research goal is to support the research hypothesis by disproving the null hypothesis, one should not consider the inability to disprove the null hypothesis as a failure. On the contrary, the failure to support the null hypothesis may actually lead to new information or additional research not previously known or conducted.

Methodological Link

To respond to the research question in the previous Methodological Link, Dantzker and Waters (1999) offered the following research hypotheses:

1. Students in criminal justice courses would have a more positive perception of policing than students in a non-criminal justice course.
2. There will be a change in students' perceptions at the end of such courses where criminal justice students' perceptions will remain more positive than the non-criminal justice students' perceptions.

Whether it is the research, null, or rival hypothesis, it must be clearly stated and consist of readily identifiable variables. Variables are factors that can change or influence change. They result from the operationalization of a concept. The two types of variables are:

1. The *dependent* variable(s), which is/are the factor(s) being influenced to change over which the researcher has no controls. Basically, the dependent variable(s) is/are the outcome item(s) or what is being predicted.
2. The *independent* variable(s), which is/are the factor(s) that will influence or predict the outcome of the dependent variable. This variable is something the researcher can control.

If one were measuring attitudes, perceptions or beliefs, these would be dependent variables because the researcher has no control over their outcome and they may be influenced by the independent variables. From the students' perceptions of policing research, the main independent variable was the course taken. Other independent variables included age, gender, ethnicity, and college major. The dependent variables were created from the perceptual statements (See Box 3-3).

Ultimately, the researcher is going to want to be sure to properly identify the variables, because misidentification can cause the research to be useless. A better understanding of variables will occur during a later discussion on measurement.

Box 3-3

Statements Used to Form Dependent Variables (Dantzker and Waters, 1999)

1. Although police officers are often called upon to do a variety of tasks, their primary role is crime fighter.

2. Most police officers do not solve more crimes because they are incompetent.

3. The motto "To Protect and Serve" is merely a public relations concept and has nothing to do with what police officers actually do.

4. At some point in their careers, all police officers commit a corrupt act.

5. Police officers are quicker to physically strike a minority group member than a white person.

6. Ignoring the needs of citizens is a common action of police officers.

7. Preventing crimes for rich white people is more important to police officers than solving crimes for or assisting any ethnic or cultural group member.

8. Police officers are only out to hurt or harass people instead of being out to help them.

9. A problem people have with police officers is that they know police are always out there, but they never know what to expect from them.

10. Many individuals who become police officers want to help society.

11. Any time you see a police officer you should try to avoid having contact with him or her.

12. The reason police officers are still primarily white males is because of politics, discrimination, and the "good old boy" system of recruitment.

13. Police officers who take drugs or drink on duty should be immediately fired instead of being offered counseling or other assistance.

14. No matter what the circumstances, if a police officer violates an individual's constitutional rights s/he should be held accountable.

Summary

Prior to starting any research effort, a topic must be chosen, keeping in mind that the research effort can explore, describe, or explain. This topic should be of interest, relevant, and have support in the literature through journals, government documents, or the Internet.

Upon choosing the topic, the research question is created, which advises others what is to be studied. From the research question comes the hypothesis(es), a statement that indicates the nature of the relationship to be studied. The three main types of hypotheses are the research, null, and rival. The goal is to disprove the null hypothesis.

Finally, for the hypothesis(es) clearly identifiable variables are required. Two types of variables are the dependent, which cannot be controlled by the researcher, and independent, which can be controlled. Failure to clarify the variables could render the research useless.

Methodological Queries:

From the following brief literature review,[1]

   (1) What are three possible research topics?
   (2) What is the hypothesis(es) for each?
   (3) What might be the null and rival hypotheses for each?
   (4) What are the possible variables?

Since the early 1900s, when Chief August Vollmer of the Berkeley, California, Police Department hired the first college-educated individual as a police officer, the value of a college degree for police officers has been debated. It was Chief Vollmer's belief that a college-educated police officer would perform more effectively and efficiently than the non-college educated officer.

In the past twenty years both our society and law enforcement have experienced many changes (Elliot, 1973; Bayley, 1977; Heaphy, 1978; Cohn, 1978; Becker and Whitehouse, 1979; Saunders, 1985). These changes are especially apparent in the area of education (More, 1985). Our society has increased the educational level of its citizenry by several years and continues to advance (Digest of Education Statistics, 1987). This same trend has not been as apparent in law enforcement (Statistical Abstract of the U.S., 1987). A much-debated topic among criminal justice practitioners and academicians is whether or not higher education, particularly a college degree, has become a necessity for today's police officer (Dailey, 1975; Finckenauer, 1975; Cascio, 1977, Dantzker, 1986b; Lynch, 1986; Scott, 1986).

---

[1]This literature review was written by one of the authors many years ago to use as a research problem example. The sources cited are real but the full citations are not provided here for purposes of efficiency.

Dr. Gerald Lynch, president of John Jay College of Criminal Justice provided the following observations on college education and policing:

> Police officers not only must understand the legal issues in their work, but also must understand human nature, the social problems they confront daily, and the thinking of those whose attitudes toward the law are different from their own. College education, regardless of the area of study, can crystallize and substitute raw experience, enlighten prejudice, and heighten tolerance for ambiguity (1986, p. 11).

Finckenauer (1975) advised that college-educated police officers seemed to respond differently from their non-college colleagues in certain discretionary situations. He found that the college-educated police officer was less likely to advocate invoking the criminal process to solve a given situation. The college-educated police officer would attempt to use all other options available before relying on arrest powers.

Cascio (1977) found that formal higher education in police officers could be associated with fewer injuries, physical confrontations, disciplinary actions from accidents, and sick times per year. He further found that officers with a higher level of formal education received fewer complaints related to brutality allegations. However, he also observed that little positive association could be found in behaviorally related indicators such as job knowledge, judgment, initiative, dependability, demeanor, and attitude.

References

Babbie, E. (1998). *The Practice of Social Research, Eighth Edition.* Belmont, CA: Wadsworth Publishing.

Berg, B.L. (1998). *Qualitative Research Methods for the Social Sciences (3rd Ed.).* Boston: Allyn and Bacon.

Brown, S. E. and Curtis, J. H. (1987). *Fundamentals of Criminal Justice Research.* Cincinnati, OH: Pilgrimage.

Dantzker, M. L. (1989). The effect of education on police performance: The education perspective. Ann Arbor, MI: University Microfilms International.

Dantzker, M. L. and Waters, J. E. (1999). Examining students' perceptions of policing:—A pre- and post-comparison between students in criminal justice and non-criminal justice courses. In M. L. Dantzker (Ed.), *Readings for Research Methods in Criminology and Criminal Justice,* pp. 27-36. Woburn, MA.: Butterworth-Heinemann.

Eck, J. E. and La Vigne, N. G. (1994). *Using Research: A Primer for Law Enforcement Managers (2nd ed.).* Washington, D.C.: Police Executive Research Forum.

Fitzgerald, J. D. and Cox, S. M. (1998). *Research Methods in Criminal Justice: An Introduction, Second Edition.* Chicago: Nelson-Hall Publishers.

Guy, R. F., Edgley, C. E., Arafat, I., and Allen, D. E. (1987). *Social Research Methods.* Boston, MA: Allyn and Bacon, Inc.

Hagan, F. (1993). *Research Methods in Criminal Justice and Criminology (3rd Ed.).* New York: Macmillan Publishing Company.

Senese, J. D. (1997). *Applied Research Methods in Criminal Justice.* Chicago: Nelson-Hall Publishers.

Singleton, Jr., R., Straits, B. C., Straits, M. M., and McAllister, R. J. (1988*). Approaches to Social Research.* New York: Oxford University Press.

The Language of Research

■ **Vignette 4-1**
Terminology??

Still pondering the instructor's comments about research papers, you remain puzzled. In many previous classes you have been asked to write a research paper and now you are being told you have never written one. You raise your hand. When called upon, you ask, "What do you mean that we have never written a research paper? I know I have written several." The instructor acknowledges expecting this query. Yet the response is not what you expected. Your instructor asks, "Have you ever studied a foreign language?" You reply that you took a few years of Spanish in high school. The instructor then asks whether you recall a word or words that have a specific meaning, yet are often used more broadly? When you reply positively, the instructor says that is what is happening here with the word *research*. It is quite common for students and teachers alike to use the term *research* to describe a paper assignment that is actually a literature review. The instructor goes on to explain that with the conducting of research comes a language that one must understand before one can proceed with the research. One might call this language researchese.

■ **CHAPTER 4**
Learning Objectives

After studying this chapter the student should be able to:

1. Define theory and explain how it relates to research.
2. Describe the conceptualization process.
3. Describe what takes place during operationalization.

4. Define what a variable is. Discuss how dependent and independent variables differ from one another.
5. Describe what a hypothesis is and how it differs from an assumption. Present and discuss the types of hypotheses.
6. Identify a population and discuss how it is related to a sample. Provide examples of some different types of samples.
7. Define validity and describe the various types of validity.
8. Define reliability. Explain how it relates to validity.
9. Describe what data are. Describe the four levels of data.
10. Discuss the steps in the research process.

The Language of Research

It is quite common for students and teachers alike to use the term *research* to describe a paper assignment that is actually a literature review. As previously noted, with respect to criminal justice and criminology there is more to research than reviewing literature. This synonymous use of the term research is just one example of the need to understand associated language. In Chapter 1, the term *research* was defined. In this chapter, various associated terms, such as *theory, hypothesis,* and *variable,* will be defined or further expanded upon.

Theory

There is an interesting debate one could have regarding the term *theory,* which is reminiscent of the age-old argument: Which came first, the chicken or the egg? With respect to theory, one side of the debate argues that theories drive the research (theory-then-research) or deductive logic. The other side would argue that research creates the theory (research-then-theory) (Berg, 1998) or inductive logic (see Figure 4-1).

In reality, as noted earlier (Chapter 1), the two types of logic are actually extensions of one another. Observation may lead to theory construction, which then leads to more observation in order to test the theory. Therefore, even research that is initially inductive in nature, ultimately becomes deductive in that the theory that is generated is tested by observation. In short, all criminal justice practice is grounded in criminological theory. Theory is defined here as *an explanation that offers to classify, organize, explain, predict, and/or understand the occurrence of specific phenomena.*

Based on the definition, a theory is a statement that attempts to make sense of reality. Reality consists of those phenomena that we can identify, recognize, and observe. For example, in criminology, criminal behavior is observed. Therefore, people breaking the law are a reality. A question that arises from this reality is, what causes people to break the law? It is here that theory comes into the picture.

The Language of Research 59

Criminology is replete with theories about criminal behavior that focus on causes that include biological, psychological, and sociological factors (see Box 4-1).

Whether theories have any merit or are truly applicable is why research is conducted. Proving that a theory is valid is a common goal of criminological and criminal justice researchers. However, in order to research a theory, the first step is to focus on a concept.

Box 4-1
Examples of Theories in Criminology

Biological
   (1)   A person's physique is correlated to the type of crime one commits.
   (2)   Criminality is genetic.
   (3)   A chemical imbalance in one's brain can lead to criminal behavior.

Psychological
   (1)   Criminal behavior is the result of an inadequately developed ego.
   (2)   Inadequate moral development during childhood leads to criminal behavior.
   (3)   Criminals learn their behavior by modeling their behavior after other criminals.

Sociological
   (1)   Socializing with criminals produces criminal behavior.
   (2)   Society's labeling of an individual as deviant or criminal breeds criminality.
   (3)   Failure to reach societal goals through acceptable means leads to criminality.

Theory-then-research	Research-then-theory
Theory =	Investigation +
Construction +	Measurement +
Selection +	Analysis +
Design +	Acceptance =
Reject/Accept	Theory

Figure 4-1 Theory Debate Models

Conceptualization

A concept is best defined as an *abstract label that represents an aspect of reality (usually in the form of an object, policy, issue, problem, or phenomena).* Every discipline has its own concepts. For example, in criminal justice and criminology some concepts include criminality, law, rehabilitation, and punishment.

Concepts are viewed as the beginning point for all research endeavors and are often very broad in nature. They are the bases of theories and serve as a means to communicate, introduce, classify, and build thoughts and ideas. To conduct research, the concept must first be taken from its conceptual or theoretical level to an observational level. In other words, one must go from the abstract to the concrete before research can occur. This process is often referred to as conceptualization. As with the definition of theory, there is more than one way to approach conceptualization. This text promotes the two-phase (theory and research levels), five-stage (conceptual level, conceptual components, conceptual definitions, operational definitions, and observational level) approach (Nachmias and Nachmias, 1987) (see Figure 4-2). In most research it is seldom specified just how the concept reaches its researchable position. This can cause readers to have problems in understanding what is being researched and why. Therefore, it is often helpful when the researcher can offer readers a clearer picture of the conceptualization of the topic.

Methodological Link

Seldom will researchers report how they conceptualized their concept. When they do, it provides a better understanding of the research. From the following excerpt, can you fit the pieces into the first phase, theoretical, of the conceptualization model?

Community empowerment is a concept used to describe individuals living in close proximity who as a group unite to combat a common problem. The focus of the group is the common problem. If a community is to be empowered, the residents must first be aware that a problem exists (community awareness) to such an extent that it is disturbing or troubling (community concern), resulting in organization of the community (community mobilization) to fight against it (community action). (Moriarty, 1999, p. 17)

To achieve the second part of the conceptualization model, the research phase, the concepts must now be measured. Although concepts can be qualitative, they are most often converted into variables through a process called operationalization.

Operationalization

The act of operationalizing is the describing of how a concept is measured. This process is best described as *the conversion of the abstract idea*

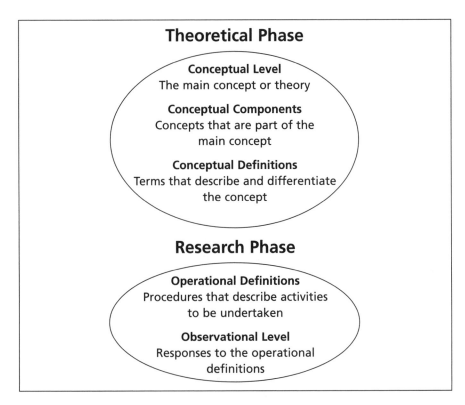

Figure 4-2 Conceptualization Process Model

or notion into a measurable item. In other words, it is the taking of something that is conceptual and making it observable, or going from abstract to concrete.

Operationalization is one of the more important tasks prior to conducting any research. Furthermore, there is no one right way. How this is accomplished is up to the researcher. Yet, it is common for researchers to publish their results without ever explaining how their concepts were operationalized. This shortcoming has made it difficult for many students to fully comprehend the notions of conceptualizing and operationalizing variables. Therefore, when research is conducted that focuses on these two terms, it can be quite useful.

Methodological Link

The following excerpt shows how a concept is operationalized.
Community awareness was conceptualized as the level of knowledge about the use of alcohol and other drugs in the community. Four variables reflected community awareness: drug usage in the neighborhood; drug dealing in the neighborhood; alcohol/drug prevention messages;

(continued on next page)

Methodological Link (continued)

and availability of certain drugs (eight different drugs in all). The following are the actual questions used to establish each variable:

- *Drug usage in the neighborhood:* Respondents were asked, "How many people in this neighborhood use drugs?" Responses included "many, some, not many or no residents use drugs."
- *Drug dealing in the neighborhood:* Respondents were asked, "How often do you see drug dealing in this neighborhood?" The responses included "very often, sometimes, rarely, never."
- *Alcohol/drug prevention message:* Respondents were asked if they had heard or seen any drug or alcohol prevention messages in the past six months.
- *Availability of certain drugs:* Respondents were asked about the difficulty or ease of obtaining specific drugs in the county. The list of drugs included marijuana, crack cocaine, other forms of cocaine, heroin, other narcotics (methadone, opium, codeine, paregoric), tranquilizers, barbiturates, amphetamines, LSD. Each drug availability represents one variable. (Moriarty, 1999, p. 18)

Variables

The primary focus of the operationalization process is the creation of variables and subsequently developing a measurement instrument to assess those variables. Variables are concepts that may be divided into two or more categories or groupings known as attributes. This ability enables us to study their relationships with other variables. Attributes are the grouping into which variables may be divided. As an example, "male" is an attribute of the variable "gender." There are two types of variables: dependent and independent.

Dependent Variables

A dependent variable is a factor that requires other factors to cause or influence change. They are factors over which the researcher has no controls. Basically the dependent variable is the outcome factor or that which is being predicted. In criminal justice and criminology, criminal behavior is a dependent variable because it requires other factors for it to exist or change. These other factors are the independent variables.

Independent Variables

The independent variable is the influential or the predictor factor. These are the variables believed to cause the change or outcome of the dependent variable and are something the researcher can control. Some better-known independent variables used in criminal justice and criminological research are gender, race, marital status, and education.

Identifying and recognizing the difference between the variables is important in research, but sometimes may get lost. Therefore, when research specifically calls attention to the variables, it can be quite informative.

Methodological Link

Researching attitudes among different criminal justice practitioners is popular. Gordon (1999) looked at the attitudes of correctional officers toward delinquents and delinquency and whether the type of institution they work in made a difference. In describing the research, she is clear as to the variables used and how they are measured. This makes the finding much easier to understand (see Box 4-2).

Box 4-2
Variables and Measurement

VARIABLE	MEASUREMENT
Dependent Variables	
PUNITIVENESS	Examines attitudes toward punitiveness.
	Higher scores indicate disagreement with punitiveness as a means to reduce crime. Range 3–12, Mean 6.38.
DELINQUENCY	Examines attitudes toward delinquency. Higher scores indicate disagreement that crime is a *result* of environmental and opportunity factors. Range 3–12, Mean 7.49.
TREATMENT	Examines attitudes toward treatment of youth*. Higher scores indicate disagreement with the ability of "treatment" programs to change offenders' behaviors. Range 4–16, Mean 10.34.
Independent Variables	
FACILITY	0 = Open-Security, 1 = Closed-Security
AGE	In years
GENDER	0 = Female, 1 = Male
RACE	0 = White, 1 = Non-White
EDUCATION	0 = Less than High School, 1 = High School, 2 = Some College, 3 = Bachelor Degree, 4 = Graduate Degree
LENGTH AT CURRENT POSITION	In months

The key to any research is to be able to operationalize the concepts into understandable and measurable variables. Failing to complete this task will make the creation and testing of the hypothesis(es) more difficult.

Hypotheses

Once the concept has been operationalized into variables fitting the theory in question, most research focuses on testing the validity of statement(s) called hypothesis(es). The hypothesis is *a specific statement describing the expected relationship between the independent and dependent variables.* As previously discussed, there are three common types of hypotheses: research, null, and rival.

Research Hypothesis

The foundation of a research project is the research hypothesis. This is a statement of the expected relationship between the dependent and independent variables. The statement may be specified as either a positive (as one increases, the other increases) or as a negative (as one increases, the other decreases) relationship.

Methodological Link

Again referring to Gordon's study of correctional attitudes, her hypotheses are clearly stated so that readers know exactly what she is attempting to discover. The three hypotheses examined are:

1. Correctional officers from the open-security facility are less likely to agree that punishing offenders reduces crime than correctional officers at the closed-security facility.

2. Correctional officers from the open-security facility are less likely to agree that crime is a result of environmental/opportunity factors than correctional officers at the closed-security facility.

3. Correctional officers from the open-security facility are more likely to agree that the treatment of offenders can produce change than the correctional officers at the closed-security facility. (1999, p. 89)

Null Hypothesis

Some would argue that the results of the research should support the research hypothesis(es). Others will claim that the goal is to disprove the null hypothesis(es), which is a statement indicating that no relationship exists between the dependent and independent variables.

EXAMPLE

The null hypotheses from Gordon's study could be:

1. the type of institution will have no effect on correctional officers' belief that punishing offenders reduces crime;
2. the type of institution will have no effect on correctional officers' belief that crime is a result of environmental or opportunity factors; and
3. The type of institution will have no effect on correctional officers' belief that the treatment of offenders can produce change.

   By rejecting the null hypotheses, the research goal has been fulfilled. However, rejecting the null hypothesis(es) does not necessarily mean that the results have established the validity of the research hypothesis(es).

Rival Hypothesis

Prior to starting the research it is customary to establish the research hypothesis, which is generally what the researcher hopes to validate or demonstrate. However, sometimes the results may reject both the null hypothesis and the research hypothesis. This allows for the creation of what is called a rival hypothesis. The rival hypothesis is a statement offering an alternate prediction for the research findings. Assume that in Gordon's study the findings were not what she expected or hoped for, instead finding that the difference was opposite. Her rival hypotheses would then be:

1. Correctional officers from the open-security facility are *more* likely to agree that punishing offenders reduces crime than correctional officers at the closed-security facility.
2. Correctional officers from the open-security facility are *more* likely to agree that crime is a result of environmental/opportunity factors than correctional officers at the closed-security facility.
3. Correctional officers from the open-security facility are *less* likely to agree that the treatment of offenders can produce change than the correctional officers at the closed-security facility.

It is usually the goal of the research to be able to reject the null hypothesis. Testing the research hypothesis becomes central to the research, making identifying the hypothesis(es) an important aspect of the research. Yet, while hypotheses often take center stage in research, there is another type of statement that can find its way into the research:

assumptions. However, these types of statements should be avoided whenever possible.

Assumptions

Hypotheses are educated guesses about the relationship between variables, and must be proven by the research. An assumption is a *statement accepted as true with little supporting evidence.* From a research perspective, assumptions are problematic. It is expected that with statements of inquiry or fact that there be research to substantiate it. Fortunately, assumptions can often lead to research. For example, because of the believed natural caring instincts of women, an assumption might be made that women would make better police officers than males. Since there is little evidence to validate this assumption, and it would not be a readily accepted statement, at least among males, there would be a need to research this assumption. In this situation, the researcher could move beyond the untestable assumption that women would be better officers because they are more caring by converting it into hypotheses that can be tested. Variables could be created to measure what is meant by caring and what is meant by officer performance.

Theory, concept, operationalize, variable, hypothesis, and *assumption* are all key words in the language of research. Still, they are just the building blocks and causes for other words with which one should be familiar.

Other Necessary Terms

There are many other terms a student should be familiar with before undertaking a research effort. Because these remaining terms are covered in greater detail in later chapters, only a brief definition will be offered, but in the same context as previous definitions.

Once the researcher has managed to conceptualize and operationalize his/her research it is then time to choose who will be targeted to respond to the dependent variables. A unit of analysis is the level at which the researcher will focus his/her attention. It could be individuals, groups, communities, or even entire societies depending upon the nature of the research. The researcher then selects (draws samples) from the population that is being studied.

Population

A population is *the complete group or class from which information is to be gathered.* For example, police officers, probation officers, and correctional officers are each a population. While it would be great if every member of a population could provide the information sought, it is usually logistically impractical in that it would be both inefficient and wasteful of the researcher's time and resources. Therefore, most researchers choose to obtain a sample from the targeted population.

Sample

A sample is *a group chosen from within a target population to provide information sought.* Choosing this group is referred to as sampling, and may take one of several forms. Sampling is important enough to warrant an entire chapter of its own later in the text. Some examples of samples follow.

Random: A random sample is one in which all members of a given population had the same chances of being selected. Furthermore, the selection of each member must be independent from the selection of any other members.

Stratified Random: This is a sample that has been chosen from a population that has been divided into subgroups called *strata.* The sample is comprised equally of members representing each stratum.

Cluster: The sample is comprised of randomly selected groups, rather than individuals.

Snowball: This sample begins with a person or persons who provide names of other persons for the sample.

Purposive: Individuals are chosen to provide information based on the researcher's belief that they will provide the necessary information. This type of sample is also known as a judgmental or convenience sample.

Once the sample has been identified, the information is collected. The various collection techniques will be covered in detail in a later chapter. In collecting this information two concerns for the researcher are the validity and the reliability of the data collection device.

Validity

Validity is a term describing whether the measure used accurately represents the concept it is meant to measure. There are four types of validity: face, content, construct, and criterion. There are some individuals who will also offer validity as internal (truthfulness of the findings with respect to the individuals in the sample), and external (truthfulness of the findings with respect to individuals not in the sample).

Face Validity

This is the simplest form of validity and basically refers to whether the measuring device appears, on its face, to measure what the researcher wants to measure. This is primarily a judgmental decision.

Content Validity

Each item of the measuring device is examined to determine whether the element measures the concept in question.

Construct Validity

This validity inquires as to whether the measuring device does indeed measure what it has been designed to measure. It refers to the fit between theoretical and operational definitions of the concept.

Criterion (or Pragmatic) Validity

This type of validity represents the degree to which the measure relates to external criterion. It can either be concurrent (does the measure enhance the ability to assess the current characteristics of the concept under study?) and predictive (the ability to accurately foretell future events or conditions).

Reliability

Reliability refers to how consistent the measuring device would be over time. In other words, if the study is replicated, will the measuring device provide consistent results? The two key components of reliability are stability and consistency. Stability means the ability to retain accuracy and resist change. Consistency is the ability to yield similar results when replicated.

Having established the validity and reliability of the measuring device, the sample can now be approached for information. The information gathered is known as data.

Data

Data are simply pieces of information gathered from the sample that describe events, beliefs, characteristics, people, or other phenomena. This data may exist at one of four levels: nominal, ordinal, interval, and ratio.

Nominal Data

This level data are categorical based on some defined characteristic. The categories are exclusive and have no logical order. For example, gender is a nominal level data form.

Ordinal Data

Ordinal data are categorical, too, but their characteristics may be rank-ordered. These data categories are also exclusive but are scaled in a manner representative of the amount of characteristics in question, along some dimension. For example, types of prisons may be broken down into the categories of minimum, medium, and maximum.

Interval Data

Categorical data for which there is a distinctive, yet equal, difference among the characteristics measured are interval data. The categories have order and represent equal units on a scale with no set zero starting point (for example, the IQ of prisoners).

Ratio Data

This type of data is ordered, has equal units of distance, and a true zero starting point (for example, age, weight, income).

As the text continues, other terms will be introduced and defined. Because a sufficient number of terms have been introduced, it is now possible to review the research process in a researchese manner.

The Research Process

Having been introduced to research and its language, the last item to be offered in this chapter is a model of the research process through terminology. This model begins with a theory usually identifying some concept. The concept is then conceptualized and operationalized creating dependent variables. Completing the identification of both the independent and dependent variables leads then to developing the hypothesis(es). Finally, a sample is chosen, measurement or information is gathered from the sample, the information is converted into the proper data for analysis, and the results are reported (see Figure 4-3). This process will become functionally clearer as the text progresses.

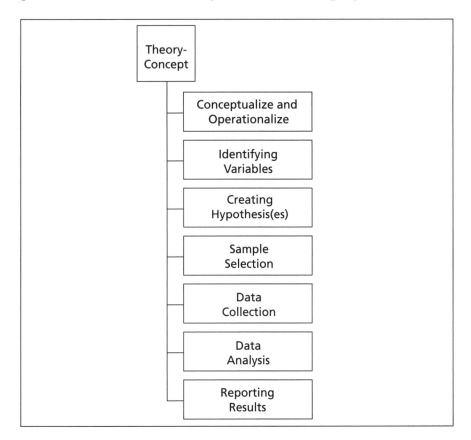

Figure 4-3 The Research Process

Summary

Becoming proficient in research requires knowing the language. Several terms have been introduced that are important to mastering research as a language. The main terms include theory, concept, operationalize, variables, hypothesis, and sample. There are two types of variables: independent and dependent. A sample may be random, stratified, clustered, snowball, or purposive. Other terms are validity (face, content, construct, and criterion), reliability, and data (nominal, ordinal, interval, and ratio). With knowledge of these terms, the research process can be taken to another level.

Methodological Queries:

(1) Taking both sides of the debate about theory, how would you apply the definition of theory to this statement: crime is a direct result of poverty?

(2) How would you convert or operationalize the following concepts: professionalism, stress, and ethnicity?

(3) What are the null hypotheses for the three research hypotheses offered in the Methodological Link?

(4) Covert this assumption into a hypothesis: Due to the natural caring instincts of women, they will make better police officers.

(5) How would you demonstrate the research process using turnover rate of federal probation officers as the concept under study?

References

Gordon, J. (1999). Correctional officers' attitudes toward delinquents and delinquency: Does the type of institution make a difference? In M.L. Dantzker (Ed.), *Readings for Research Methods in Criminology and Criminal Justice*, pp. 85-98. Woburn, MA: Butterworth-Heinemann.

Moriarty, L.J. (1999). The conceptualization and operationalization of the intervening dimensions of social disorganization. In M.L. Dantzker (Ed.), *Readings for Research Methods in Criminology and Criminal Justice*, pp. 15-26. Woburn, MA: Butterworth-Heinemann.

Nachmias, D. and Nachmias, C. (1987). *Research Methods in the Social Sciences*. New York: St. Martin's Press.

PART III

Research Design

Qualitative Research

◼ Vignette 5-1
Must It Always Be a Question of Numbers?

As a student worker, you spend more time around the departmental office than you really care to, but it is how you earn that extra spending money. Furthermore, it can have its perks, such as becoming better acquainted with professors and learning more about criminal justice and criminology than you might just sitting in a classroom. There is also the downside, like hearing a couple of professors arguing over what type of research is more acceptable, qualitative or quantitative. You have heard this debate on a couple of occasions but never really paid much attention before. Now that you are taking the research methods course, however, the debate piques your interest.

The professor arguing in favor of quantitative research proclaims to be a socio-criminologist schooled in some strong theoretical, yet numbers-oriented background. The other professor is an ex-practitioner whose Ph.D. is in criminal justice, but claims to have come from a program that favored qualitative work. The debate, as usual, is about which form of research is more appropriate to criminal justice, especially as its continues its drive toward being accepted as a pure social science. Both professors appear to be making reasonable arguments for their positions. Still, you are not sure who is right, if either. Perhaps it will become clearer after this debate is discussed in your research methods course.

■ **CHAPTER 5**
Learning Objectives

After studying this chapter the student should be able to:

1. Compare and contrast quantitative and qualitative research.
2. Define qualitative research.
3. Discuss the strengths and weaknesses of qualitative research.
4. Explain how qualitative research differs from a literature review.
5. Describe the types of field interviews and give examples.
6. Describe the different roles that may be utilized in field observation.
7. Describe ethnographical research.
8. Describe sociometry.
9. Describe historiography.
10. Describe how a content analysis may be qualitative.

Because of its long-standing image of being an applied social science, some of the criminal justice research conducted and published has had detractors. This is primarily the result of what is perceived as the research's lack of statistical sophistication. This perception is central to the continuing debate over what is more "academic," qualitative or quantitative research. Since the remainder of the text focuses on elements more commonly associated with quantitative research (although very applicable to qualitative research) this chapter offers a closer look at qualitative research.

Qualitative versus Quantitative Research

In Chapter 1 it was briefly noted that the debate over qualitative versus quantitative research simply comes down to a question of "concepts as ideas or terms versus numerical values." Broadening this distinction in easy terms finds that quantitative research merely refers to counting and measuring items associated with the phenomena in question. Qualitative research focuses on "the meanings, concepts, definitions, characteristics, metaphors, symbols, and description of things" (Berg, 1998, p. 3). Based upon these statements one might easily understand why quantitative research appears more popular. However that does not mean that it is always the best method to use.

In recent years there has been a trend among scholarly journals to demand more quantitative than qualitative research. This preference is because qualitative research is often criticized as not being scientific (Berg, 1998; Denzin and Lincoln, 1994; Patton, 1990; Senese, 1997). That debate will not be continued here because we believe that both methods are appropriate and necessary to criminal justice and criminology. This view is not unique as is demonstrated in the following:

> Qualitative and quantitative research can be complementary, together yielding better results than only one approach would. Furthermore, qualitative data collected through observations can be used while planning quantitative research. Such observations can help define the research subject and indicate the issues that need further study. (Eck and La Vigne, 1994, pg. 5)

Qualitative Research Defined

Qualitative research is defined as "the nonnumerical examination and interpretation of observations for the purpose of discovering underlying meanings and patterns of relationships. This is most typical of field research and historical analysis" (Babbie, 1999, p. 458). In this type of research "the interpretation of action or representations of meanings tend to be expressed in the researcher's own words" (Adler and Clark, 1999 p. 495) rather than through numerical assignments. Such analysis enables researchers to verbalize insights that quantifying of data would not permit. It also allows us to avoid the trap of "false precision" which frequently occurs when subjective numerical assignments are made. These quantifications are misleading in that they convey the impression of a precision that does not really exist.

Merits and Limitations of Qualitative Research

The insights gained from qualitative research and its usefulness in designing specific questions and analyses for individuals and groups make it invaluable in the study of criminal justice and criminology. However, the costs and time involved in such studies may not be logistically feasible (Ford and Williams, 1999). One of the major complaints about qualitative research is that it takes too long to complete. Other complaints about qualitative research include that it requires clearer goals and cannot be statistically analyzed (Berg, 1998; Maxwell, 1996; Senese, 1997). There may also be problems with reliability in that replication may prove quite difficult. Lastly, validity issues may arise from the inability to quantify the data.

What You Have Done Before

Before we proceed further let us deal with an issue that may be developing in your mind as you read about qualitative research. We have stressed that most, if not all, of the "research" that you have done in the past was not true research but merely an extended literature review.

Now we are telling you that research does not have to use numbers. Therefore, we were obviously wrong and you have been doing research all along. This would be a false assumption. Unless you have used the scientific method to structure your inquiry so as to yield results that logically extend from your analysis, you have not conducted qualitative research. A mere reciting of what others have done does not qualify as research. However, if you actually used the prior research to compare or assess an issue or event you may actually have done so.

The distinction we are making between true qualitative research and the literature review "research" will become clearer after you review the various types of qualitative research that are available for use. There are a variety of methods available for conducting qualitative research. They include field interviews, focus groups, field observation, ethnography, sociometry, and historiography (Berg, 1998; Denzin and Lincoln, 1994; Maxwell, 1996; Senese, 1997).

Types of Qualitative Research

Conducting qualitative research may be time-consuming, but because it better reflects the actual being of something, the time factor becomes moot for the qualitative researcher. Therefore, the bigger issue becomes what method to employ. Obviously, this will depend on the goals of the research and from where the information is to be sought. When information is wanted directly from individuals, the most common method to use is interviewing.

Field Interviewing

Simply, interviewing is the asking of questions by one individual of another in order to obtain information. If the interview consists of specific questions for which designated responses may be chosen, this would qualify as quantitative research. (Quantitative interviews will be discussed in the next chapter.) Generally, even if a field interview is structured the answers are open-ended. By this we mean that the response given by the interviewee is recorded exactly as stated rather than assigned to a predetermined category.

There is no one agreed way to conduct a field interview. Consensus could probably be found that a major key to interviewing is asking the right questions. A reflection on the questions would be based on the type of interview being conducted and the information sought. Although there may be debate as to what the differing ways of interviewing are called, three types of interviews are possible: structured, semi-structured, and unstructured[1].

---

[1] Berg (1998) refers to the three methods as standardized, unstandardized, and semi-standardized.

Structured Interviews

A structured interview entails the asking of pre-established open-ended questions of every respondent. As stated above, if the questions asked are closed-ended (respondents select from a choice of predetermined answers for which a numerical value can be assigned) this would qualify as quantitative survey research. The majority of structured interviews are quantitative in that they consist entirely or predominantly of closed-ended questions. Responses are recorded as given and the interview pace is such that all the questions can be asked and responded to in a timely fashion, but neither the interviewer nor the respondent are rushed. The following have been suggested as guidelines for conducting a structured interview. Never . . .

> get involved in long explanations of the research,
>
> deviate from the study introduction, sequence of questions, or question wording,
>
> let another person interrupt the interview, or respond for the person being questioned,
>
> suggest, agree to, or disagree to, an answer,
>
> interpret the meaning of a question, or
>
> improvise. (Fontana and Frey, 1994, p. 364)

The structured interview is geared toward limiting errors and ensuring a consistency of order in the responses even though the responses themselves may vary. Still, there are factors that could cause problems eventually affecting the outcome. Some errors include, but are not limited to, the respondent's behavior (for example, is the respondent being truthful or only saying what he or she believes the interviewer wants to hear), the setting of the interview (for example, face-to-face or telephonic), question wording (for example, uncommon terms), and poor interviewer skills (for example, the interviewer does not clearly enunciate or changes the question's wording). In addition, if an interviewer is not familiar with the respondent's background, culture, education, or other factors, this can be detrimental to the interview.

EXAMPLE

A researcher interested in gang membership decides to interview all juveniles arrested during a certain month without knowing anything about why any particular person was arrested or his or her life leading up to the arrest. This individual may find it very difficult to receive cooperation or truthful responses because his or her questions may not be appropriate (for example, asking every juvenile how long he or she has been in a gang assumes gang affiliation without actually knowing if it exists).

Overall, the structured interview can elicit rational, legitimate responses. Unfortunately, it does not consider the emotional aspect. This is where a semi-structured interview might be more useful.

Semi-Structured Interviews

This type of interview primarily follows the same ideas or guidelines of a structured interview. The major difference is that in this type of interview, the interviewer can go beyond the responses for a broader understanding of the answers. This is known as "probing for more detail." Probing may consist of asking for more explanation of an answer than has been given or following up with an additional question or questions depending upon the answers given. Semi-structured interviews are commonly used as a qualitative research strategy.

Methodological Link

In order to study how academic researchers gain access to data, Flanyak (1999) used the qualitative research method of in-depth interviewing, but in a semi-structured manner. This method provided a high response rate and allowed the interviewer to have personal contact with and observation of her subjects. Using an interview guide instrument permitted the researcher to maintain a general outline and framework of questions to ensure specific topics were investigated, yet provided the researcher with the opportunity and discretion to explore or probe respondents for detail in specific areas.

Semi-structured interviews allow for deeper probing into the answers given to structured, close-ended questions. Still, there are limitations to this type of interview. If a researcher wants to really explore a topic through interviewing without having specific question boundaries, then the unstructured interview would best serve this purpose.

Unstructured Interviews

The unstructured interview is far less rigid than either of the previous two methods. Seldom is a schedule kept or are there usually any predetermined possible answers. Often the questions are created as the interaction proceeds (Adler and Clark, 1999, p. 248). The most common form of unstructured interview makes uses of open-ended (ethnographic or in-depth) questions. In many cases, this style interview is done in conjunction with participant-observation (Fontana and Frey, 1994).

EXAMPLE

To gain a better understanding of what police detectives find stressful, a researcher chose to spend several days with detectives from a particular police agency. While the primary role was to observe how detectives responded to certain situations or events, during "down times" (for example, between calls, meals, after the shift) the researcher was able to ask open-ended questions pertaining to what the detectives found stressful. One such question might be "What do you find stressful about being a detective?"

Because of the nature of an unstructured interview, the researcher must be able to complete the following for the study to be successful:

> Gain access to the setting
>
> Understand the language and culture of respondents
>
> Decide how to present oneself
>
> Locate a contact or informant
>
> Gain the respondent's trust
>
> Establish rapport
>
> (Berg, 1998; Fontana and Frey, 1994, Maxwell, 1996; Senese, 1997).

By meeting the above requirements, the researcher should be successful in his or her efforts.

Obviously, interviewing can be a tedious means of gaining data, especially if it is of the one-on-one variety. However, sometimes research requires interviewing more than one person at a time. This qualitative method is often called focus groups or group interviewing (Berg, 1998; Fontana and Frey, 1994).

Focus Groups

Perhaps the best way to define a focus group is the interviewing of several individuals in one setting. While not meant to replace individual interviews, focus groups have long been in use in marketing and politics (Fontana and Frey, 1994). The focus group is basically an information gathering method where the researcher/interviewer directs the interaction and inquiry. This can occur in either a structured (for example, pretesting a questionnaire) or unstructured (for example, brainstorming) manner. In either case the researcher-interviewer must meet the same guidelines offered for conducting any interview. But, why would someone use this method?

The use of focus groups has its advantages and disadvantages. The advantages include limited expenses, flexibility, and stimulation. The disadvantages include group culture, dominant responder, and topic sensitivity (Berg, 1998; Fontana and Frey, 1994; Patton, 1990; Senese, 1997). The focus group can be a useful qualitative method for gathering information and can be particularly interesting. However, there may be times when the researcher may wish to take part in the activities or just observe the subjects of the research in their natural setting, a method of research referred to as observational.

Field Observation (or Participant-Observer)

The method of observation is interesting because of the context in which it places the researcher. While this method of qualitative research has not received the same attention as interviewing (Adler and Adler, 1994; Atkinson and Hammersly, 1994), it is still a very viable tool especially in criminal justice and criminology. Usually this method of study has only focused on two means: observer and participant-observer.

The observer method is where the researcher gathers information in the most unobtrusive fashion by simply watching the study subjects interact, preferably without their knowledge. With participant-observation, the subjects not only are aware of the researcher but actually interact as the researcher takes an active role in activities under study. While these two methods are quite fitting, Senese (1997) has offered what appears to be a more useful description of the options for this type research. His model includes four types: full participant, participant researcher, researcher who participates, and the complete researcher.

The Full Participant

Sometimes it may be fitting or perhaps even essential that a researcher become part of the study. The full participant method allows the researcher to carry out observational research, but does so in a "covert" manner (for example, to study the workings of a gang, the researcher takes an active role as a gang member, where other members are unaware of the research agenda). Of course, some problems with this method include the researcher possibly facing ethical and moral dilemmas that could adversely affect the research if the wrong decision is made, for example, having to compromise one's beliefs, or even place the person in legal jeopardy (for example, being in a car during a drive-by shooting). To avoid ethical and moral dilemmas (discussed in Chapter 2), a researcher may decide to move one step down, and become a participant researcher.

The Participant Researcher

Because participating in the activities of the research subjects can offer insights and information not attainable through other forms of research, and to avoid dilemmas facing full participation, there is the participant research method. This method is where the researcher participates in the activities of the research environment but is known to the research subjects to be a researcher (for example, to study the behavior of males in a reformatory, the researcher goes in and participates in all activities, but everyone knows he or she is there collecting information). The biggest negative of this research method is that by the subject knowing the researcher's role, behaviors other than those being studied can be influenced. The subjects may not act as they would under unobserved conditions, either over- or under-exaggerating their actions. This is known as "subject reactivity" to the research. Furthermore, by being part of the activities, the researcher can influence outcomes and behaviors that may not have existed without his or her presence. This then gives way to the third method of observation.

The Researcher Who Participates

Rather than taking part in activities, the researcher who participates method requires nothing more than observation by the researcher whose status as a researcher is known to the research subjects. For example, to study whether a particular treatment offered to incarcerated juveniles is working, the researcher enters the environment where his or her status as a researcher is known, but does nothing more than observe. While this method eliminates many of the problems of the previous two methods, the mere presence of the researcher who participates can still influence behavior and activities. How does one avoid this dilemma?

The Complete Researcher

The way for a researcher to minimize the problems generally associated with observation-participatory research is to avoid all possible interaction with the research subjects. Data collection may involve "covert" methods of observation (for example, from some disguised vantage point such as a guard tower in a maximum level prison or the review of records). As can be imagined, the benefits that are gained by covert observation or assumption of a non-interacting role are countered by possible resentment and denial of access by those being observed.

Regardless of which form is used, observational research can be time-consuming, and may not provide the results ultimately sought. Still, it can be a very interesting means for gathering data.

Methodological Link

To study the implementation of community policing, Memory (1999) conducted research as the "researcher as participant." His methodology took the form of "ridealongs," where he spent 180 hours riding with police officers from selected cities or counties. Departmental contact persons arranged the ridealongs ahead of time. Because six law enforcement agencies had agreed to be involved in a larger overall research project, the researcher did not need to "gain access," but still had to fully comply with agency and officer directions, to maintain access. Memory rode during both daylight and darkness in each jurisdiction but rode nearly none between 1:00 a.m. and 1:00 p.m. As a "researcher as participant," he dressed in slacks, a dress shirt, and a sport coat. He observed everything that occurred concerning the officers ridden with. The data collection involved taking notes on the front and back of data-collection forms. The researcher recorded observations, words of officers and citizens, and his own impressions and ideas.

Despite the respective problems of observational research it does provide a perspective that is often missed through quantitative research. Furthermore, it can be an important part of another form of qualitative research, ethnography.

Ethnographical Study

Ethnographical study or field research (ethnography) overlaps with field observation in that the researcher actually enters the environment under study, but does not necessarily take part in any activities. While the defining of ethnographical study has been controversial (Atkinson and Hammersly, 1994; Berg, 1998), it is a form of qualitative research in which the researcher looks at various "sociological, psychological, and educational variables in real social structures" (Kerlinger, 1964, p. 387). It consists of several attributes that include:

> a strong emphasis on exploring the nature of particular social phenomena, rather than setting out to test hypotheses about them;
>
> a tendency to work primarily with "unstructured" data, that is, data that have not been coded at the point of data collection in terms of a closed set of analytic categories;
>
> investigation of a small number of cases, perhaps just one case, in detail;
>
> analysis of data that involves explicit interpretation of the meanings and functions of human actions, the product of which mainly takes the form of verbal descriptions and explanations, with quantification and statistical analysis playing a subordinate role at most (Atkinson and Hammersly, 1994, p. 248)

Not a particularly popular means of conducting research, ethnography, like observation, can provide insights not found through quantitative research. For example, the study of gang graffiti from a quantitative perspective might simply identify the differing types of symbols drawn and how many of each. However, an ethnographic study could provide what the symbols mean, why they have been placed where, and who is placing them. This information gives a different slant to the information than the quantitative approach. One of the interesting aspects of ethnographical study is the possibility for the researcher to examine social interactions, which leads to another form of qualitative research, sociometry.

Sociometry

Sociometry is a technique by which the researcher can measure social dynamics or relational structures such as who-likes-whom (Philliber, Schwab, and Sloss, 1980). Information can be gathered through interviews or by observation and will indicate who is chosen and the characteristics about those who do the choosing. With respect to criminal justice, a sociometric study might involve prosecutor-defense attorney relationships, where the researcher observes the interaction of prosecutors with defense attorneys noting how each treats and is treated by the other and how that affects outcomes such as plea bargains. This study might show whether there is a hierarchy among lawyers or among potential defendants (the accused).

As with observation and ethnography, the researcher's presence, attitudes, biases, etc., can influence the outcomes of sociometric research. Because the mere presence of the researcher can be problematic, a less obtrusive means of conducting qualitative research is available.

Historiography

Historiography (also known as Historical/Comparative Research) (Berg, 1998) is basically the study of actions, events, and phenomena that have already occurred. This type of research often involves the study of documents and records with information about the topic under study. This type of study is generally inexpensive and unobtrusive. It can assist in determining why or how an event occurred and whether such an event could happen again. It is also a means by which researchers may compare and contrast events or phenomenon that have occurred. Historiography can be either qualitative or quantitative in nature depending on the materials being utilized and the focus of the research. Historians as well as Marxist scholars utilize this method.

EXAMPLE

To study sentencing patterns of individuals convicted of Driving Under the Influence (DUI), a researcher chose to review court cases for a specific period of time. The methodology required the reading of the formal court recordings from a particular court from which the researcher noted the name of the individual and the sentence given. From this information, the researcher could then go to the arrest records and find demographic information about the subject. To this point all the data is qualitative. However, to see whether any relationships existed between sentence type and demographic characteristics, the information was quantified for computer analysis. What was missing from this research that other forms of qualitative methods would have provided was information directly from the subjects involved and observations of interactions.

Content Analysis

Like historical research, content analysis is the study of social artifacts to gain insights about an event or phenomenon. It differs in that the focus is upon the coverage of the event by the particular medium being evaluated (books, magazines, television programs, news coverage, etc.) rather than the event. Depending upon how the research is conducted, this may be either qualitative or quantitative in nature. Qualitative content analysis would emphasize verbal rather than statistical analysis of various forms of communication. For example, Maguire, Sandage, and Weatherby (1999) examined the development of perceptions of policing by citizens based on news stories aired by three different television stations. Their main focus was on the types of stories about policing being aired, that is, positive or negative.

Overall, qualitative research offers a perspective that contrasts, yet can compare to that which is discovered through quantitative research. Perhaps Berg (1998) best summarizes qualitative research:

> Qualitative research properly seeks answers to questions by examining various social settings and the individuals who inhabit these settings. Qualitative researchers, then, are most interested in how humans arrange themselves and their settings and how inhabitants of these settings make sense of their surroundings through symbols, rituals, social structures, social roles, and so forth (p. 7).

Whether it is qualitative or quantitative, the research can serve a purpose in criminal justice and criminology. Thus, the debate should not be over which is better, but over what should be studied. How the selection of research impacts upon the research design will be discussed in a later chapter.

Summary

There is a continuing debate between criminal justice and criminology researchers as to what type of research is best, qualitative or quantitative. This chapter argues that they complement each other and have appropriate roles in related research. To that end, this chapter explores what qualitative research is by noting that it is the research of ideas and concepts not of numbers. While there are many forms of qualitative research, the more popular include:

1. Field interviewing: structured, semi-structured, and unstructured
2. Field observation: the full participant, participant researcher, the researcher who participates, and the complete researcher
3. Ethnography
4. Sociometry
5. Historiography
6. Content analysis

Methodological Queries

(1) You are interested in interviewing probation officers about their jobs. For each type of interview structure, what are some questions you would ask?

(2) There has been some discussion about implementing a Drug Awareness and Reduction Education program in the local elementary school. However, before this happens, a qualitative study of other programs has been ordered. What method would you suggest? Why?

(3) To better understand the workings of a boot camp, you are asked to conduct an observational study. What form would you use and why?

(4) What method of qualitative research would you use to study: (1) police dispatcher job satisfaction, (2) correctional officers' interaction with individuals awaiting trial versus those who have been convicted, and (3) a particular judge's sentencing patterns? Explain how you would conduct each study.

(5) How might ethnographical research be best employed in criminal justice? Criminology?

References

Adler, P. A. and Adler, P. (1994). Observational techniques. In N. K. Denzin and Y. S. Lincoln (Eds.), *Handbook of Qualitative Research,* pp. 377-392, Thousand Oaks, CA: Sage Publications.

Adler, E. S. and Clark, R. (1999). *How It's Done: An Invitation to Social Research.* Belmont, CA: Wadsworth Publishing.

Atkinson, P. and Hammersly, M. (1994). Ethnography and participant observation. In N. K. Denzin and Y. S. Lincoln (Eds.), *Handbook of Qualitative Research,* pp. 248-261, Thousand Oaks, CA: Sage Publications.

Babbie, E. (1999). *The Basics of Social Research.* Belmont, CA: Wadsworth Publishing.

Berg, B. L. (1998). *Qualitative Research Methods for the Social Sciences (3rd ed.).* Boston: Allyn and Bacon.

Denzin, N. K. and Lincoln, Y. S. (Eds.) (1994). *Handbook of Qualitative Research.* Thousand Oaks, CA: Sage Publications.

Eck, J. E. and La Vigne, N. G. (1994*). Using Research: A Primer for Law Enforcement Managers (2nd ed.).* Washington, D.C.: Police Executive Research Forum.

Flanyak, C. M. (1999). Accessing data: Procedures, practices, and problems of academic researchers. In M. L. Dantzker (Ed.), *Readings for Research Methods in Criminology and Criminal Justice,* pp. 157-180. Woburn, MA: Butterworth-Heinemann.

Fontana, A. and Frey, J. H. (1994). Interviewing: The art of science. In N. K. Denzin and Y. S. Lincoln (Eds.), *Handbook of Qualitative Research,* pp. 361-376, Thousand Oaks, CA: Sage Publications.

Ford, M. and Williams, L. (1999). Human/cultural diversity training for justice personnel. In M. L. Dantzker (Ed.), *Readings for Research Methods in Criminology and Criminal Justice,* pp. 37-60. Woburn, MA: Butterworth-Heinemann.

Kerlinger, F. N. (1964). *Foundations of Behavioral Research.* New York: Holt, Rinehart and Winston, Inc.

Kimmel, A. J. (1988). *Ethics and Values in Applied Social Research.* Thousand Oaks, CA: Sage Publications, Inc.

Maguire, B., Sandage, D., Weatherby, G. A. (1999). Television news coverage of the police: An exploratory study from a small town locale. *Journal of Contemporary Criminal Justice,* 15(2), pp. 171-190.

Maxwell, J. A. (1996). *Qualitative Research Design: An Interactive Approach.* Thousand Oaks, CA: Sage Publishing Company.

Memory, J. M. (1999). Some impressions from a qualitative study of implementation of community policing in North Carolina. In M. L. Dantzker (Ed.), *Readings for Research Methods in Criminology and Criminal Justice,* pp. 1-14. Woburn, MA: Butterworth-Heinemann.

Patton, M. Q. (1990). *Qualitative Evaluation and Research Methods (2nd ed.).* Newbury Park, CA: Sage Publications.

Philliber, S. G., Schwab, M. R., and Sloss, G. S. (1980). *Social Research: Guides to a Decision-Making Process.* Itasca, IL: F.E. Peacock Publishing, Incorporated.

Senese, J. D. (1997). *Applied Research Methods in Criminal Justice.* Chicago, IL: Nelson-Hall Publishers.

Quantitative Research

■ **Vignette 6-1**
The Debate over Numbers-Oriented
Research Continues

Last week you observed two faculty members in your department debate which form of research is better: qualitative or quantitative. The last time your methods course met, qualitative research was discussed. You are a little clearer as to the purpose and means of conducting qualitative research but you find yourself still skeptical about its relevance over quantitative. Knowing that the next course topic is quantitative, you hope it will finally make both sides clear. As you enter the classroom, you are handed a questionnaire by the instructor's assistant who advises you that you are being asked to participate in the most important and most often used type of research in criminal justice, a survey. A quick review of the questionnaire finds that there are 20 questions with responses that are categorical or have a numeric choice. Now normally this might not make an impression on you but the survey is being conducted by your current instructor, the same person who strongly supported qualitative research. Now you are really confused.

When the instructor finally comes into the classroom, you immediately offer a challenge as to why this type of research is being conducted. An answer, you are told, will be clearer, by the end of this night's class.

■ **CHAPTER 6**
Learning Objectives

After studying this chapter the student should be able to:

1. Define quantitative research.

2. Define empiricism and discuss how it relates to quantitative research.
3. Contrast the two types of causality.
4. Identify and discuss the three criteria for causality.
5. Contrast necessary and sufficient cause.
6. Describe what is meant by false precision.
7. Identify and explain the four levels of measurement.
8. Recognize and describe the types of survey research.
9. Explain the strengths and weaknesses of survey research.
10. Describe field research and give an example.
11. Discuss the types of unobtrusive research.
12. Describe evaluation research.

Quantitative Research

As was stressed in Chapter 5, qualitative research is a valuable tool that provides many insights in the study of crime, criminality, and society's responses to crime. It is not only an excellent means of conducting primary research but is highly useful in complementing quantitative research. However, to be a complete criminological researcher, one must be able to move beyond qualitative research. Quantitative research is the means to do so.

Quantitative Research Defined

Quantitative research is defined as "the numerical representation and manipulation of observations for the purpose of describing and explaining the phenomena that those observations represent" (Babbie, 1998, p. G5). This means that research is not based upon a possibly subjective interpretation of the observations but is (hopefully) a more objective analysis based upon the numerical findings produced from observations.

Qualitative versus Quantitative Research, Part II

In the previous chapter we stated that *quantitative research refers to counting and measuring items associated with the phenomena in question whereas qualitative research focuses on "the meanings, concepts, definitions, characteristics, metaphors, symbols, and description of things"* (adapted from Berg,

1998, p. 3). Because of the potential for bias as well as the criticisms of qualitative research as being unscientific, the majority of criminological research tends to be quantitative in nature. A quick review of the leading journals that publish criminal justice and criminology research would support this assertion.

There are many issues that are not suitable for numerical assignments. To do so would be both inaccurate and misleading. Some of the more intense theoretical debates, such as the merits of the death penalty, are based upon personal beliefs about human nature that are shaped by deep-seated religious, political, and moral convictions. As a result, perceptions of these tend to frequently be more influenced by emotion and ideology than by scientific study. This does not mean that quantitative research cannot be conducted, but to do so is difficult at best.

What You Have Not Done Before

As a developing researcher you may feel that you have done qualitative research through the literature reviews and comparative/historical research that you have done for previous courses. If done in a systematic and logical manner consistent with the scientific method, perhaps you have. But have you actually assigned numerical values, collected data utilizing that assignment, and then analyzed the results? We doubt that you have unless you have a strong background in math and science or have been fortunate enough to have been involved in an empirical research project. (For those who are still struggling with methods phobia, we define fortunate here as having benefited from the knowledge and insights of the experience rather than from the pleasure of the experience.) This is a deficiency that we hope to aid your instructor in correcting. As a college graduate who values and is capable of critical thinking and independent learning, you need to be able to conduct quantitative research. It will serve you not only in your academic career but in future work tasks or civic duties. You will be surprised to find how many things there are in life that warrant "looking into." You will also find that in some ways, quantitative research is actually easier than qualitative research.

Empirical Observation

If you think back to your introductory course in criminology/criminal justice and/or your course in criminological theory, you have already received an introduction to empiricism. Cesare Lombroso, the founder of the Positive School of Criminology, used empiricism in his study of criminals. Earlier scholars (for example, Quetelet and Guerry in their independent area studies of crime rates in France) also used empirical techniques.

Empiricism is use of sensations and experiences (observations) to arrive at conclusions about the world we live in (Jeffery, 1990, p. 30). The use of the scientific method with its focus on causation rather than casual observation is what makes empiricism important. It is this emphasis upon empiricism rather than idealism that is the basis upon which positive criminology is founded. Rather than just quoting an "eye for an eye," we can use empirical techniques to gather and evaluate data as to the effectiveness of correctional programs; or to decide which patrol strategy is more cost effective; or to determine whether extra-legal factors influence conviction rates. Quantitative research is based upon empiricism.

Causality

In applying empirical observation to criminal justice research we focus upon causal relationships. Simply stated, what behaviors or events leads to other behaviors or events? When we try to answer that question, we seek to determine causality.

Idiographic and Nomothetic Causes

When we try to examine numerous explanations for why an event occurred this is known as *idiographic* explanation. Historians and Marxist criminologists tend to use the method in their qualitative analyses. Idiographic causation may also be quantitative in that many causes may be compared and contrasted using numerical assignments. When researchers focus upon a relatively few observations in order to provide a partial explanation for an event this is known as *nomothetic* causation (Babbie, 1999, p. 70-71).

Rather than trying to provide a total picture of every influence in a causal relationship, nomothetic explanation focuses on one or a few factors that could provide a general understanding of the phenomena being studied. Nomothetic explanations of causality are based upon probabilities (which will be discussed in Chapter 9). It is this use of probability that enables us to make inferences based upon a relatively few observations.

The Criteria for Causality

In investigating to determine if there is a causal relationship between the events or issues that we are studying there are three criteria that we must observe. The first criteria is that the independent variable (the variable that is providing the influence) must occur before the dependent variable (the variable that is being acted upon). The second criteria is that a relationship between the independent and dependent variable must be observed. The third criteria is that the apparent relationship is not explained by a third variable (Adler and Clark, 1999, p. 160). As an example, you see individual A struck by another person, B. Person A then falls down. Using the criteria for causality you would conclude that the striking (independent variable) led to the falling (dependent variable). It occurred prior to the falling and was clearly related to that which you witnessed. If no other event (a third variable such as a blow having also been struck by a Person C) occurred, then it is reasonable to assume that the criteria for causality have been met.

Necessary and Sufficient Cause

In investigating causality we must meet the above criteria but we do not have to demonstrate a perfect correlation. In probabilistic models, such as those used in most inferential research, we will often find exceptions to the rule. If a condition or event must occur in order for another event to take place, that is known as a *necessary cause*. As an example, despite Hollywood dramatizations, one must be female to give birth to a child (Babbie, 1998, p. 76). The cause must be present for the effect to occur.

When the presence of a condition will ordinarily cause the effect to occur, this is known as a *sufficient cause*. The cause will usually create the effect but will not always do so. Playing golf in a thunderstorm may not result in your being struck by lightning, but the conditions are sufficient for it to occur. In social science research we prefer to identify a necessary cause for an event but to do so is often impossible. Instead we are more likely to identify causes that are sufficient.

False Precision

We have discussed the issue of *false precision* earlier but it warrants another visitation. When quantifying data it is imperative that the numerical assignments are valid. If you arbitrarily assign numbers to variables without a logical reason for doing so, the numbers have no true meaning. This assignment is known as false precision. We have quantified a concept but that assignment is subjective rather than objective. The precision that we claim really does not exist. In those cases a qualitative analysis would be more appropriate.

Quantitative Measurement

On many occasions in our lives we are confronted with some form of measurement. Based upon our earlier definition of quantitative research, measurement, as it is applied here to criminal justice and criminological research, is viewed as *the assignment of numerical values or categorical labels to phenomena for the expressed purpose of quantifiable identification or analysis*. With respect to quantifying something, there is more than one means or level.

Levels of Measurement

What can often be a very confusing part of conducting quantitative research is determining what level of measurement to use. There are four levels of measurement from which to choose: nominal, ordinal, interval, and ratio. The level that is chosen will have an extremely important impact upon how the data are collected and analyzed. The researcher can move down from a higher level of data to a lower level during data analysis but they cannot move up to a higher level from a lower level. You will see why this is so as we discuss the various levels of measurement.

Nominal Level Data

The simplest level of measurement is the nominal level. At this level, measurement is categorical where each is mutually exclusive. There is neither a quantitative nor statistical value assigned except for the expressed need to describe the results or to code it for data analyses. Most often nominal measures are used to represent independent variables that describe characteristics of the sample, but may also be used to describe dependent variables, too (see Box 6-1).

Ordinal Level Data

The second level of measurement is the ordinal level. This level moves beyond being merely categorical by assigning a rank or a placement of order to variables. Although in using this level numbers are assigned for ranking purposes (for example, 1-10), these numbers are not meant to, or

---

Box 6-1
Examples of Nominal Measures

Gender—Male, Female
Ethnicity—American, African, Hispanic, Asian
Religion—Catholic, Jewish, Protestant, Baptist
Education—High School, B.S., M.S., Ph.D.
Marital Status—Single, never married
               Single, divorced
               Married
               Widow/Widower
Criminal Offense—Murder, Sexual Assault, Robbery, Theft, Burglary.
Sentence Disposition—Probation, Jail, Prison
Prison Security Level—Maximum, Medium, Minimum

are unable to explain the response, but are simply viewed as a demonstration of where the respondent believes the item to fall. For example, in looking at the difference between the seriousness of criminal offenses where murder is labeled as a nine, robbery a five and theft a one, there is a four-unit difference between each but again, we cannot explain what that difference truly represents.

Most often ordinal measures are found in attitudinal surveys, perceptual surveys, quality of life studies, or service studies. Figure 6-1 offers a list of occupations that respondents could be asked to rank in order of how stressful they perceive each to be, from most stressful to least stressful. Although they would write any number between one and ten, the listed order would only tell us what the individuals perceive. There is no way to determine how much difference there is in the perceived stressfulness between each occupation. Despite being assigned numerical values and being useful in data analysis, ordinal level data are limited in providing explanation (see Figure 6-1).

Interval Level Data

The third highest level of measure is interval, which provides far better opportunity for explanation than data collected at the nominal and ordinal levels. Within interval data there is an expected equality in the distance between choices on the continuum. This allows us to use more sophisticated techniques during data analysis.

Unlike ratio level data (discussed below), there is no set zero or starting point for interval data. Since numbers assigned have an arbitrary

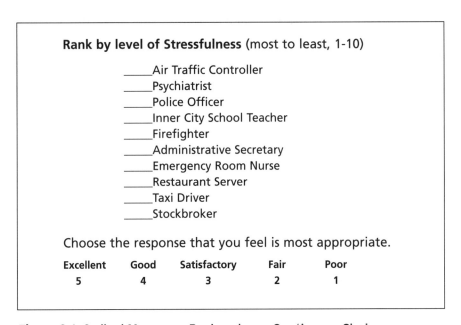

Figure 6-1 Ordinal Measures: Rank order or Continuum Choice

beginning, the usefulness of the information may be limited. For example, the difference between an IQ of 135 and 150 is the same 15 unit difference as between 150 and 165. However, there is no distinction as to what the difference means. We can comment on the differences but cannot explain what that difference means. To be able to do so would require ratio level data.

Ratio Level Data

The highest and most quantifiable level of measure is ratio. This level is primarily characterized by an absolute beginning point of zero and the differences between each point are equal and can be explained. Two of the more common ratio measures are age and money. With respect to research, ratio measures can be collapsed into nominal or ordinal measures. Age and family income are often ratio level, independent variables that for analysis purposes are collapsed into a nominal measure (for example, under 18, 18–25, 26–34, over 34; and under $10,000, $10,000–$24,999, $25,000–$49,999, over $50,000). The benefits of doing so will be discussed in a later chapter.

Obviously, choosing a level of measurement is just one of the first steps in conducting quantitative research. Probably the most important step is deciding what type of method or design to use.

Types of Quantitative Research

There are a variety of designs available to the justician and criminologist for conducting quantitative research. Yet, despite all the possibilities, there is one form of research that is both a research method and a research tool, the survey. Because of its dual nature, it will be discussed briefly here as a quantitative research design and in Chapter 9 as a data collection device.

Survey Research

The survey is one of the most popular research methods in criminal justice. The survey design is used when researchers are interested in the experiences, attitudes, perceptions, or beliefs of individuals, or when trying to determine the extent of a policy, procedure, or action among a specific group. Most often a researcher will contact a sample of individuals presumed to have participated in a particular event, who belong to a certain group, or who are part of a specific audience having experienced similar events. Of the identified group, certain questions pertaining to the topic under study will be asked, either verbally or in written form. The solicited responses to the questions comprise the data used to test the research hypothesis(es). The three primary survey methods are personal interview, mail questionnaire, and telephone survey.

Personal Interviews

Personal interviews are surveys that are administered by face-to-face discussions between the researcher and the survey respondent. Unstructured interviews in which the researchers questions are developed during the conversation are qualitative and were discussed in Chapter 5. Structured interviews in which the researcher asks only open-ended questions would also be qualitative.

Interviews in which the researcher reads from a previously developed questionnaire to which responses are numerically assigned are quantitative. Such interviews may in fact be nothing more than the reading of a questionnaire that could have been mailed out to respondents. Personal interviews permit the researcher to obtain not only responses to the questions asked but permit probing on open-ended questions and observation as to the respondents' demeanor and nonverbal responses to the questions asked. They are however, more costly and time consuming as well as less safe than other strategies that do not bring researchers into physical contact with respondents.

Mail Questionnaires

Mail questionnaires are survey instruments that are mailed to selected respondents to complete on their own rather than being directly interviewed by the researcher. They are much cheaper and safer to administer. In addition they enable researchers to easily survey large numbers of people very quickly.

Mail questionnaires may be administered three ways. The questionnaire may be mailed with a request for it to be completed and returned in a self-addressed stamped (or metered) envelope to the researcher. To provide a more personal touch the researcher may drop off the questionnaire in a face-to-face contact with the respondent with the request that it be mailed back to them. Or, in a strategy designed to intimidate people into completing the questionnaire (which we do not recommend) the researcher may mail out the questionnaire and advise that he/or she will come by at a later time to retrieve it. Either of the later two strategies will greatly increase the time and costs involved in conducting the survey.

Telephone Surveys

The last form of survey has rapidly become popular among pollsters. Telephone surveys are quick and easy to do, enabling the researcher to contact large numbers of people in an efficient manner. They are safe in that verbal abuse is about the worst that researchers can incur from their dealings with respondents. Telephone surveys may be more efficient in that they may utilize random digit dialing to sample the population. They may also have the added advantage of actually imputing data into a computer as the surveyor asks the questions. The biggest disadvantage is that people who are sick of telephone solicitors will often refuse to participate. The means of administering survey research will be discussed more in Chapter 10.

Pros and Cons of Survey Research

There are numerous reasons why the survey design is popular:

1. It uses a carefully selected probability sample and a standardized questionnaire, one can make descriptive assertions about any large population.
2. Survey research makes it feasible to use large samples.
3. It offers more flexibility to the researcher in developing operational definitions based on actual observations.
4. It generally uses standardized questionnaires, which from a measurement perspective, offers a strength to the data because the same question is being asked of all respondents, thus requiring credence to the same response from a large number of respondents.

Yet, despite the positives, the survey design also has its share of negatives:

1. A standardized questionnaire is limited with respect to whether the questions are appropriate since it is designed for all respondents and not for a select group.
2. It can seldom allow for the development of the feel for the context in which respondents are thinking or acting.
3. Survey research is inflexible in that it typically requires that no change occur throughout the research, thus often requiring a preliminary study to be conducted.
4. The survey tool is often subject to artificiality.

Even with the negatives, the survey design remains one of the most popular methods for conducting research. Furthermore, it is an extremely popular tool for collecting data. The issues involved in conducting survey research will be discussed in more detail in the following chapters.

Field Research

In Chapter 5 we discussed *ethnography* as a qualitative research method. In that discussion it was indicated that such research may often be quantitative in nature. When *structured interviews* are used that permit closed-ended questions to be answered, this would become a personal interview as described above. If *field observations* were made (such as observing how many vehicles ran a certain stop sign in a given time period or how many times members of the group being observed exhibited specific behaviors) allowing for numerical assignments then this would be quantified field research. When quantified, field research becomes an even more valuable tool for criminological researchers.

EXAMPLE

Standardized field sobriety tests (SFST) were developed during the 1980s to enable traffic officers to accurately estimate drug and alcohol impairment. These SFSTs consist of Walk-and-Turn (WAT), One-leg Stand (OLS) and Horizontal Gaze Nystagmus (HGN). Traffic officers in all fifty states have been trained to administer these tests to individuals suspected of impaired driving and to numerically score their performance on them. It has been claimed that the SFST test battery is valid for detection of low blood alcohol concentrations (BACs) and that no other measures of observations offer greater validity for BACs of 0.08% and higher.

 To study the legitimacy of these claims Burns and Dioquino (1997) set up a field research in Pinellas County, Florida. Eight sheriff's deputies, with years of experience in traffic control, each having made hundreds of DUI arrests, and all having extensive training in DUI enforcement including certification in SFST were selected to participate. A rigorous observation procedure was established in which both officers and observers assigned to each officer carefully recorded the SFST scoring and the actual outcome of measured BACs. 379 traffic stops were evaluated. In 313 cases SFSTs were administered. Drivers refused to take breath tests in 57 of these cases. In 256 cases, a breath test was administered to verify the accuracy of the SFST. The traffic officers were found to have an accuracy level of 97% in their arrest decisions based upon the use of SFSTs.

Unobtrusive Research

As was mentioned in Chapter 5, unobtrusive research does not require the researcher to be directly involved with the subjects of his/her study. There is no observation or interaction with the individuals or groups involved because the data has already been gathered by someone else or the data is available in a format that does not require such interaction. Examples of quantitative unobtrusive research include analysis of existing data, historical/archival research, and content analysis.

Analysis of Existing Data

Analysis of existing data is a very efficient way to conduct criminological research. The data has already been gathered by a governmental organization, a research foundation, or an independent researcher. Rather than gathering new data, the researcher obtains the existing data and reanalyzes it. This may include a reevaluation of the data from a prior study using a new method of analysis. Or it could be the use of government-generated data such as Uniform Crime Reports or census data in a new research analysis.

EXAMPLE

Hunter (1988) studied the effects of environmental factors upon the incidence of robbery at convenience stores in Florida (this is shown as a Methodological Link later in this chapter). The data from this study were reanalyzed several years later by Amandus et al (1995). Using the existing data from the 1988 research, logistic regression was utilized to reassess the findings. The findings were similar to Hunter's but not identical. Some environmental influences were found to have more significance than in the Hunter study while others were found to have less.

Quantified Historical Research

Historical or archival research involves the review of prior research, documents, or social artifacts to gain insights about an event or era in history. The majority of these types of research are qualitative. However, much of this research can be quantified and empirical assessments are becoming more common on the part of historians and neo-Marxist criminologists.

Quantified Content Analysis

Like historical research, content analysis is the study of social artifacts to gain insights about an event or phenomenon. It differs in that the focus is upon the coverage of the event by the particular medium being evaluated (books, magazines, television programs, news coverage, etc.) rather than the event. Depending upon how the research is conducted, this may be either qualitative or quantitative in nature. Quantitative content analysis would emphasize statistical rather than verbal analysis of various forms of communication. Instead of reading to understand the general emphasis or nature of the communication the researcher would either count the number of occurrences in which a topic or issue was presented or numerically assess the presentations based upon a predetermined scale or ranking.

Evaluation Research

To this point, almost all the research designs discussed are used after an event, situation, or other unexplained phenomenon occurs and we want to understand it better. They are designs that are quite useful to the academic researcher, but what about the practitioner who wants to know how something will work or what might occur when something not previously done is attempted? In particular, what about the manager or administrator who is interested in making a change that could have sweeping policy implications? Oftentimes the best type of research design for this situation is evaluation research.

Evaluation research is a quantified comparative research design that assists in the development of new skills or approaches. It aids in the solving of problems with direct implications for the "real world." This type of research usually has a quasi-experimental perspective to it.

EXAMPLE

A police agency is debating whether to add a non-lethal weapon, a stun gun, to what is available to its officers. To see how these might work and the outcome of their use, an action design would use a select group of officers who are issued the stun gun for a set period of time. Each time it is used, a report explaining why and the results must be filed. At the end of the experimental period, the reports are analyzed and depending on the results, stun guns would be issued to all officers, certain officers, or not at all.

Evaluation research is important for the criminal justice practitioner-researcher because it assesses the merits of programs or policies being used (or under consideration for use) in the field. Whereas more basic research seeks to develop theoretical insights and much applied research seeks to determine if a theory can actually be applied in the field, evaluation research allows practitioners to determine the costs and effectiveness of the program or project that is being or has been implemented. For this reason evaluation research that studies existing programs is frequently referred to as *program evaluation*.

Combination Research

Each of the methods presented above is an excellent means of conducting quantitative research. However, you have even more strategies available to you. Frequently in criminological research a combination of strategies are utilized. A research design is, in actuality, a combination of qualitative and quantitative research in that a serious review of the prior research is expected to have been conducted and its contributions to the development of the quantitative research. This is demonstrated in scholarly works in the problem statement and literature review.

Combinations of different quantitative methods are also commonly used. They may include the use of survey research and field observation, survey research and unobtrusive research, unobtrusive research and field observation, or a combination of all three.

EXAMPLE

In order to study the effects of environmental factors upon a convenience store's vulnerability to robbery, Hunter (1988) conducted a statewide study of convenience stores. In order to conduct this study, a combination of quantitative research designs were utilized. From records provided by the Florida Department of Business Regulation 7,740 convenience stores were found to be operating in the State of Florida during 1987. Two hundred stores were selected at random from this listing. Letters were sent from the Florida Attorney General to the heads of the law enforcement agencies within which the stores were located. These letters contained a survey instrument seeking to obtain the number of times that each store had been robbed during the years 1984, 1985, and 1986. Hunter then visited each store to observe and rank them on a listing of environmental factors thought to be related to robbery vulnerability. Uniform Crime Report Data from the Florida Department of Law Enforcement were obtained regarding the crime rates, clearance rates, percent of sworn police personnel, and population numbers for each jurisdiction within which the sampled stores were located. By using a variety of statistical analyses, Hunter was able to identify several environmental factors as having an influence upon a convenience store's vulnerability to robbery.

Overall, quantitative research offers a perspective that contrasts, yet can compare to that which is discovered through qualitative research.

Summary

This chapter explores what quantitative research is by noting that it is the research based upon the assignment and assessment of numbers. Quantitative research is based upon empiricism. It uses causality and probability to describe and explain relationships among variables. In order to construct a proper quantitative design, the level of measurement (nominal, ordinal, interval, and ratio) must be considered.

While there are many forms of quantitative research, the more popular include:

1. survey research: personal interviews, mail questionnaires, and telephone surveys
2. field research (quantified field observation)
3. quantified unobtrusive research: existing data, historical research, and content analysis
4. combination research, which uses a mixture of research methodologies

Methodological Queries

(1) What level of measurement would you use for the following variables: gender, race, perceptions of stress, convicted felons, courts' sentences, and average prison stay for burglars?

(2) For the following research queries, identify what type of research design you would use and why.

Stress among correctional officers

Probation officer caseloads

Police-involved shootings

(3) Why is causality an important issue?

(4) What type of research should never or could never be conducted quantitatively?

(5) When is necessary or sufficient cause not important in conducting research?

References

Amandus, H. E., Hunter, R. D., James, E., and Hendricks, S. (1995) Reevaluation of the effectiveness of environmental designs to reduce robbery risk in Florida convenience stores, *Journal of Occupational and Environmental Medicine.* June, Vol. 37 No. 6.

Babbie, E. (1989). *The Practice of Social Research (5th Ed.).* Belmont, CA: Wadsworth Publishing.

Berg, B. L. (1998). *Qualitative Research Methods for the Social Sciences (3rd Ed.).* Boston: Allyn and Bacon.

Burns, M. and Dioquino, T. (1997). *A Florida Validation Study of the Standardized Field Sobriety Test Battery.* Tallahassee, FL: Florida Department of Transportation.

Hunter, R. D. (1988) *The Effects of Environmental Factors Upon Convenience Store Robberies in Florida.* Tallahassee, FL: Florida Department of Legal Affairs.

Jeffery, C. R. (1990). *Criminology: An Interdisciplinary Approach.* Englewood Cliffs, MA: Prentice Hall.

Research Designs

■ **Vignette 7-1**
Choosing the Plan

Having been a student in the Criminal Justice and Criminology department since your freshman year, and a work study there during your sophomore and junior years, you are quite comfortable around the faculty. It has been common for you to drop by and visit with one faculty member or another either to ask specific questions about classes or just to "pick their brains." This particular afternoon you are walking through the halls when you overhear your faculty advisor in a friendly, yet heated debate with a doctoral student over the student's dissertation research design. Being on friendly terms with both, you stick your head in the office and ask about the debate.

It seems that the doctoral student wants to do a qualitative historical study while the faculty advisor is pushing for something with a more empirical orientation. Since you will soon have to decide what research methodology you will employ for your senior paper, you ask if you may sit in and listen to what both sides have to say about research designs. You soon discover there are many from which to choose.

■ **CHAPTER 7**
Learning Objectives

After studying this chapter the student should be able to:

1. Discuss the issues to consider in selecting a research design.
2. Describe how a historical research design is conducted.
3. Explain the merits of a descriptive research design.
4. Discuss developmental or time-series research. List the various types of time-series designs.

5. Compare and contrast longitudinal and cross-sectional research designs.

6. Compare and contrast trend studies, cohort studies, and panel studies.

7. Compare and contrast case studies with correlational and causal-comparative studies.

8. Discuss the strengths and weaknesses of experimental and quasi-experimental designs.

Research Designs

In order to successfully complete any type of research, it is important to establish a feasible plan or blueprint, the research design. This plan primarily responds to the common five W's (who, what, where, when, and why) and H (how) of investigation. Because the justician and criminologist have a choice of research designs, it is important to be able to properly match the design to the desired outcomes. In selecting a research design there are a number of issues that should be considered. It is recommended that an outline be created to ensure that all relevant issues have been considered. Box 7-1 is an example of such an outline. The reader will note that most of these issues were discussed in previous chapters. The remainder will be covered in detail in later chapters.

This chapter discusses the more common forms of research designs applied to criminal justice and criminology. They include historical, descriptive, developmental, case, correlational, and causal-comparative. A brief mention will be made of experimental and quasi-experimental action designs. The main focus will be on what appears to be the most popular research design, survey research.

Historical

Probably one of the most debated topics in criminal justice and criminology is the deterrent effect of capital punishment. A common hypothesis for pro-capital punishment supporters is *the death penalty serves as a better deterrent for homicides than life imprisonment*. To study this hypothesis a historical, sometimes referred to as records, research design would be appropriate.

Historical designs allow the researcher to systematically and objectively reconstruct the past. This is accomplished through the collection, evaluation, verification, and synthesis of information, usually secondary data already existing in previously gathered records, to establish facts. The goal is to reach a defensible conclusion relating to the hypothesis. So, using the above hypothesis about the death penalty, a historical design could include a study of homicide rates in the United States

---

Box 7-1
Issues to consider in selecting a research design.

Purpose of Research
The purpose of the research project. It should be clearly indicative of what will be studied.

Prior Research
Review similar or relevant research. This will promote knowledge of the literature.

Theoretical Orientation
Describe the theoretical framework upon which the research is based.

Concept Definition
List the various concepts that have been developed and clarify their meanings.

Research Hypotheses
Develop the various hypotheses that will be evaluated in the research.

Unit of Analysis
Describe the particular objects, individuals, or entities that are being studied as elements of the population.

Data Collection Techniques
Determine how the data are to be collected. Who will collect it, who will be studied, and how will it be done.

Sampling Procedures
Sample type, sample size, as well as the specific procedures to be utilized.

Instrument(s) Used
The nature of the measurement instrument or data collection device that is used.

Analytic Techniques
How the data will be processed and examined. What specific statistical procedures will be used.

Time Frame
The period of time covered by the study. This will include the time period examined by research questions as well as the amount of time spent in preparation, data collection, data analysis, and presentation.

Ethical Issues
Address any concerns as to the potential harm that might occur to participants. Also deal with any potential biases or conflicts of interest that could affect the study.

---

between 1950 and 1997. Although just studying the numbers might provide an interesting conclusion, the true historical study requires inclusion of possible intervening factors, which in this case could include U.S. Supreme Court decisions, sentencing patterns, social episodes (for example, a war), and population growth. A successful historical study will consider all relevant information in order to provide proper conclusions.

Methodological Link

To determine the role of women in gambling (numbers running) in New York City, Liddick (1999) used a historical or records design. From various police records, detailed information was gathered about the personnel involved in the delivery of numbers gambling services. It included residences, areas of illegal operation, ethnic identity, gender, organizational affiliation, roles in the given numbers enterprise, age, and classification numbers assigned by the police. In some instances, other information available included relatives, legal employment or businesses, automobiles used, dates and places of birth, places frequented, criminal and non-criminal associates, aliases, and physical descriptions were also provided. Additional information, which was important to the research, were arrests made by the investigative teams, the dates of the arrests, the names of the arrested individuals, the locations of the arrests, the arresting officers, and the number of slips, ribbons, plays, envelopes, cash, and personal property seized in each arrest. The only information that was not readily available was the disposition of arrests and the sentences given to those convicted.

The historical design is an economically efficient means for conducting research. Considering the vast array of records available related to criminal justice, there is no shortage of possible research topics. A shortcoming of this design is the difficulty of expanding beyond what is documented, therefore limiting the scope of the research. Researchers are limited to the information in the files and seldom have any means of following up or getting clarification of the available information. This may render it unfit for the purpose that you wish to utilize it. In addition, there is the old computer maxim of "garbage in garbage out." Your research is only as good as the data that is contained in the records. If there is inaccurate information or missing data in the original, your research will suffer.

Descriptive

Assume you want to know the composition of a particular jail population. A descriptive research design would be very appropriate because it focuses on the description of facts and characteristics of a given population, issue, policy, or any given area of interest in a systematic and accurate manner. Like the historical design, a descriptive study can also rely on secondary or records data. It is also similar in that much historical research is descriptive in nature.

Methodological Link

One of law enforcement's more popular tools against drug dealers and organized crime has been the use of forfeiture. Yet, despite its popularity, little is known about how forfeiture has been used. Using a descriptive study design, Warchol and Johnson (1999) conducted a study which "contributes to the current literature by examining the different types of federal asset for-

(continued on next page)

Methodological Link (continued)

feiture, and their application cross-nationally. The interest is in the types of seized assets, their economic values, the manner in which they are proceeded against, and the disposition of the proceeding" (p. 140). The data were obtained from the federal forfeiture data maintained by the United States Marshals' Service (USMS), whose role in the federal forfeiture program is that of a property custodian. Detailed data on each seized asset, the date of seizure, the seizing agency, the asset's owner(s), the economic value, the legal proceeding used to forfeit the asset, and the asset's final disposition must be collected. These records also contain detailed records of the population of individual properties seized and disposed of in the United States by fiscal year for all of the federal judicial districts.

The information obtained in descriptive studies can provide insights not recognized in prior research. It can also lead to the study becoming inferential. An inferential study generalizes findings from a sample group and applies it to a larger population. However, descriptive design findings are not always accurate or reliable because of other elements not in the sample that are present in other parts of the population. Therefore, if one is going to make inferences from this type of study, they must be sure that the population is well represented within the sample studied.

Methodological Link

In the Warchol and Johnson (1999) study, they examined data from four federal judicial districts: the Southern Districts of California and Florida, the Northern District of Illinois, and the Eastern District of Michigan. These districts were distinct from one another in terms of their geographic location and level of drug trafficking. The Southern District of Florida and the Southern District of California have been identified as "high-intensity drug trafficking areas" and serve as ports of entry, being border districts on different coasts, while the centrally located districts of Northern Illinois and Eastern Michigan were not identified as ports of entry or major drug distribution centers and were selected because they may exhibit different characteristics from the border districts. This cross-section of districts was included in the analysis to develop an initial profile of how the use of forfeiture varies across districts rather than to draw specific conclusions about forfeiture activities by district.

Both historical and descriptive research can be cost-effective and logistically easier to conduct than other designs. However, they present researchers with limitations as to what variables can be examined and the extent of the information available. They may also be more time sensitive, which means that data may only be available for a certain time frame, and the information obtained may be limited in its usefulness. Thus, what if a researcher wants to control the information to be studied over a period of time that he or she controls? The answer is to use a longitudinal design.

Developmental or Time Series

Perhaps you are interested in following the activities of members from a rookie police class from graduation through their first five years of service. In particular you are interested in turnover rate, promotions, injuries, accommodations and complaints, and their levels of job satisfaction. The best research design for this type of study is developmental, more commonly referred to as *time series studies*. This type of research design allows for the investigation of specifically identified patterns and events, growth, and/or change over a specific amount of time. Unfortunately, this type of research can be very costly and time-consuming so it is not readily used. There are several time-series designs that are available: cross-sectional studies, longitudinal studies, trend studies, cohort studies, and panel studies.

Cross-sectional Studies

The primary concept of the cross-sectional design is that it allows for a complete description of a single entity during a specific time frame. In this instance an entity might include an individual, agency, community, or in the case of the U.S. Census, an entire nation. These studies are best used as exploratory or descriptive research.

Methodological Link

An innovative differential police response protocol offering citizens the option of problem-solving with an officer over the telephone was developed. To determine citizen satisfaction with this program, a cross-sectional approach was employed. Because an evaluation research component was built into this program, data collection was much easier. The particular data examined included perceived deputy demeanor, departmental problem-solving skills, and overall citizen satisfaction. The data analyses revealed that "most socio-demographic factors make no significant difference in the degree to which citizens are satisfied with problem-solving services offered by the department. The exception is found in age and education. Age makes a difference in the degree to which citizens are satisfied with the overall service received, and overall satisfaction from beginning to end of the problem-solving process is dependent on education but only for those receiving telepolicing service." (Fitzpatrick, 1999, p. 100)

Longitudinal Studies

Where cross-sectional studies view events or phenomena at one time, longitudinal studies examine events over an extended period. For this reason, longitudinal studies are useful for explanation as well as exploration and description. Most field research projects tend to be longitudinal studies (Babbie, 1998, p. 101).

EXAMPLE

Hunter and Wood (1994) were interested in the relationship between severity of sanction and unarmed assaults upon police officers. They obtained assault data on officers for all fifty states. They compared this data with the sanctions applied for unarmed assaults on police officers within each respective state during 1991. They then compared the rates in states that had felony sanctions for weaponless assault upon police officers with their neighboring states during the years 1977 through 1991. This resulted in the longitudinal analysis of four groups of states. Analysis of results in these groupings did not reveal support for the hypothesis that more sanctions would decrease the incidence of weaponless assaults upon police officers.

Trend Studies

Trend studies examine changes in a general population over time. For example, one might compare results from several census studies to determine what demographic changes have occurred in that population. Surveys might indicate that opinions on the death penalty fluctuate over time depending upon social conditions not related to crime as well as changes in the incidences of murder and the occasional occurrences of sensational murders.

Cohort Studies

Cohort studies are trend studies that focus upon the changes that occur in specific sub-populations over time. Usually cohort studies employ age groupings. For example, in a famous criminological study, Wolfgang, Figlio, and Sellin (1972) examined delinquency among a cohort of juveniles. The findings from this study significantly impacted future research and practice in juvenile justice.

Panel Studies

Panel studies are similar to trend and cohort studies except that they study the same set of people each time. By utilizing the same individuals, couples, groups, etc., researchers are able to more precisely examine the extent of changes and the events that influenced them. However, due the effects of deaths, movements from the area, refusal to continue as subjects and other factors that cause the sample to lose members, these studies are logistically difficult to continue over an extended period of time.

Case Studies

The *case* (sometimes referred to as *case and field*) research design allows for the intensive study of a given issue, policy, or group in its social context at one point in time even though that period may span months or years (Adler and Clark, 1999, p. 167). It includes close scrutiny of the background, current status, and relationships or interactions of the topic under study. Case studies often focus upon a specific phenomenon such as Williams's (1989) study of a group of juvenile cocaine dealers over a four-year period.

Case studies may also be longitudinal in that they sometimes observe repeated cases over a certain length of time. These observations are closely linked with the observing of potential independent variables that may be associated with changes in the dependent variables. There are three basic features to this design:

1. Qualitative and/or quantitative descriptions of a variable over the extended period of time.
2. Provides a context wherein the researcher can observe the changes in the variables.
3. Can be used for developing measurement instruments and the testing of their reliability over time.

Case research designs are not limited as to what can be studied. However, they can be costly and time prohibitive and may not provide an explanation for why the results turned out as they did. If one wants to know why something is or has occurred and possible correlating factors, then a correlational design may be more appropriate.

Correlational

A popular research design is one that allows researchers to investigate how one factor may affect or influence another factor, or how the one factor correlates with another—the *correlational* design. In particular, this type of design focuses on how variations of one variable correspond with variations of other variables. An example might be a study of the level of education of police officers and promotion rates, arrest rates, or job satisfaction. The goal of this research design is to obtain correlational coefficients at a statistically significant difference.

Causal-Comparative

Why do men rape? Teens turn to gangs? Individuals become serial killers? To answer these types of questions, a *causal-comparative* (or *ex post facto*) design is useful. This design allows the researcher to examine relationships from a cause-and-effect perspective. This is done through the observation of an existing outcome or consequence and searching back through the data for plausible causal factors.

Each of the previously discussed designs can be found relatively frequently in the criminal justice and criminological research. However, there are three other designs that could be used, but are much more difficult to employ because of costs, logistics, and the fact that they cannot be easily applied to topics in criminal justice and criminology. They are the true experimental, quasi-experimental, and action designs.

Methodological Link

Interested in the relationship between drug addiction and criminal activity among incarcerated women who were in a prison drug rehabilitation program, Stevens' (1999) study could be viewed as a causal-comparative design. In this study, it was believed that drug addiction gave rise to criminality among females. Yet the results of the data did not support this belief. One implication of this finding was that drug addiction in itself is not necessarily a causal factor for producing crimes of violence, especially among females.

True or Classic Experimental

Although it is most often used in the natural sciences, occasionally social scientists may attempt research requiring a *true experimental* design. This type of design allows for the investigation of possible cause-and-effect relationships where one or more experimental units will be exposed to one or more treatment conditions. The outcomes are then compared to the outcomes of one or more control groups that did not receive the treatment. This design includes three major components: (1) independent and dependent variables, (2) experimental and control groups, and (3) pre- and post-testing.

The primary advantages of the experimental design are the isolation of the experimental variation and its impact over time; individual experiments can be limited in scope and require little time, money, and number of subjects; and it is often possible to replicate the results. The major disadvantage is artificiality. Processes that occur in a controlled setting may not actually occur in the natural setting.

With respect to criminal justice and criminology, this type of research is often expensive and logistically difficult to perform. Probably one of the most difficult issues is obtaining consent when the research involves human test subjects. However, sometimes consent is easier to obtain if the experiment could prove useful to the subjects.

EXAMPLE:

A new drug has been created that could suppress sexual desires. A group of convicted pedophiles are asked if they will participate in a study in which part of the group will receive the new drug while the other half are given a placebo. After a certain number of weeks, both groups are tested for sexual response to certain stimuli. The results are compared.

Another major problem in conducting true experimental research is the difficulty in being able to maintain and control the environment where the experiment is conducted. The environment in which criminal justice and criminology research is conducted is often far from stable and filled with possible interfering or intervening variables. As a result of the control and consent issues, along with costs and other logistical problems, it is rare to see a justician or criminologist conduct true experimental research. This has not stopped some efforts to conduct this form of research. Some examples found in criminal justice include the Kansas City Preventive Patrol Experiment, the Minneapolis Domestic Violence study, and San Diego's one- versus. two-person patrol units.

Reality dictates that few exprimental research projects are possible in criminal justice and criminology. The limitations, however, can be addressed to some degree with a quasi-experimental design.

Quasi-Experimental

Unlike the true experimental design where the researcher has almost complete control over relevant variables, the *quasi-experimental* design allows for the approximation of conditions similar to the true experiment. However, the setting does not allow for control and/or manipulation of the relevant variables.

Methodological Link

To examine the level of citizen satisfaction with a telepolicing response, Fitzpatrick (1999) conducted research that combined case study (cross-sectional) with a quasi-experimental design. The research design used provided randomly selected citizens, who had phoned the department for assistance, an opportunity to express feedback on their experiences with the department. The results from this group were then compared to a group of citizens who had received an in-person response.

Although easier to implement than the true experimental design, the quasi-experimental design has its difficulties, too, making it less appealing to most social scientists. The main difficulty lies in the interpretation of the results, that is, being able to separate the effects of a treatment from the effects due to the initial inability to make comparisons between the average units in each treatment group. As with experimental designs, the quasi-experimental design is rare in theoretical criminological research. It is more commonly utilized in evaluation research (previously discussed in Chapter 6) to evaluate new approaches in the criminal justice system and to solve problems with direct application to justice system operations.

Overall, there are a number of research designs to choose from. The design chosen will depend largely on what the researcher is seeking to discover, explain, or describe. Other considerations include economics, logistics, and time. Ultimately, the researcher must decide which design will allow for the best results.

Summary

Selecting a topic and creating the research question are just the beginning of conducting research. One of the most important steps becomes the choosing of an appropriate research design. While one of the most popular designs is survey research, which is also a means of collecting data in the other designs, there are a variety of other possible methods. These include:

Historical—reconstructing the past objectively and accurately, often in relation to the tenability of a hypothesis.

Descriptive—describing systematically a situation or area of interest factually and accurately.

Developmental—investigating patterns and sequences of growth and/or change as a function of time.

Case—studying intensively the background, current status, and environmental interactions of a given social unit, such as individual, group, institution, or community.

Correlational—investigating the extent to which variations in one factor correspond with variations in one or more other factors based on correlation coefficients.

Causal-comparative or "ex post facto"—investigating possible cause-and-effect relationships by observing some existing consequence and searching back through the data for plausible causal factors.

True experimental—investigating possible cause-and-effect relationships by exposing one or more experimental groups to one or more treatment conditions and comparing the results to one or more control groups not receiving the treatment (random assignment being essential).

Quasi-experimenta—approximating the conditions of the true experiment in a setting that does not allow the control and/or manipulation of all relevant variables. The researcher must clearly understand what compromises exist in the internal and external validity of his design and proceed within these limitations.

The chosen design should best meet the needs of the research goals.

Methodological Query:

What type of research design would you use to study the following topics? Why?

  (1) Gang activity in prisons

  (2) Sentencing patterns of a particular court

  (3) The effect of a treatment program for drug users

  (4) Perceived job stress of police officers

  (5) Caseload of parole officers

  (6) The effect of a community policing program on crime

(7) Recidivism and first-time Driving Under the Influence/While Intoxicated offenders

(8) Race and sentencing of drug offenses

References

Adler, E. S. and Clark, R. (1999). *How It's Done: An Invitation to Social Research*. Belmont, CA: Wadsworth Publishing.

Babbie, E. (1998). *The Practice of Social Research, Eighth Edition*. Belmont, CA: Wadsworth Publishing.

Fitzpatrick, C. (1999). A survey of citizen perceptions of treatment and satisfaction with a telephone service option in a rural sheriff's department. In M.L. Dantzker (Ed.), *Readings for Research Methods in Criminology and Criminal Justice*, pp. 99-122. Woburn, MA: Butterworth-Heinemann.

Hunter, R. D. and Wood, R. L. (1994) Impact of felony sanctions: An analysis of weaponless assaults upon American police. *American Journal of Police*, XII (1):65-89.

Liddick, Jr., D. R. (1999). Women as organized criminals: An examination of the numbers gambling industry in New York City. In M. L. Dantzker (Ed.), *Readings for Research Methods in Criminology and Criminal Justice*, pp. 123-138. Woburn, MA.: Butterworth-Heinemann.

Stevens, D. J. (1999). Women offenders, drug addiction, and crime. In M. L. Dantzker (Ed.), *Readings for Research Methods in Criminology and Criminal Justice*, pp. 61-74. Woburn, MA: Butterworth-Heinemann.

Warchol, G. L. and Johnson, B. R. (1999). A cross-sectional quantitative analysis of federal asset forfeiture. In M. L. Dantzker (Ed.), *Readings for Research Methods in Criminology and Criminal Justice*, pp. 139-156. Woburn, MA: Butterworth-Heinemann.

Williams, T. (1989). *The Cocaine Kids*. Reading, MA: Addison-Wesley.

Wolfgang, M. E., Figlio, R. M., and Sellin, T. (1972). *Delinquency in a Birth Cohort*. Chicago: University of Chicago Press.

PART IV

Data Collection

Questionnaire Construction

■ **Vignette 8-1**
A Matter of the Right Questions

You are beginning to see some light at the end of the tunnel. The concept of conducting research is making sense. Maybe the senior project is not going to be so bad after all. Then you meet with your supervising professor. You were originally planning on using archival data to examine the type of crimes for which students at your university are most frequently arrested. You were planning to look at arrest records for the past five years. Your supervising professor approves of the topic, but not the approach. She seems to think it would be more interesting if you did a survey of self-reported criminal behavior. She believes there is probably more criminal activity among the students than what appears in arrest records and it would be interesting to see what might be going undetected or unpunished. Furthermore, her position is that this type of research project will be helpful to you when you have to write a master's thesis, and should you pursue a Ph.D., a dissertation (both of which you have acknowledged as a possibility).

After some discussion you reluctantly agree to pursue your research using a survey, which you decide to call "The College Students' Criminality Survey." Now, the problem is, what questionnaire will you use? Your professor is encouraging you to design your own. It does not have to be fancy or something everyone will want to use, but it will still need to meet specific research criteria. So, once again you look toward your research methods class for guidance.

■ CHAPTER 8
Learning Objectives:

After studying this chapter the student should be able to:

1. Describe what is involved in listing the items you are interested in knowing about the group, concept, or phenomenon.
2. Explain how to establish validity and reliability.
3. Discuss why the wording in the questionnaire must be appropriate for the target audience.
4. Explain why who should answer the questions should be clearly identifiable.
5. Discuss why to avoid asking any questions that are biased, leading, threatening, or double-barreled in nature.
6. Explain why prior to construction, a decision must be made whether to use open- or close-ended questions, or a combination.
7. Discuss how the respondents may not have all the general information needed to complete the questionnaire.
8. Explain why a questionnaire should be pretested whenever possible before it is officially used.
9. Discuss why to set up questions so that the responses are easily recognizable whether it is self-administered or interview.
10. Explain why the questionnaire should be organized in a concise manner that will keep the interest of the respondent, encouraging him or her to complete the entire questionnaire.
11. Define scales and explain their purpose. Identify the different types of scales available for use.
12. Compare and contrast Thurstone Scales, Likert Scales, and Guttman Scales.

Questionnaire Development

When conducting survey research, a well-recognized research "rule of thumb" or perhaps "golden rule" is to *use a questionnaire that has previously been developed and tested.* The primary reason for this is that it eliminates the worries of validity and reliability, two major concerns of questionnaire development. However, an instrument may not exist for a particular research question or, if it does exist, it may not meet the researcher's specific needs. Therefore, the researcher must resort to creating a research-specific questionnaire.

In creating a new survey instrument there are several things to consider, including reliability and validity, and the level of measurement to use. Every textbook offers a different way to approach this task, but in the end, the basic elements are similar. To make understanding this task as easy as possible, a set of guidelines, offered in the manner of rules, is provided that can make questionnaire construction easier.

Rules for Questionnaire Construction

When possible, many of us would prefer not to follow rules, or at least would like to bend them to our satisfaction. The rules you are about to be presented with do not have to be followed in a strict manner, but complete failure to follow them will lead to a failed questionnaire.

■ Rule One

Start with a list of all the items you are interested in
knowing about the group, concept, or phenomenon.

How many times have you gone grocery shopping without a list? When that happens, it is common to end up with many things you do not want and missing things you really need. Questionnaire development should be approached with a "grocery list" mentality. List all the things you want to know, things you would like to know, and things that would be interesting to know about each item you are seeking information about.

Consider the situation in the opening vignette. The student is interested in unreported criminal activity among college students. To collect this information a questionnaire should be developed that will ask the respondents to provide certain identifying characteristics (the independent variables) along with their responses to questions about criminality (dependent variables). What is asked about the students will depend on what type of comparisons or analysis will be conducted. Assume that the researcher is interested in reported behavior by age, year in college, ethnicity/race, gender, and major. Therefore, questions pertaining to this information will be necessary. This information will also aid in describing the sample. Regardless of the nature of the sample, similar questions in various formats should be asked.

Methodological Link

In Dantzker and Waters (1999) study of students' perceptions of policing, the data for their sample was gathered in this manner and included:

Gender: Male_____ Female_____

Race/Ethnicity: White_____ African American_____ Hispanic_____ Other_____

Age: _____

Year in College: Freshman_____ Sophomore_____ Junior_____ Senior_____
Other_____

Major: _____ **Minor**: _____

Last four digits of social security number (for analyses purposes only)
_____

FOR CRIMINAL JUSTICE STUDENTS ONLY

Other than Intro to Criminal Justice, have you taken any other courses with a police component? Yes_____ No_____

If Yes, how many?_____

Employment Goal: Law Enforcement_____ Probation_____ Courts_____
Corrections_____ Law_____ Other_____

Are you related to a police officer? Yes_____ No_____

If Yes, what is the relationship?_____

Note the similarity in information, yet the differing format used in Ford and William's (1999) study of police and correctional officers' perception of a cultural diversity course.

Personal Information

Sex: ( ) M	Race: ( ) **American Indian** ( ) **Hispanic**	Age: ( ) **18-21** ( ) **35–39**
( ) F	( ) **Asian** ( ) **White**	( ) **22-24** ( ) **40–44**
	( ) **Black** ( ) **Other**_____	( ) **25-29** ( ) **45–49**
		( ) **30-34** ( ) **50+**

Number of years in policing/ Corrections: _____	Rank: **Patrol** OR _____**Supervisor**	Ed: ( ) **High school/GED** ( ) **2 yr AA degree** ( ) **4 yr BS/BA degree** ( ) **Grad school or degree**

Listing the characteristics for the sample is the easier phase. Often researchers get into trouble because they failed to list everything they know or want to know about the subject. This failure could cause a shortage of very important data. The key is to decide what is of interest and what is needed. The questions will then take care of the rest, regardless of how they are asked, in statement form or as a question.

Methodological Link

Dantzker and Waters preferred to use a statement format to obtain students' perceptions of policing. The statements were believed to offer enough diversity about policing to give the researchers confidence that they were getting the information they wanted (refer back to Box 3-3). Ford and Williams used the question approach in their survey instrument:

---

1. When did you take the human diversity course? **Year_____**

2. How would you rate your understanding of other cultures prior to taking the course?

3. How would you rate your understanding of other cultures after taking the course?

4. Has there been a difference in your on-the-job behaviors (beliefs, the way you think about others, or your actions) since you took the course? **Can you give an example?** *[Use the reverse side if you need more room.]*

5. Has there been a difference in your off-duty behavior or your personal life since you took the course? **Can you give an example?** *[Use the reverse side if you need more room.]*

6. What do you feel is the single most important thing you learned from the course? *[Use the reverse side if you need more room.]*

7. What, if anything, was the worst thing about the course? *[Use the reverse side if you need more room.]*

8. Would you recommend/have you recommended the course to others?

Regardless of which approach is used, the key is to ask all the questions or create all the statements believed necessary to obtain the information desired. You can always cut data out, but it is difficult to go back and get what was missed. In sum, Rule One suggests making a list of information desired prior to creating any questions or statements.

■ Rule Two

Be prepared to establish validity and reliability.

After the "golden rule," this may actually be the next most critical rule for questionnaire construction. These two concepts will establish whether the data collected will be acceptable to others who may be interested in using your findings, or perhaps even trying to replicate them.

Validity refers to whether the questionnaire is in fact measuring what it claims to measure. That is, it is imperative that the questions or statements are a true measure of the topic under study. This requires that the researcher be able to determine and establish the questionnaire's validity, which can be accomplished through one or more of the following ways: face, content, construct, and criterion validity.

Face

The simplest means of establishing validity is *face* validity. This requires the researcher to accept that the questionnaire is measuring what is being attempted to be measured because the researcher believes it is. This makes it a very judgmental process, lacking empirical support, and requiring the researcher to demonstrate why he or she believes it measures what is expected. For example, in creating the questionnaire to measure perceptions of policing by students, Dantzker and Waters offered face validity as the means of supporting the questionnaire's validity because it yielded expected responses. The statements were developed based on one researcher's anecdotal and observational experiences. Although this is an acceptable means of validation, it is the least acceptable because it is empirically weak.

Content

The second form of validation, *content* validity, also suffers from being judgmental and usually nonempirical. Unlike face validity where the belief in validity focuses on the questionnaire as a whole, content validity emphasizes each individual item's ability to measure the concept in question. Now instead of simply supporting the complete questionnaire's ability to measure what is expected, the researcher must be able to explain why each item measures what is expected. Again, the responsibility falls to the researcher to support why it is believed that each item measures what is expected.

In a study of the perception of job satisfaction among police officers, one question may simply ask the respondent to indicate how satisfied he or she is with being a police officer. While there is no empirical evidence to support this question, it can be argued that because the goal is to measure perceived job satisfaction directly asking someone how satisfied he or she is would be indicative of how he or she perceives his or her job satisfaction level.

While this is an acceptable means of validation, it is not recommended to rely solely on this method.

Construct

Although you are seeking to measure a particular phenomenon, there may be related concepts that are equally important to understanding the phenomenon in question. *Construct* validity (sometimes referred to as *concept* validity) seeks to demonstrate that the questions do actually measure what they have been designated to measure in relation to other variables. It is interested in establishing the fit between the theoretical and operational aspects of the item. With respect to the job satisfaction study, it was expected that individuals with a college degree would indicate a higher level of satisfaction with some items than individuals without a college degree. If the responses to those particular questions support this, than you have established construct validity. However, if the responses from both groups indicate equal satisfaction, then the validity may be challenged. Construct validity can be reinforced through empirical measures.

Criterion

Criterion, also called *pragmatic* or *empirical*, validation is concerned with the relationship between the questionnaire and its results. The assumption is that if the questionnaire is valid, a certain empirical relationship should exist between the data collected and other recognizable properties of the phenomenon. Most often the evidence to support this is garnered from correlational measures consistent with the level of measure. The key requirement, however, is that a reliable and valid measure must already exist to make the comparison. To apply criterion validity to the previously mentioned job satisfaction measure, one group of officers is given the job satisfaction measure which is then compared to the results of a reliable and validated job stress measure (because it has been established that job stress is linked to job satisfaction). With the two sets of scores, a correlation coefficient can be computed providing what is called the validity coefficient. The more common form of criterion validity is predictive validity, which rests upon the questionnaire's ability to accurately predict future conditions or responses.

There may be debates over the best type of validity. Failing to establish any type of validity will devalue your data. Obviously, the more ways you can establish validity the better. Still, validity alone is not enough. It must be accompanied by reliability.

Everyone who lives in a climate where there are several days of extremely cold weather wants a car battery that will start the vehicle day in and day out. Perhaps the battery was purchased because of its reliability to do just that. When it does not start as expected, it is no longer considered reliable. A questionnaire has the same expectation: that it be reliable each time it is used. If the questionnaire is consistent over time and yields similar results each time it is employed, it is reliable. To further establish reliability, one must demonstrate stability and consistency.

Stability occurs when, under similar conditions, a respondent will provide the same answers to the same questions on a second testing. Consistency is determined when the set of questions is strongly related and is measuring the same concept. There are three standard ways to test reliability: test-retest (pretesting), split-half technique, and using multiple forms.

Pretesting is the most fundamental method, yet perhaps the most inconvenient in terms of time and money. The test-retest method requires distributing the questionnaire to the same population twice. If the results are the same, then reliability is accepted. Another method is to distribute the questionnaire to similar samples and look for consistent results between the samples.

A popular and widely used method is the split-half technique. Here the questionnaire is divided into sections or halves. Both sections are given to the same group or among similar groups. A similarity of scores between both halves supports stability.

Using several variations or formats of the same questionnaire, the multiple forms method can support stability. As with the previous methods, if scores on each format are similar, one can assume stability.

All these methods are acceptable; however, it is suggested, when possible, to employ the test-and-retest method. In addition, many statistical packages offer methods for statistical comparison by item-to-item and item-to-scale analyses, and the use of Cronbach's alpha, a commonly used reliability coefficient.

Overall, there are a number of ways to establish validity and reliability. Therefore, there is no reason to fail meeting Rule Two, being able to establish both validity and reliability.

■ Rule Three

The wording in the questionnaire must be appropriate for the target audience.

Everyone is required to complete questionnaires of one type or another at some point in their lives. Sometimes the questions are quite clear, and other times they may befuddle the respondent. When developing a questionnaire, the first guideline is to be sure to use language geared toward the target population. Obviously, you do not want to use words or phrases with which the respondent is not familiar. Otherwise, it can cause confusion and misunderstanding and probably lead to tainted data. For example, on the questionnaire for college students and criminal behavior, in a question about drug use you would want to use the slang or more common usage rather than the scientific one.

Have you ever smoked cannabis? (Wrong)

Have you ever smoked marijuana? (Right)

Therefore, Rule Three suggests that the questions or statements be written in a manner that the target audience can understand.

■ Rule Four

Be sure that it is clearly identifiable who should answer the questions.

How many times have you received a questionnaire in the mail addressed to Dear Occupant and upon opening it discover that it is not clear who should be completing this questionnaire. At least it may not be clear who should fill out which parts. Referring back to the Methodological Link demonstrating the Dantzker and Waters' sample's identifying questions, did you note that there was a section that was specifically for criminal justice students? Anyone not majoring in criminal justice was to avoid answering those questions. All it takes is a simple statement advising who should complete which questions. Thus, for Rule Four the idea is to be sure to clarify who fills out or responds to which questions.

■ Rule Five

Avoid asking any questions that are biased, leading, threatening, or double-barreled in nature.

Does it not feel great to get high? How often do you get high and do you enjoy it? Do you cheat on exams and if you do, do you know you are only cheating yourself? Questions like these are considered biased, double-barreled, or leading. The basic premise is to create questions where there is no confusion for the respondent on how to answer nor is there a push toward a particular answer.

Questions or statements that confuse respondents can cause ambiguous responses. Questions that seek to "guide" the respondent can create blatantly false responses. In addition, the structure of the questionnaire may be such that preceding questions will influence the responses to later questions. If any of the above occur, the findings will not be valid.

Ultimately, the wording of questions and questionnaire format can influence responses. Be aware of that when responding to surveys conducted by ideological groups or organizations that hold particular positions on controversial issues (such as the opposing views of Handgun Control, Inc. and the National Rifle Association). Potential biases may also be observed among the questionnaires of scholars and students who are trying to support a favored hypothesis. If those administering a survey have an interest in or might benefit from the outcome of the survey, they may word the questions or structure the format so as to enhance the likelihood of desired responses. Be skeptical of survey findings by such individuals or groups.

■ Rule Six

Prior to construction, a decision must be made whether to use open- or closed-ended questions, or a combination.

Because the goal of the questionnaire is to ascertain specific information related to the topic and to readily analyze it, deciding on what type of questions should be asked is important. Open-ended questions can make data analyses somewhat more difficult, but can provide more in-depth responses. On the other hand, well-constructed closed-ended questions can provide sufficient data that is more readily analyzable. The more popular method is to combine the types of questions in an effort to collect the most pertinent information about the topic.

Examine Box 8-1. This questionnaire was created as a telephone survey to investigate community satisfaction with its police department.[1] Observe how the questionnaire is composed of both closed- and open-ended questions. Notice how the open-ended questions are worded so that responses could be more readily coded for statistical analysis.

■ Rule Seven

Consider that the respondents may not have all the general information needed to complete the questionnaire.

Under any circumstances, making assumptions could be problematic. This is especially true in questionnaire development. It is a common error to believe that would-be respondents have all the information needed to respond to the questionnaire. For example, several questions about drug and alcohol programs on campus might be asked in the Student Criminality study simply because it is assumed that all students are familiar with these programs. This assumption might result in few responses, causing another incorrect assumption about the results. To avoid this dilemma, always provide an "escape" response such as "unknown" or "no prior knowledge." Refer back to Box 8-1 and the use of the "Unable to respond" choice.

---

[1] This questionnaire was created as part of a proposal to evaluate a police agency. To date, it has neith been tested nor published elsewhere.

Box 8-1
Questionnaire: Open- and Closed-ended Questions

POLICE COMMUNITY TELEPHONE SURVEY

(1) Have you had any official contact (by telephone or in person) with any member of the XXXXX Police Department during the past 18 months?_____Yes_____No

IF YES, what was the reason/circumstance?

_____ Traffic stop	_____ Traffic accident	_____ Victim of a crime
_____ Arrested	_____ Witness to accident	_____ Witness to a crime
_____ Informational	_____ Telephone contact	_____ Other

How would you rate the performance of the person you had contact with?

Wholly Unsatisfactory	Less than Satisfactory	Adequate	Completely Satisfactory	Unable to Respond
1	2	3	4	0

Providing Assistance	1 2 3 4 0
Knowledge	1 2 3 4 0
Courtesy	1 2 3 4 0
Sensitivity	1 2 3 4 0
Friendliness	1 2 3 4 0
Handling of Situation	1 2 3 4 0
Overall Conduct	1 2 3 4 0

IF NO, what is your opinion, perception, or attitude of the XXXXX Police :

Wholly Unsatisfactory	Less than Satisfactory	Adequate	Completely Satisfactory	Unable to Respond
1	2	3	4	0

Providing Assistance	1 2 3 4 0
Courtesy	1 2 3 4 0
Sensitivity	1 2 3 4 0
Friendliness	1 2 3 4 0
Handling of Situation(s)	1 2 3 4 0
Competence	1 2 3 4 0
Attitude	1 2 3 4 0
Behavior	1 2 3 4 0
Traffic Enforcement	1 2 3 4 0
Crime Prevention	1 2 3 4 0
Enforcing Laws	1 2 3 4 0
Solving Crimes	1 2 3 4 0
Dealing with Citizens	1 2 3 4 0
Dealing w/Arrested Persons	1 2 3 4 0
Overall Performance	1 2 3 4 0

continued on next page

continued from previous page

(2) In your opinion, what is the main problem needing police attention in your neighborhood?

(3) In your opinion, what is the main problem needing police attention in the city of XXXXX?

(4) In your opinion, what is the BEST thing about the XXXXX Police?

(5) In your opinion, what is the WORST thing about the XXXXX Police?

(6) In your opinion, what is one change you would make that could improve the XXXXX Police?

For Analysis Purposes Only:

Gender _____Male _____Female

Race/Ethnicity _____Caucasian _____African-American _____Hispanic _____Asian _____Native American _____Other

Age _____18-29 _____30-49 _____50-65 _____Over 65

Employment _____Professional (i.e., doctor, lawyer, etc.) _____Education _____Retail Business _____Food Service _____Clerical _____Laborer _____Other

Education _____High School _____Some College _____Two-yr Degree _____Four-yr Degree _____Graduate Degree _____Other

Live/Area of City _____North _____South _____East _____West _____Central

THANK YOU FOR YOUR ASSISTANCE.

■Rule Eight

Whenever possible pretest the questionnaire before it is officially used.

A reinforcement to Rule Two (stability), and one of the most difficult of the rules to follow, this rule is undoubtedly very legitimate and should be employed whenever possible. With the Student Criminality questionnaire example, after completing the first draft of the questionnaire you might have members in one of your classes complete the questionnaire. By pretesting it you can find errors in construction, language, or other errors that may cause the data to be useless if not corrected. Keep in mind, this does not necessarily require anything more than a few individuals from the target population willing to complete the questionnaire and provide you feedback. While this process might take a little more time and effort, it is well worth it in the long term.

■Rule Nine

Set up questions so that the responses are easily recognizable whether it is self-administered or interview.

The fastest way to jeopardize research is through a questionnaire in which the respondents are not clear on how to respond. Be sure to provide adequate, clear instructions and establish recognizable means for responding. Also, try not to make the format too busy (hard to read due to squeezing too many questions in on a page). If at all possible, avoid using small print.

Methodological Link

Returning to both the Dantzker and Waters and the Ford and Williams' questionnaires, specific instructions are provided and the way and means for answering are quite clear.

Dantzker and Waters:

This survey was designed to examine students' perceptions of policing prior to taking and after completing an introductory level police course. Please read each statement and without spending too much time "analyzing" the statement, indicate your level of agreement/disagreement using the scale provided. Thank you for your cooperation.

Strongly	Not Strongly Disagree	Disagree	Sure Agree	Agree
-2	-1	0	1	2

Question Response Example:
Many individuals who become police officers want to help society.

-2	-1	0	1	2

Ford and Williams:

Introduction: This study is being conducted by two professionals who work in the law enforcement and correctional fields. We are conducting the survey to understand your reactions to the Human Diversity Training course that was required in the Academy for initial certification or in later retraining. While this survey is being distributed at your work site through the courtesy of your Chief/Director, it is not intended to be shown/used there. We would appreciate your help — and your honesty — about this course. You do not have to put your name on the survey; it is anonymous. The personal questions at the end of the survey may help us interpret differences in survey responses. Thank you for your time!

Question Response Example:
How would you rate your understanding of other cultures prior to taking the course?
( ) Good   ( ) Fair   ( ) Poor

Regardless of the format, it should be clear to respondents what you want them to do and how to accomplish it.

■ Rule Ten

The questionnaire should be organized in a concise manner that will keep the interest of the respondent, encouraging him or her to complete the entire questionnaire.

How often have you started a novel only to find that you didn't make it past the first few chapters because it was boring? If you had continued to read, it might have become more pleasurable, but you had lost interest. This same concept is applicable to questionnaire development. If the beginning questions are not interesting and do not hold the respondents' attention, chances are that they may not complete the rest of the questions, which leaves you with missing data. Therefore, it is beneficial to have questions that may pique the respondent's interest in the beginning and at the end. In addition, if respondents see several pages of questions, they are less likely to begin the survey. While it is tempting to try to "cover everything," a clear and concise survey that consists of a few easy-to-read questions will receive more responses. While specialized questionnaires that target a specific population (that has a vested interest in the subject matter) may be longer, we recommend that most surveys be kept to two pages of questions using normal size type.

Rules and guidelines are fallible, but the ten rules offered for questionnaire construction, if followed, will certainly improve the chances of obtaining good, analyzable data. Still, keeping all the rules in mind might not keep us from creating a poor questionnaire. Consequently, these rules are not the only thing that must be known to create a usable questionnaire. A key aspect in questionnaire construction is measurement.

Scales

A common element of survey research is the construction of scales. A scale can either be (1) a measurement device for responding to a question or statement or (2) a compilation of statements or questions used to represent the concept studied. For example, in the previous Methodological Link the responses' to Dantzker and Water's statement is a scale that ranges from –2 to +2. Each statement is a separate variable of perception. Putting all the statements from their questionnaire together (attaining a numerical result for responses to all statements) gave them what they refer to as the Student's Perceptions of Policing Scale. Scales, as compilations, are particularly important and a relevant part of research for three primary reasons (Nachmias and Nachmias, 1987).

1. They allow the collapsing of several variables into a single variable that produces a representative value, thus reducing the complexity of the data.
2. They offer measures that are quantifiable and more open to precision and statistical manipulation.
3. They can increase the measurement's reliability.

To accomplish these things, a scale must fit the "Principle of Unidimensionality" (Nachmias and Nachmias, 1987). This principle suggests that the items making up the scale need to represent one dimension befitting a continuum that is supposed to be reflective of only one concept. For example, if you are measuring job satisfaction, the scale should not be capable of measuring job stress, too. The representativeness of any scale will rely greatly on the level of measurement used.

Scaling Procedures

Ultimately, to conduct research we are looking to complete a measurement. Yet what is the actual purpose of this measurement? We use measurement in research as a means of connecting phenomena with numbers for analytical purposes. Scaling is identified as a means of assisting in making the necessary and proper connections. Despite the existence of numerous scales, there will be times when the researcher must create his or her own. The key is to understand that you are trying to explain a phenomenon and that the scale must meet this criterion. There are two primary types of scaling procedures to choose from.

Arbitrary Scales

An arbitrary scale is designed to measure what the researcher believes it is measuring and is based on face validity (discussed earlier) and professional judgment. While this allows for the creation of many different scales, it is easily criticized for its lack of substantive support. Still, this type of scale does provide a viable starting point for exploratory research, even though it is the less recommended method of scaling.

Attitudinal Scales

More commonly found in criminal justice and criminological research are the attitudinal scales. There are three primary types available: Thurstone, Likert, and Guttman.

Thurstone Scales

The construction of a Thurstone scale relies on the use of others (sometimes referred to as "judges") to indicate what items they think best fits the concept. There are two methods for completing this task. The first method is paired comparisons. Here the judges are provided several pairs of questions or statements and asked to choose which most favorably fits the concept under study. The questions or statements picked most often by the judges become part of or comprise the complete questionnaire.

Which question might best fit the concept of job satisfaction.

1. I enjoy going to work every day.
2. Sometimes I am very tired when I get home from work.

The second method and one more often used is equal appearing intervals. For this method, the researcher will submit a list of questions or statements to the judges who are then asked to give each a number, which will depend on how large a scale is desired, indicating the strength of the question or statement to the concept. The researcher would then keep those items where judges were in the strongest agreement and eliminate those with the weakest indicator scores.

EXAMPLE

In designing the College Students' Criminality Questionnaire, you want the questions to form a 15-point item criminality scale. You submit 50 questions to judges asking them to score each question from 1 (strongest indicator) to 15 (weakest indicator). The top fifteen questions become your scale.

Consequently, Thurstone scaling is not very popular because of the time it takes for the judges to complete their tasks. Furthermore, since the judges have to be experts in the area of study, finding an adequate pool of qualified judges could also be problematic for the researcher.

Likert Scales

Probably the most commonly used method in attitudinal research is the Likert scale. This method generally makes use of a bipolar, five-point response range (i.e., strongly agree to strongly disagree). Questions where all respondents provide similar responses are usually eliminated. The remaining questions are used to comprise the scale.

Guttman Scales

The last scale, the Guttman scale, requires that an attitudinal scale measure only one dimension or concept. The questions or statements must be progressive so that if the respondent answers positively to a question, he or she must respond the same to the following.

There are various other types of scaling procedures. However, because so few are used in criminal justice and criminological research they will not be discussed. Furthermore, advanced statistical techniques, such as factor analysis and Chronbach's alpha, are much faster and simpler to use to determine a scale's composition. For example, the Student's Perceptions of Police scale (Dantzker and Waters, 1999) was originally 20 items before a factor analysis and Chronbach's alpha eliminated six items, bringing it to its current 14-point scale. The question at this point might be, why use scales at all?

There are three primary reasons or advantages to using scales. First, a scale allows for a clearer and more precise measure of the concept than individual items. Second, scales can be replicated and used as longitudinal measures. Finally, scales require more thought. The disadvantages to scales are twofold: (1) there is concern as to whether true attitudes can be measured on a scale, and (2) the question of validity and reliability. Despite the shortcomings, overall, scales can be quite useful in measuring data and should be used where and when it is appropriate and necessary.

Summary

To conduct research, data must be collected. Generally this means that some type of tool (a questionnaire) must be available to assist in collecting the data. The golden rule is to try to use a questionnaire that has previously been tested. However, when that is not possible and a questionnaire must be constructed, following the suggested rules will help create an acceptable tool. These rules are:

1. Start with a list of all the items you are interested in knowing about the group, concept, or phenomenon.
2. Be prepared to establish validity and reliability.
3. The wording in the questionnaire must be appropriate for the targeted audience.
4. Be sure that it is clearly identifiable as to who should answer the questions.
5. Avoid asking any questions that are biased, leading, threatening, or double-barreled in nature.
6. Prior to construction, a decision must be made whether to use open- or closed-ended questions, or a combination.
7. Consider that the respondents may not have the general information needed to complete the questionnaire.
8. Whenever possible pretest the questionnaire before it is officially used.
9. Set up questions so that the responses are easily recognizable whether it is self-administered or interview.
10. The questionnaire should be organized in a manner that will keep the interest of the respondent, encouraging him or her to complete the entire questionnaire.

In addition to the rules, questionnaire development requires familiarity with issues such as reliability, validity, measurement level, and scales. Scales can be either arbitrary or attitudinal in nature. Three primary attitudinal scales are Thurstone, Likert, and Guttman. The most popular scale is Likert, which makes use of a bipolar set number of points.

Methodological Queries:

Referring to the opening vignette,

(1) What type of questionnaire would you develop to measure student criminality? Give some examples of the information you would seek.

(2) What are some questions you would ask?

(3) How would you develop the questions? Would you hope to create a scale? Why?

References

Dantzker, M.L. (1993). Designing a measure of job satisfaction for policing: A research note. *Journal of Crime and Justice*, 16(2), 171-181.

Dantzker, M.L. and Waters, J.E. (1999). Examining students' perceptions of policing—A pre- and post-comparison between students in criminal justice and non-criminal justice courses. In M.L. Dantzker (Ed.), *Readings for Research Methods in Criminology and Criminal Justice*, pp. 27-36. Woburn, MA.: Butterworth-Heinemann.

Ford, M. and Williams, L. (1999). Human/cultural diversity training for justice personnel. In M.L. Dantzker (Ed.), *Readings for Research Methods in Criminology and Criminal Justice*, pp. 37-60. Woburn, MA.: Butterworth-Heinemann.

Nachmias, D. and Nachmias, C. (1987). *Research Methods in the Social Sciences.* New York: St. Martin's Press.

Sampling

■ Vignette 9-1
Would You Like to Sample . . . ?

Finally, it is the weekend, time to do some chores other than school. In particular, you would like a break from your research class and your pending project. It seems more and more everything you do has research-related implications and you would like to get away. So, the first thing you decide to do is some grocery shopping. Having shopped at the same store for a few years you are quite familiar with where everything is and any unusual activities. Only now, for the first time, you pay some attention to the individuals at the end of each aisle offering samples of a product to shoppers. You decide to watch one of the "vendors" for a few minutes taking note of who is being solicited to sample this particular product and who accepts. You observe that not everyone is offered and of those who are approached, not everyone accepts. You make the same observation of several of the other vendors.

Later that day, you are at the mall. While walking among the stores, you have observed several "vendors" attempting to get passersby to sample their goods. At one point you are approached by an individual who asks if you could take a few minutes to participate in a marketing survey. After responding to a few personal questions, you are advised that you do not fit the demographics being sought and are thanked for your time. By the end of your shopping day you realize that you witnessed or took part in several "research" efforts where sampling was a very important component. Yet, you wonder whether the sampling efforts you observed were appropriate and whether you could try the same methods for your research. Could you just stand out in the quad and stop every other student? Were there certain demographics you might need to screen for? Would this method be acceptable? Representative? Even on the weekend, you cannot escape thinking about your research project. However, while every phase is important, a poor job of sampling would make all other efforts useless. The question then is, what type of sample should you use?

■ CHAPTER 9
Learning Objectives

After studying this chapter the student should be able to:

1. Discuss the purpose of sampling in criminological research.
2. Define what is meant by population, sampling frame, and sample. Describe their relationships. Give examples of each.
3. Explain how probability theory enables the researcher to obtain representative samples.
4. Identify and describe the various types of probability samples.
5. Compare and contrast probability sampling with nonprobability sampling.
6. Identify and discuss the various types of nonprobability samples.
7. Explain the importance of sample size. Include confidence intervals, confidence levels, and sampling error in your discussion.
8. Determine how many observations would be necessary to obtain a sample with an error tolerance of +3 at the 95 percent confidence level. Explain how many more observations you would add to this number and why you would do so.

Sampling

Conducting research requires the gathering of information about a specific concept, phenomenon, event, or group. Although there are some types of research that require gathering information about every element associated with the topic, a natural science necessity, in the social sciences, this is neither feasible nor necessary. In conducting criminal justice and criminological research the primary focus is usually on some population.

Recall from Chapter 3 that a population is the complete group or class from which information is to be gathered. For example, police officers, probation officers, and correctional officers are each a population. Again, although it would be great if every member of a population could provide the information sought, it is just not practical. Therefore, sampling the population is a necessity. Before one can begin to sample, the first step is to identify the group from which the sample will come. This is called the sampling frame:

That list or quasi-list of units composing a population, from which a sample is selected. If the sample is to be representative of the population, it is essential that the sampling frame include all (or nearly all) members of the population. (Babbie, 1998, p. G6)

For example, keeping with the idea of the College Students' Criminality study (introduced in Chapter 8), it is obvious that college students are the population. However, not all college students could be surveyed. Even surveying all the college students at one university could prove to be quite burdensome. Therefore, a sampling frame must be chosen. For discussion purposes, under the above circumstances, the sampling frame will be freshmen students at the university.

Having identified the sampling frame, the next decision is to choose the type of sample to be used. Again, recall from Chapter 3 that a sample is a group chosen from a target population to provide information sought. That sample will either be of the probability or nonprobability nature. It is appropriate at this point to provide an overview of probability theory.

Probability Theory

A friend of ours frequently buys lottery tickets. On a number of occasions individuals (usually whom he does not know) have taken it upon themselves to inform him that, "You are wasting your money. The odds of you being hit by lightning are higher than of you winning the lottery." To which he honestly replies, "Thank you for your concern. I have been hit by lightning. This is more fun." The individuals who are warning our friend are statistically correct: his chance of winning the lottery is extremely small and actually is less likely than being hit by lightning. However, since he doesn't really care if he wins (he amuses himself by checking them several days later, asserting that he is potentially a winner until he discovers otherwise) and since his investment only averages about $2.00 per week, statistical probabilities don't mean much to him. Unfortunately, many people who wager far more than they can afford also disregard statistical probability. These individuals tend to either believe that "it is time for their luck to change" or that "God (or fate, depending on their religious orientation) will intervene in their lives." While we do not question the benevolence of a Supreme Being, we do feel that if God or even luck preordained such an event, the purchase of one ticket would be adequate. If not preordained, the sincere gambler might want to seriously consider the statistical probability of success.

Probability theory is based on the concept that over time there is a statistical order in which things occur. If you flip an unaltered coin ten times, it is possible that it will land on heads five times and tails five times. However, it might land on heads eight times and tails only two. This is because each time the coin is flipped it has an equal chance of being heads or tails. What happened previously has no influence on what will happen in the future. We cannot accurately predict what will happen on the next coin toss. Yet, we can accurately assume that over a lengthy period of time the number of heads and the number of tails will be about the same. This is the basis of statistical probability. Anything can happen, but over the long run there will be a statistical order.

The knowledge that over time things tend to adhere to a statistical order allows us to chose samples that are representative of a population in general. While we cannot say in advance that a sample is representative, we can follow a procedure that "should" lead to a representative sample being selected. Since every number (representing people, items, or events) has the same chance of being chosen, then most of the time the sample drawn will be representative. On occasion it will not be.

Probability Sampling

The general goal when choosing a sample is to obtain one that is representative of the target population. By being representative, the results can be said to be applicable to the whole population and would be similar no matter how many different samples were surveyed. Representation requires that every member in the population or the sampling frame have an equal chance of being selected for the sample. This is a probability sample. Four types of probability samples exist: simple random, stratified random, systematic, and cluster.

Simple Random Samples

As previously stated, a random sample is one in which all members of a given population have the same chance of being selected. Furthermore, the selection of each member must be independent from the selection of any other member. To assist in selecting a random sample, a device known as a table of random numbers is often used (which can be found in almost every statistics book published). You select a numeral at random and then use the subsequent numerals provided within the table until you have selected the appropriate number of population members needed. Today using the computer to randomly generate a sample is

---

Methodological Link

Moriarty (1999) and Moriarty, Pelfrey, and Vasu (1999) made use of random sampling to conduct a telephone survey. The sampling element was telephone numbers belonging to a sampling frame of North Carolina's estimated phone households. The initial sample pool of telephone numbers was 35,000; however, only 16,800 numbers were necessary to generate the required sample size. The sample was computer-generated and purchased from a company that specializes in generating samples: Survey Sampling, Incorporated of Fairfield, Connecticut.

becoming more popular. In either case, the researcher must have a complete list of every member of the sampling frame, which is one of the disadvantages of random sampling. Yet, even with this obstacle, random sampling is very popular, partly because it has become easier for researchers to obtain statistically acceptable, random samples.

Stratified Random Samples

Chapter 3 defines a stratified sample as one that has been chosen from a population that has been divided into subgroups called strata. These strata are selected based upon specified characteristics that the researcher wishes to ensure for inclusion in the study (Adler and Clark, 1999; Babbie, 1998; Fitzgerald and Cox, 1998). This type of sample requires the researcher to have knowledge of the sampling frame's demographic characteristics. These characteristics (selected variables) are then used to create the strata from which the sample is chosen. Depending on the interests or needs of the researcher, a proportionate selection will be made from each strata (in a random manner) or oversampling (disproportionate) may be necessary.

EXAMPLE

There are approximately 700,000 police officers in the United States divided between more than 14,000 police agencies. A large portion of these agencies may employ less than 10 officers while a small number employ a large percentage of all police officers (that is, New York, Chicago, and Los Angeles account for employing close to 60,000 police officers). Therefore, when a study of police agencies is conducted, often it requires dividing them into some form of strata, more commonly by size (number of sworn personnel employed). Then to be representative of policing, there must be a disproportionate number of smaller agencies selected.

Systematic Samples

There seems to be some debate over this type of sampling. It has been discussed as both probability and nonprobability sampling. It is offered here as a probability sample because it includes random selection and initially allows inclusion of every member of the sampling frame. With a systematic sample, every nth item in the sampling frame is included in the sample. Where to begin selecting the nth item is derived from a sampling interval established based on the ratio of the sample size to the population. A warning should be given when using systematic sampling. If you are sampling an organization, such as a police patrol division, ensure that your selection procedure (for example every 20th officer) does not result in a rhythm with the organization's bureaucratic structure (Babbie, 1998) that would cause a particular type of individual (patrol squad sergeant) to be selected each time. This would negate the purpose of such a sample.

| **Methodological Link** |

To conduct her study of citizen perceptions of treatment and satisfaction with the telephone service option in Larimer County, Colorado, Fitzpatrick (1999) made use of systematic random sampling. A comprehensive listing of citizens who called the department for help each month served as the sampling frame. Callers were then randomly selected by going through the sampling frame systematically using a sampling interval based on a predetermined percentage of the population needed for inclusion in the study and the total size of the monthly population. For example, if the population for a given month was 200 callers and the sample size needed was 10 percent of the population, then the sampling interval became the proportionate sample size multiplied by the monthly population total (that is, $[.10][200] = 20$ which is the minimum sample size needed; the sampling interval became $200/20 = 10$, therefore every 10th element was selected until reaching the sample size of 20).

Cluster Samples

The last of the probability sampling methods is the cluster sample (also known as area probability sample). This sample consists of randomly selected groups, rather than individuals. Basically, the population to be surveyed is divided into clusters (for example, census tracts). This is a multi-stage sample (sampling occurs two or more times) in which groups (clusters) are sampled initially (Fitzgerald and Cox, 1998). Subsequent sub-samples of the clusters are then selected. For example, a sampling may be taken of correctional institutions nationwide. Employee information from each of the sampled institutions might then be obtained. From these lists, a sample of correctional employees from each institution may be drawn. This method is popular for national victimization or other national interest topics. It is a particularly useful tool for political scientists.

Usually, the researcher wants to make use of probability samples primarily because they are often more statistically stable. However, random sampling can be very expensive and logistically difficult to complete. Therefore, it is common to find nonprobability sampling in criminal justice and criminological research.

Nonprobability Sampling

The major difference between probability and nonprobability sampling is that one provides the opportunity for all members of the sampling frame to be selected while the other does not. This shortcoming of nonprobability sampling often leads to questions and concern over the representativeness of the sample. However, when the sample produces the requisite information, representativeness is often not as much of a concern (although its limitations must still be noted). Furthermore, a nonprobability sample could be perceived as representative if enough characteristics of the target population exist in the sample. There are four types of nonprobability samples: purposive, quota, snowball, and convenience.

Purposive Samples

Among the nonprobability samples, the purposive sample appears to be the most popular. Based on the researcher's skill, judgment, and needs, an appropriate sample is selected (Fitzgerald and Cox, 1998). When the subjects are selected in advance based upon the researcher's view that they reflect normal or average scores, this process is sometimes referred to as typical-case sampling. If subgroups are sampled to permit comparisons among them, this technique is known as stratified purposeful sampling (Adler and Clark, 1999, p. 111). A major factor of purposive sampling is accessibility to units or individuals that are part of the target population.

Methodological Link

Dantzker and Waters (1999) chose specific classes of students, both criminal justice and American government, to comprise their sample of college students. Accessibility to these classes played a major role in their selection. Stevens (1999), to better study women, drugs and criminality, made use of a group of women in a particular prison at which he was teaching. Gordon (1999) surveyed all the employees of three different institutions to examine the attitudes of correctional officers among the three different types of institutions. Finally, Ford and Williams's (1999) sample consisted only of those individuals who had taken the diversity class and were employed by two area police agencies and a local department of corrections.

In all of the studies from the preceding Methodological Link, the researchers chose their samples because they believed they best fit the needs of the study. The selection was based on their knowledge of the topic, the target populations, and accessibility. Although the samples may not have been representative, they did provide the requisite data to complete the studies. In most cases, because the purposive sample is not representative, findings cannot be generalized to complete populations. This does not mean that a purposive sample cannot be generalizable, but it must conform to some similar elements of the population.

EXAMPLE

As previously noted, one of Dantzker's research interests is job satisfaction among police officers. In his studies of this subject he has used purposive sampling, choosing police agencies he perceived as being representative of a "typical municipal police agency." Since he has surveyed only fourteen agencies to date, one might easily suggest that only the job satisfaction for each agency could be discussed and that the findings could not be applied to all police agencies. However, when the data from all the agencies are combined, he has a sample whose characteristics are quite similar to the police population in terms of gender, race, age, and educational composition. As a result, he would have no qualms about generalizing the findings.

Despite statistical concerns about the sample, purposive sampling can offer researchers a legitimate and acceptable means of collecting data.

Quota Samples

Recall from the opening vignette that one of the observations dealt with a marketing researcher who decided that the individual did not fit the sampling needs. These types of research efforts often rely on quota sampling. For this type of sample, the proportions are based on the researcher's judgment for inclusion. In other words, does the individual or unit fit the needs of the survey? Selection continues until enough individuals have been chosen to fill out the sample.

Assume that for the College Students' Criminality study only second-semester freshman students at the university are being targeted. Since you have no means of identifying these individuals, you set up a booth in the student union where you stop students as they come by and inquire as to their status at the university. You survey only those who advise you that they are second-semester freshman students and continue this approach until you have reached your desired sample size or your quota.

To assure some level of representativeness by gender and race, you set your quota at a percentage equivalent to what the university claims to have in its population. For example, by gender, the university is 45% female and 55% male while racially it is 43% White, 37% African American, and 20% other.

Reaching some minimal level of representativeness requires you to continue selecting students until your quota sample appears to be comprised in similar fashion to the university. Obviously, this can be a painstakingly long method and does not guarantee representation.

Snowball Samples

Although not a highly promoted form of quantitative sampling, snowball sampling is commonly used as a qualitative technique. The snowball sample begins with a person or persons who provide names of other persons for the sample. This sample type is most often seen used in exploratory studies where an appropriate target population is not readily identifiable, making a sampling frame more difficult to select, but does not eliminate the existence of an identifiable sampling frame (Senese, 1997). Additionally, despite the issue of representation, snowball sampling requires the researcher to rely on the expertise of others to identify prospective units for the sample. Snowball sampling is frequently used in field research when the researcher must rely on introductions from group members in order to access other group members.

Methodological Link

Flanyak (1999), conducting a qualitative, exploratory research study, utilized both snowball and convenience sampling methods. Through this method she obtained twenty-two subjects for the study. While her sampling frame consisted of lists of sociology and criminal justice department faculty members in several universities in Illinois, it was the result of initial interviews during a pilot study with respondents at her academic institution, that other potential subjects were identified. Furthermore, other subjects were chosen from the faculty of her undergraduate institution to ensure a high response rate.

Obviously, the snowball method may lead to an elite sample that has no representative or generalizable attributes. Consequently, if the data addresses the research question, then these shortcomings are acceptable.

Convenience Sample

Undoubtedly the last choice for a sample is the convenience sample or available subjects sample. Here there is no attempt to ensure any type of representativeness. Usually this sample is a very abstract representation of the population or target frame. Units or individuals are chosen simply because they were "in the right place at the right time."

EXAMPLE

To study officer opinions on police misconduct, Hunter (1999) developed a survey instrument based upon the findings of prior research on police ethics and misconduct. Before administering this survey to a sample of several hundred officers in the southeastern United States, he sought feedback from a convenience sampling of currently serving officers. One group consisted of officers on a patrol shift from a mid-sized metropolitan police agency. A second group was composed of officers taking college courses at a regional college. A third group was made up of officers in their final phase of training at a regional police academy. Findings from this convenience sample not only permitted Hunter to refine the questionnaire, but he was also able to gain insights as to how officers felt about different forms of police misconduct and a variety of proposed solutions aimed at curbing such behaviors. Obviously the results were only indicative of this sample's opinions and could not be construed to be representative of the opinions of officers outside the sample. However, as an exploratory study it was quite useful.

Analysis of data from a convenience sample is extremely limited. The sample selected may or may not represent the population that is being studied. Therefore generalizations that are made about the population cannot be considered to be valid (Adler and Clark, 1999). Because of this limitation, convenience samples are not useful for explanation or even for description beyond the sample surveyed. They are often useful as explorations upon which future research may be based.

The quality and quantity of the data are dependent on the sampling technique. Statistical support is stronger for probability samples. However, there are times when nonprobability samples are fruitful. Regardless of which type is used, an important element of each is the sample size.

Sample Size

It is claimed that the "quality of a sample depends largely upon its size" (Vockell, 1983, p. 111). The belief is that the larger the sample, the more likely the data will more truly reflect the population. An interesting aspect about sample size seems to be that there is no set size that a sample should be. Usually, the sample size is the result of several elements:

1. how accurate the sample must be,
2. economic feasibility (how much do you have to spend),
3. the availability of requisite variables (including any subcategories), and
4. accessibility to the target population.

Confidence Levels

Deciding how large the sample should be requires an understanding of confidence intervals, which indicates a range of numbers (for example, ±15). Since a sample is merely an estimated reflection of the target population, a confidence interval suggests the accuracy of the estimate (Vockell, 1983). The smaller the confidence interval the more accurate the estimated sample. The estimated probability that a population parameter will fall within a given confidence interval is known as the confidence level (Adler and Clark, 1999, p. 494). Thus to reduce sampling error the researcher would desire a smaller confidence interval. To do so, he or she would select a smaller confidence level. Consider Box 9-1, which offers an excerpt from a grant proposal in which job satisfaction of both sworn and nonsworn personnel in a municipal police agency is to be measured. Specifically, note the difference in confidence levels and the reasons why.

Methodological Link

Moriarty (1999) made a total of 809 complete telephone interviews. Considering the size of the target population, her sample size represented a ± 5 point margin of error with a 95 percent confidence level.

Box 9-1
Confidence Level Example[1]

FOR SWORN OFFICERS

(B) After the data from the surveys have been tabulated, interviews could then be held with a stratified-random sample (by rank and assignment) of 50 officers. (The sample of 50 officers has been calculated to have a ±3.65 confidence level, which is statistically, a very good level. This would mean that if 56% of the officers interviewed indicated the same reason for satisfaction with a given item, then it would be safe to say that if all 167 officers were interviewed the chances are that a confidence interval between 52% to 59% would give the same response.)

FOR NONSWORN EMPLOYEES

(B) After the data from the surveys have been tabulated, interviews could then be held with a random sample of 30 nonsworn employees. (The sample of 30 has been calculated to have a ±15.12% confidence level. This would mean that if 56% of the employees interviewed indicated the same reason for satisfaction with a given item, then it would be safe to say that if all 94 employees were interviewed the chances are that between 41% to 71% would give the same response.) In the case of the nonsworn, a higher number could be interviewed, which would improve the confidence level, should the City so desire to spend the additional funds to complete these interviews. However, it is believed that the combination of the surveys and the interviews will be sufficient to offer reliable findings and recommendations.

In social science research, confidence levels are very important, although they are rarely explained or identified. In many cases readers are expected to accept that samples are statistically acceptable, or an accurate estimate of the target population. This does not mean that the findings should be ignored. It simply means that their application must be more conservative and judicious.

---

[1] This excerpt is from a grant proposal written by Dantzker in response to a Request for Proposals (RFP) to conduct a study of a police department in Texas. The proposal was not accepted and is not published anywhere.

Sampling Formulas

The key aspect to selecting appropriate confidence levels is the sample size. As previously suggested, the larger the sample the more accurate the estimate. Therefore, it would be beneficial to know just how large a sample is required to attain the best confidence level. There are several mathematical formulas to assist in determining sample size. Unless you are a good mathematician, it is suggested that pre-existing tables or computer statistical packages be used to make that determination. Should those means not be available to you, in the following paragraphs we shall demonstrate how such a formula may be utilized.

A Commonly Used Sampling Formula

When you select a sample size you are seeking to draw a large enough number of observations from the target population to ensure that the sample accurately represents that population. As was discussed above, the larger the sample size, the more likely that it will be representative. However, since the costs in time and money of sampling large numbers are prohibitive, we rely upon probability theory to estimate the proper sample size. We are guided in our selection by our knowledge of acceptable sample sizes. Generally, in social science research, we seek a sample size that would 95 times out of 100 vary by 5 percent or less from the population. In some cases we may use less stringent requirements and in others we may wish to have (and be able to afford) a higher level of accuracy.

Assuming that we wish to have a sample of a large population that is at the 95 percent confidence level and has a sample error within 5 percent of the population, we could use the following formula:

$$n = \left(\frac{(1.96)2}{se} \right) \left[p(-p) \right]$$

where n = sample size needed
$\quad$ p = assumed population variance
$\quad$ SE = standard error

1.96 = represents a normal curve z score value at a confidence level of 95%

For an error tolerance of 5 percent at the 95 percent confidence level we would use .05 as the SE. The formula would then become:

$$n = \left(\frac{(1.96)2}{.05} \right) \left[.5(-.5) \right]$$

$$n \quad = 384.16$$
$$n \quad = 385$$

Thus we would find that a sample size of 385 would provide us with a sample that had an error tolerance of ±5 percent at the 95 percent confidence level. If we wished to change confidence levels and/or error tolerance, we would then adapt the formula to do so. For example if you wanted to ensure that your sample was representative, and had the money and time to do so, an error tolerance of ±1 percent at the 99 percent confidence level would result in the following:

$$n = \left(\frac{(4.2930175)2}{.01} \right) \left[.1(1-.1) \right]$$

$$n \quad = 16586.99$$
$$n \quad = 16,587$$

A Sampling Size Selection Chart

Having read how the above formula was used to obtain the desired sample size, you may decide that you have no desire to ever do so. To save you from such an exercise, we have included a simple chart that will make sample size selection much easier. Simply determine the confidence level and error tolerance that you desire in your survey sample and look it up in Table 9-1. The number indicated is how many observations from the study population that you would need to randomly select in order to have a representative sample.

Table 9-1 provides you with the sample size you will need based upon the error tolerance and confidence level desired. However, those are the numbers of observations needed in the sample. To ensure that those numbers are obtained, we recommend that you always oversample by twenty percent. If this isn't enough, you can always add more observations as long as they are randomly selected from the same population and any time differences do not affect responses. Remember, the sample must be selected randomly if it is to be representative of the population.

Summary

Gaining data from a complete population is usually impossible. In most cases, research data is best obtainable through a sample. Before a sample is chosen, identifying the sampling frame is necessary. Having an identifiable sampling frame leads to a decision as to what type of sample to select: probability or nonprobability. Probability samples include random, stratified random, strata, and cluster sampling. Purposive, quota, snowball, and accidental are forms of nonprobability sampling.

Regardless of the type of sampling, there is a question of sample size. Although no magical number exists, confidence levels provide a statistical means for establishing legitimacy of the sample. The smaller the confidence level the more representative is the sample. As can be seen,

Table 9-1   Sample Size Selection Chart

Error Tolerance (percent)	Confidence Levels	
	95%	99%
1	9,604	16,587
2	2,401	4,147
3	1,068	1,843
4	601	1,037
5	385	664

Adapted from: Richard L. Cole, *Introduction to Political Science and Policy Research* (New York: St. Martin's Press, Inc.), p. 83.

careful thought should be given prior to choosing a sample type and a sample size.

Methodological Queries:

Referring to the College Students' Criminality Study,

(1) Briefly describe how you could use each type of sample to conduct the survey.

(2) What would be the best sample type? Why?

(3) What size sample would you need?

(4) Discuss what roles that confidence level and error tolerance would play.

References

Adler, E. S. and Clark, R. (1999). *How It's Done: An Invitation to Social Research.* Belmont, CA: Wadsworth Publishing.

Babbie, E. (1998). *The Basics of Social Research.* Belmont, CA: Wadsworth Publishing.

Cole, R. L. (1996). *Introduction to Political Science and Policy Research.* New York: St. Martin's Press, Inc.

Dantzker, M. L. and Waters, J. E. (1999). Examining students' perceptions of policing—A pre- and post-comparison between students in criminal justice and non-criminal justice courses. In M. L. Dantzker (Ed.), *Readings for Research Methods in Criminology and Criminal Justice,* pp. 27-36. Woburn, MA: Butterworth-Heinemann.

Fitzgerald, J. D. and Cox, S. M. (1998). *Research Methods in Criminal Justice: An Introduction* (3rd Ed.). Chicago, IL: Nelson-Hall Publishers.

Fitzpatrick, C. (1999). A survey of citizen perceptions of treatment and satisfaction with a telephone service option in a rural sheriff's department. In M. L. Dantzker (Ed.), *Readings for Research Methods in Criminology and Criminal Justice,* pp. 99-122. Woburn, MA: Butterworth-Heinemann.

Flanyak, C. M. (1999). Accessing data: Procedures, practices, and problems of academic researchers. In M. L. Dantzker (Ed.), *Readings for Research Methods in Criminology and Criminal Justice,* pp. 157-180. Woburn, MA: Butterworth-Heinemann.

Ford, M. and Williams, L. (1999). Human/cultural diversity training for justice personnel. In M. L. Dantzker (Ed.), *Readings for Research Methods in Criminology and Criminal Justice,* pp. 37-60. Woburn, MA: Butterworth-Heinemann.

Gordon, J. (1999). Correctional officers' attitudes toward delinquents and delinquency: Does the type of institution make a difference? In M. L. Dantzker (Ed.), *Readings for Research Methods in Criminology and Criminal Justice,* pp. 85-98. Woburn, MA: Butterworth-Heinemann.

Hunter, R. D. (1999). Officer opinions on police misconduct. *Journal of Contemporary Criminal Justice,* Vol. 15 No. 2, May 155-170.

Moriarty, L. J. (1999). The conceptualization and operationalization of the intervening dimensions of social disorganization. In M. L. Dantzker (Ed.*), Readings for Research Methods in Criminology and Criminal Justice,* pp. 15-26. Woburn, MA: Butterworth-Heinemann.

Moriarty, L. J., Pelfrey, W. V., and Vasu, M. L. (1999). Measuring violent crime in North Carolina. In M. L. Dantzker (Ed.), *Readings for Research Methods in Criminology and Criminal Justice,* pp.75-84. Woburn, MA: Butterworth-Heinemann.

Senese, J. D. (1997). *Applied Research Methods in Criminal Justice.* Chicago: Nelson-Hall Publishers.

Stevens, D. J. (1999). Women offenders, drug addiction, and crime. In M. L. Dantzker (Ed.), *Readings for Research Methods in Criminology and Criminal Justice,* pp. 61-74. Woburn, MA: Butterworth-Heinemann.

Vockell, E. L. (1983). *Educational Research.* New York: Macmillan Publishing.

Data Collection

■ **Vignette 10-1**
Obtaining the Data

Despite the fact that the spring break is several months away, you learned the hard way that if you do not start planning early, you might end up spending your break in a wading pool in your backyard. So you and a few friends start discussing where to go. There are several possibilities and, so, it is helpful to obtain information. The debate begins as to "how and where" to get the information. The "how" is always an interesting question. One person suggests that someone call travel agencies, another person suggests looking through travel sections of newspapers, and another says that letters of inquiry should be sent to the Chambers of Commerce of the prospective vacation sites. Each is a good idea, but they all seem to present a problem; none of the methods will provide all the required data, such as room availability and rates, airfares, special activities, and so forth.

While the discussion continues on the best way to collect the required information, your research methods class comes to mind. You recognize that the current situation could be viewed as a form of a research problem, and therefore, if you follow the steps associated with conducting research, the answers will become clear. However, you have only made it up through designing the research effort. Collecting the data is the next part of the course.

■ **CHAPTER 10**
Learning Objectives

After studying this chapter the student should be able to:

1. Identify the four primary data collection techniques that are available.

2. Explain the strengths and weaknesses of mail surveys.
3. Describe the strengths and weaknesses of self-administered surveys.
4. Compare and contrast structured, unstructured, and in-depth interviews.
5. Compare and contrast face-to-face and telephone interviews.
6. Discuss the strengths and weaknesses of observational research.
7. Explain the strengths and weaknesses of archival research.
8. Describe the strengths and weaknesses of content analysis.
9. Compare and contrast the advantages of survey, interview, observational, and unobtrusive research.
10. Identify and explain the disadvantages of survey, interview, observational, and unobtrusive research.

Data Collection

One of the most crucial aspects of the research effort is the collection of the data. Improperly collected or incorrect data can delay or even cause the cancellation of the research effort. Therefore, before the researcher begins any type of data collection, the individual must be sure to choose the right data collection technique. While one of the best means of collecting data is through the experimental design, as previously noted, this method is not very conducive to social science research. However, there are other alternatives that are very effective and efficient especially for the justician and criminologist. There are four primary data collection techniques available: survey, interview, observation, and unobtrusive means. (Note that we have broken interviews out of survey research for discussion purposes in this chapter. But please keep in mind that interviews are usually considered to be a component of survey research.) This was evident in Chapter 8's discussion of questionnaire development. These research methods have been discussed in detail in previous chapters. Our focus in this chapter will be on the issues involved in data collection utilizing these strategies.

Survey Research

Probably the most frequently used method for data collection is the survey, despite the fact that the research may be formed around invalid assumptions (Talarico, 1980). Although an excellent tool for gathering primary data, the survey is often misunderstood. It is quite useful in both descriptive and analytical studies. In criminal justice and criminology some of the uses include measuring attitudes, fears, perceptions, and victimizations. There are two primary means for collecting data through surveys: self-completing questionnaires and interviews. A common means of distributing questionnaires is through the mail or by direct distribution. Interviews can be conducted in person or via telephone.

Mail Surveys

Although there are many means available for conducting surveys, one of the most popular approaches is distributing surveys through the mail. This method allows for use of fairly large samples, broader area coverage, and minimized cost in terms of time and money. Additional advantages include that no field staff is required, the bias effect possible in interviews is eliminated, and the respondents are allowed greater privacy, fewer time constraints are placed on the respondents so that more consideration can be given to the answers, and finally, the chance of a high percentage of returns improves the representativeness of the sample.

Methodological Link

Crime and victimization are interesting topics for research. In 1992 a team of researchers was hired to examine violent crime in North Carolina. One of their data collection tools was a mail survey. The survey, entitled "Survey of Crime and Justice in North Carolina, 1992" was sent to a random sample of two thousand respondents selected from a roster of North Carolina licensed drivers. All two thousand were sent a postcard notifying them that they would be receiving a survey approximately one week later. Respondents received a complete survey packet that included an introduction letter explaining the purpose of the survey and how the respondents were selected, the survey, a pre-stamped, self-addressed envelope, and a golf pencil. After seven to ten days, if a response had not been received, the researchers sent follow-up reminders. If by the end of an additional seven days, a response had still not been received, the full survey packet with a new letter emphasizing the importance of the research and the citizen's participation was sent again. Finally, after approximately three weeks, if there was still no response, a final postcard was sent to the respondents asking that they complete the survey and call a number if they misplaced the survey and needed another one. Ultimately, this method yielded a response rate of 75 percent. (Moriarty, Pelfry, and Vasu, 1999)

The mail survey method is extremely advantageous, but it has numerous disadvantages, too. Probably one of the most frustrating disadvantages is the lack of response, or nonresponse. As shown in the previous methodological link, to combat the nonresponse problem, the researchers sent several follow-ups. Despite the fact this will help increase the number of respondents, it also can add costs not part of the original research plan.

A second disadvantage is the possible differences that might exist between the respondents and nonrespondents. For example, what if only individuals who were pleased with the way their police agency performed its duties responded to a citizen's satisfaction survey? Although the findings would be very pleasing to the police agency and city management, would it really be a true indication of citizen satisfaction?

Still another disadvantage depends on the type of survey sent. A lack of uniformity in responses could present problems when open-ended questions are used. Since each respondent will answer in a different manner (for example, paragraph, listing, or single word), this could make data compiling more difficult. In addition to the lack of uniformity is the problem that misinterpretation of the question could also create glitches in the data. Finally, slow return rates can delay the project. It took several weeks before the researchers in the previous example could move to the next phase of the study.

Obviously, the disadvantages of mail surveys can be disconcerting, but they are not difficult to overcome. The key to this type of data collection is to attain the highest response rate possible. The follow-up is just one way. Other ways to increase response rates include:

1. Offering some type of remuneration or "reward" for completing the survey. One popular method is to offer a cash incentive (for example, sending a dollar bill with the survey).

2. Appealing to the respondent's altruistic side. Advising the perspective respondent that his or her response would be extremely helpful in learning more about the subject of the research, and would be greatly appreciated.

3. Using an attractive and shortened format. Although this may sound silly, it is amazing how much more likely someone is to respond to a questionnaire that is eye-catching. This tends to show the respondent that some time and thought were given to this questionnaire and may be more inspiring to complete than designs that are very lackluster. Furthermore, keeping the format short and simple is more likely to generate a better response than a lengthy questionnaire.

4. Indicating that the survey is sponsored or endorsed by a recognizable entity. Respondents may be more encouraged to respond to a survey when they recognize and, hopefully, respect an entity supporting the research.

5. Personalizing the survey. Addressing the questionnaire to a specific person often adds more legitimacy to the research as opposed to receiving something that simply says "Dear occupant or resident."

6. The timing of the survey. When a survey is sent could be extremely important. For example, many individuals spent hours and hours watching the O.J. Simpson trial. Research geared

toward public perceptions of the court process as observed in this trial probably would have received much better response immediately following the completion of the trial than if such a study were to be conducted today.

Acceptable Mail Survey Response Rates

The previous section discussed the frustration of dealing with low response rates and provided recommendations for enhancing return rates. Perhaps the best way to cope with low return rates is (in addition to following the recommendations that were provided) to allow for them in your research design. As you may recall from Chapter 9, we recommend that you oversample in order to meet sample size requirements. In mail surveys the twenty percent oversampling rate may not be enough. Babbie (1998, p. 260) provides the response rates for mail surveys:

40% within two weeks

20% within two weeks of a follow-up letter

10% within two weeks of the final contact

Babbie (1998, p. 262) further states that response rates of 50 percent are adequate for analysis and reporting, that 60 percent is good and that 70 percent is very good. These numbers are consistent with our own experiences. Note that based upon the return rate indicated above, it may require several follow-ups to obtain a good or even adequate response rate. In the survey described in the Methodological Link above, strenuous efforts on the part of the researchers (that were just short of badgering respondents) provided a 75 percent return rate. While this was an excellent rate overall, the researchers worked very hard to get it.

The response rate will vary depending upon the type of survey (we already discussed the importance of brevity and clarity) and the targeted respondents. Ordinary citizens are far less likely to respond to a general survey than are members of a constituent group being polled by an organization in which they hold membership. In some situations, a 100 percent response rate may be possible.

EXAMPLE

In the Hunter (1988) research of convenience store robbery discussed in a preceding chapter, mail surveys were sent to approximately 130 law enforcement agencies seeking robbery data on the 200 stores in the sample. The letter requesting assistance was from the Florida Attorney General to the Sheriff or Chief of Police of the agency stating their mutual interest in combating robbery and requesting assistance. The letter from a high-ranking state official, the brevity of the survey, and the mutual interest in the survey topic resulted in an initial response of about 67 percent. A follow-up packet containing the original letter from the attorney general and a new survey was sent after one month. (Note with large bureaucracies, particularly if the data requested must be looked up or calculated, a one-month response rate is not unreasonable.) The follow-up resulted in a return rate of 92 percent by the end of the second month. A follow-up telephone call was then made to the 8 percent of agencies that had not responded. In the telephone calls respondents were asked to either respond by mail or by telephone in the next week. All but two agencies did so. Another follow-up call to those agencies finally resulted in the information. (The records manager in one agency stated that neither store in his jurisdiction had been robbed in the preceding three years. However, over a year later, after the research had been published, the records manager returned the forms indicating two robberies at one store and three at the other.) A survey from a student or a professor without the connection with the Attorney General's Office would have been fortunate to have achieved a 60 percent response rate.

In all, a mail survey can be very effective and efficient. Yet, there are situations where a mail survey is not feasible but the survey method is still necessary to complete the research. Self-administered surveys help fill this need.

Self-Administered Surveys

More and more, personal or telephone access to particular populations is becoming increasingly difficult for researchers. Some populations might need to be kept restricted (for example, prison inmates), while others wish to remain anonymous or do not want to allow personal contact with researchers (for example, police officers). However, these types of populations can offer vital data regarding numerous research topics. This is where the self-administered survey is applicable.

The self-administered survey is generally a written questionnaire that is distributed to the selected sample in a structured environment. Respondents are allowed to complete the survey within a given time period and then return it to the researcher, often through an emissary of the sample. The advantages to this method include targeting large samples, covering wide geographical areas, cost efficiency, ease of data processing, and the ability to address a wide variety of topics. The disadvantages include a low return rate, nonresponse to some questions, and misinterpretation or misunderstanding of the questions. Disadvantages aside, self-administered surveys allow for greater diversity in criminal justice and criminological research.

Overall, self-administered surveys offer economic and efficient means of collecting data. Still, this type of survey does not typically allow for in-depth responses or for the researcher to follow-up on why a particular response was given. This is where interviewing is appropriate.

Methodological Link

Dantzker and Waters (1999) used self-administered surveys to study students' perceptions of policing. The survey instruments were distributed by instructors to all students attending the first day of class in several courses, at several universities, where they were given approximately 15 to 20 minutes to complete. Completed questionnaires were collected by the instructors, who returned them to the researchers.

Ford and Williams (1999) employed a self-administered survey to collect data about cultural diversity training for police and correctional officers in Florida. This survey was distributed and collected at the officers' places of employment during a two-week period. To complete this research, the researchers had to (1) obtain cooperation from the top executives of participating agencies, (2) obtain cooperation from the supervisors in disseminating the questionnaires, (3) obtain cooperation from those who were to complete the survey, and (4) ensure that those who did respond did so fully, freely, and honestly.

Studying women offenders, Stevens (1999) made use of a self-administered survey, which was distributed to 68 women incarcerated in a high custody prison in North Carolina. These women had all been part of a drug program at the prison. Correctional officers, counselors, and student-inmates assisted distribution and collection.

To examine correctional officers' attitudes toward delinquents and delinquency and whether the type of institution they worked in made a difference, Gordon (1999) used a self-administered survey distributed to all correctional staff members at three juvenile institutions. Respondents were provided with an envelope containing a cover letter, the survey, and a separate return envelope to be used upon completion of the survey. Completed surveys were returned in the sealed envelopes to a designated person at each institution.

Interviews

For the purpose of this text, interviewing is viewed as *the interaction between two individuals where one of the individual's goals is to obtain recognizable responses to specific questions.* Interviewing is not an easy task and often requires years of training to be reasonably good at it. This does not preclude many researchers from trying this method, however. There are three types of possible interviews: structured, unstructured, and in-depth. Each can be conducted in person or by telephone.

Structured Interviews

Probably the most used type of interview in criminal justice research is the structured interview. This requires the use of closed-ended questions that every individual interviewed must be asked in the same order. Responses are set and can be checked off by the interviewer. The advantage to this type of interview is that it can be easily administered, has high response rates, and makes data processing much easier. It is in reality a questionnaire that is being administered orally with the interviewer completing the form for the respondent. Disadvantages include that it does not allow for further exploration of the responses attained, it is time-consuming and costly, and it can limit the types of responses given.

Unstructured Interviews

The unstructured interview offers respondents open-ended questions where no set response is provided. While this allows for more in-depth responses, it is much more difficult to quantify the responses. It is also more susceptible to intervening or biasing elements. Unstructured interviews are, as discussed in previous chapters, often conducted in a field research. They require a very experienced and disciplined interviewer in order to be successful.

In-depth Interviews

Finally, the in-depth interview can make use of both fixed and open-ended questions. The difference from the other types is that the interviewer can further explore why the response was given and can ask additional qualifying questions. The advantage to this method of interviewing is that a substantial amount of information can be obtained. The disadvantages include that it is time-consuming, requires small samples, and can limit the topics researched. Like the unstructured interview, this technique is best left to experienced researchers who are very familiar with the issue being studied as well as how to conduct in-depth interviews.

Methodological Link

In order to study how academic researchers gain access to data, Flanyak (1999) used in-depth interviewing. This method provided her with a high response rate, and allowed her to have personal contact with her subjects and to observe them during the interview. To assist in conformity, she made use of an interview guide instrument, which provided her with the opportunity and discretion to explore or probe respondents for detail in specific areas. Each interview lasted from 45 minutes to 75 minutes, with the longest being two hours in length. Follow-up interviews were completed as needed and lasted approximately 15 minutes.

Face-to-Face Interviews

In general, there are many advantages to using interviewing as a data collection tool. However, they differ slightly when the interview is completed face-to-face rather than by telephone. With face-to-face interviews, it provides contact between the researcher and the respondent. This contact can be positive reinforcement for participating in the research. Oftentimes simply receiving a questionnaire in the mail can be very sterile, and because of that lack of personal touch would-be respondents may simply ignore the survey. The interview can usually guarantee a higher response rate, too.

Another advantage to this type of interview is that any misunderstandings or confusion can be cleared up. This helps ensure that the responses are truer to the question. It also allows for the researcher to act as an observer, giving the interviewer the opportunity to focus on nonverbal cues. The other advantages to the face-to-face interview include being able to use audiovisual aids, schedule additional interviews, making use of language the respondent can relate to, and discretion.

Although the advantages clearly outweigh the disadvantages, they cannot be ignored. There are four basic disadvantages to face-to-face interviews. The first is that interviews can be extremely time-consuming and costly. Second, a major concern is interviewer effect or bias. Even if the interviewer attempts to remain completely neutral, there is a good chance that he or she could have some influence on the respondent perhaps through body language or voice inflections that may bias the response. Interviewer error is the third disadvantage. Not asking a question correctly, skipping a question and having to return to it, completely eliminating a question, or misinterpreting the answers, are examples of errors by the interviewer that could skew the data. Finally, the interviewer's skills or lack of them could be detrimental.

It is common for researchers to make use of graduate students to assist in conducting interviews. Unfortunately, few graduate students come equipped with the skills required to conduct a good interview. Failing to provide or hone the necessary skills will negatively affect the data. Therefore, to avoid interviewer errors it is important to properly train those who will be conducting the interview. Furthermore, interview results can be enhanced through the use of audio and video taping.

The face-to-face interview can be a very useful data collection technique. However, there are times when it is not possible to conduct face-to-face interviews, but the interview method is still necessary. This is when the telephone survey is useful.

Telephone Surveys

The advantages of telephone surveying begin with being able to eliminate a field staff and can allow for the creation of a very small in-house staff. It is also easier to monitor interviewer bias; specifically, it eliminates being able to send any nonverbal cues. Although not common, long in-depth interviews could be completed via the telephone. Finally, the telephone interview is less expensive and can be quick. The disadvantages to the telephone interview include (1) the limiting of the scope of research, (2) the difficulty in obtaining in-depth responses, (3) the elimination from the sample parameters of anyone without a telephone, and (4) the chance for high refusal to respond rates.

Comparison of Survey Strategies

Essentially, there are three common ways to collect data through surveys: mail, personal interviews, and telephone interviewing. A comparison of similar criteria finds that there are advantages and disadvantages to each (see Table 10-1). Ultimately, it is up to the researcher to determine which might best meet the needs of the research topic. Furthermore, it is possible to combine methods. For example, Moriarty et al. (1999) made use of both mail and telephone surveys in their study of violent crime in North Carolina.

Even though combinations are possible, there are times when none of these methods may be practical, yet a survey technique may still be necessary to obtain the data. Survey data collecting, regardless of the means, is very popular. However, it is not always the most appropriate and best means to collect data. Therefore, other ways of collecting data must be available and, as discussed in the qualitative chapter, there are several other methods.

Other Data Collection Techniques

Assume you want to understand the inner workings of a gang or how particular patrol techniques are affecting citizen satisfaction. You could probably conduct interviews or create a self-administered survey, but neither of these may be able to give you a complete picture because you may not know everything you need to ask. In some instances, observation is the best method for collecting data.

Observation/Field Research

Observation, as discussed in Chapters 5 and 6, can fall into one of four approaches: (1) the full participant, (2) participant researcher, (3) the researcher who participates, and (4) the complete researcher (Senese, 1997). Regardless of which approach is employed, observation allows

Table 10-1   Comparing Three Survey Methods

Criteria	Personal Interview	Mail	Telephone
Cost	High	Low	Moderate
Response Rates	High	Moderate	High
Control	High	None	Moderate
Diverse Populations	Moderate	High	Moderate
In-depth information	High	Low	Moderate
Timeliness	Slow	Slow	Fast

the researcher to see firsthand how or why something works. It provides an opportunity to become aware of aspects unfamiliar to those who do not have firsthand experience. To conduct observational data collection, the researcher needs to (1) decide where the observations are to be done, (2) decide on the focus of the observations, and (3) determine when the observations will be conducted.

A choice of where observations are to be done may be quite limited. While the idea is to determine whether the observations should take place in public or private, in many instances that choice does not exist. For example, to observe how incarcerated juveniles respond to a particular treatment program may only be possible in the institutional setting. However, if the program is provided to non-incarcerated juveniles, then the observations may take place in a public setting (for example, school). Regardless of the choice, it is still an important one. The wrong setting will generally mean an unsuccessful research venture.

What is it that we want to know? Deciding what aspect to observe is another important element. If we know absolutely nothing about a phenomenon or entity, we may end up observing everything about it. The researcher needs to have an idea of what aspects are to be studied and how to do so.

Methodological Link

As part of a 1995 to 1996 study of implementation of community policing in five cities and one county in North Carolina, Memory (1999) rode along with community policing and patrol officers in each jurisdiction. His goal was to attain firsthand knowledge of officers' attitudes and behaviors in their natural setting as they relate to the implementation of community policing. Considering all the different things one might observe while riding with police officers, without that specific focus, Memory might have ended up with all kinds of information, but not necessarily what he required to complete his research.

If the research is quantitative, a checklist will need to be prepared in advance rather than relying on field notes (for an example, see Figure 10-1).

Finally, the period or time frame when the observations are to be conducted should be determined to provide the best possible opportunity of collecting the desired data. For example, in Memory's study he only had 180 hours to make observations in six different jurisdictions. Therefore, he had to decide how many shifts he would ride in each area. Furthermore, to get the greatest amount of diversity he rode shifts that ended no later than 1:00 a.m. and did not start before 10:00 a.m.

Like survey research, observational research has its advantages and disadvantages. One of the greatest advantages is the direct collection of the data. Rather than having to rely on what others have seen, here the researcher relies only on his or her observations. However, that could also serve as a disadvantage due to researcher misinterpretation or not

On-Site Evaluation Form

Store: _____

Location: _____

City (if applicable): _____

County: _____

Law Enforcement Jurisdiction: _____

Variable Score: 1   2   3

1. Location of cashier:	Cent.	Side		____
2. Number of clerks:	Three	Two	One	____
3. Visibility within:	Good	Poor		____
4. Visibility from outside:	Good	Poor		____
5. Within two blocks of major street:	No	Yes		
6. Amount of vehicular traffic:	Heav.	Mod.	Light	____
7. Type of land use nearby:	Com.	Res.	Unused	____
8. Concealed access/escape:	No	Yes		____
9. Evening commercial activity nearby:	Yes	No		
10. Exterior well lighted:	Yes	No		____
11. Gas pumps:	Yes	No		____
12. Security devices in use:	Yes	No		____
13. Cash handling procedures:	Good	Poor		____
14. Hours of operation:	Day	6-12	24 hr	____

Source: Hunter (1988, Appendix C). Note that the checklist provides for either circling answers or edge coding as an aid in the later inputting of data. Also, the order of attributes: Yes No, No Yes are reversed in some questions to ensure that the numerical coding 1, 2, or 3 is consistent with increasing vulnerability to robbery.

Figure 10-1 Checklist Example for a Quantitative Field Research Effort

understanding what is seen. An extremely important facet is recording the observations either in field notes, with an audio recorder, or by video as quickly and as accurately as possible. This will also help reduce inaccuracy and inconsistency. It is further recommended that you transcribe your field notes as soon as possible afterwards to ensure that you can interpret your hurried handwriting and any abbreviations that were used while they are still fresh in your mind.

The fact that the research is being conducted in the phenomenon's natural environment is a bonus. Recall that a shortcoming of experiments is that the environment is controlled, perhaps biasing the results. Observational research takes place in the real world, legitimizing the observations. "This is what actually happened rather than this is what should happen."

Observational data collection, too, may not be used in all circumstances. What happens when a topic deals with a phenomenon that has already occurred and can no longer be observed or surveyed? This type of data collection would rely on using archival data.

Unobtrusive Data Collection

The last means for collecting data is through what is referred to as unobtrusive measures. These are any methods of data collection where the subjects of the research are completely unaware of being studied and where that study is not observational. It is a method that prevents the researcher from direct interaction or involvement with what is being studied. Two of the more commonly used types of unobtrusive data collection are the use of archival data (analyzing existing statistics and/or documents) and content analysis.

Archival Data

In criminal justice and criminology using official statistics or records is viewed as a form of archival collection. For example, one of the most common means of studying crime is through the use of the Uniform Crime Reports (UCR) (published yearly by the Federal Bureau of Investigation). Data in the UCR is collected monthly from police agencies, on a voluntary basis. Because it provides crime data from all over the country, and includes arrest and offense information, a researcher could do an in-depth analysis of crime patterns or arrest characteristics without the arrestees or victims knowing the research is being done.

Another use of archival data is historical research. Rather than a quantitative analysis of existing statistics, historical analysis is generally a qualitative analysis of documents and prior research. Archival data is often found in two types of records, public and private. Public records include actuarial, political, judicial, and other governmental documents, and the mass media. Private records include diaries, letters, foundations, and autobiographies. One of the biggest problems with archival data is proving the authenticity of the data. Still, archival collection allows researchers to be less intrusive than other means, and usually offers sufficient data to assess the phenomenon even though it can no longer be observed.

EXAMPLE

Assume you are interested in seeing whether race, age, gender, and occupational status influenced dispositions in cases of Driving While Intoxicated (DWI). Having not been able to see the hearings and trials, you might look at the final court dockets for the information desired. Using arrest record information to create a list of those arrested for DWI you could then go to the court dockets to find how the cases were disposed. The information could then be easily coded for analysis.

One of the benefits of archival data is that there are many possible sources for information. Police records appear to be a very popular archival record.

Methodological Link

As cited earlier, Liddick, Jr. (1999) used police records to look at the role of women in organized numbers gambling in New York. These records offered an abundance of information. Similarly, Warchol and Johnson (1999) examined records kept by the U.S. Marshals to analyze federal asset forfeiture.

Regardless of what types of records are used, archival collection can offer the researcher a wide array of topics and data. The biggest problem to overcome is access.

Content Analysis

The other unobtrusive means that we will discuss is content analysis. This technique has been discussed in previous chapters and is a favorite strategy among researchers who wish to compare social events from different eras. Analysis of the contents of archival documents could be included in this research. Generally the focus of the research is on publications and presentations (particularly media documents such as newspapers, magazines, and television programs). Depending upon how the research is structured, the analysis may be qualitative or quantitative in nature.

We recommend that when engaging in content analysis you try to create a quantifiable instrument to utilize. This requires serious thought about the issue that you are researching and the creation of a code sheet or checklist to record observations on a daily, weekly, or yearly basis (depending on the nature of the research). A summary sheet or form that permits the code sheets to be easily totaled is also recommended. These summary forms can then be used to input data for analysis. However, a checklist, in and of itself, is not as important as having a list of those items you want to collect or observe.

EXAMPLE

Dantzker (1994) conducted a content analysis of advertisements for Police Chiefs as advertised in *The Police Chief* (1985-1993). Although a checklist form was not created, every advertisement was examined for the following information: population size that the agency served, budget, number of sworn and nonsworn personnel, education requirement, required years of police experience, required years of police management experience, and any other additional requirements (for example, graduation from the FBI national academy). Once all this information was collected, it was then a matter of collapsing it into quantifiable categories for data entry and analyses.

There are a variety of means for collecting data. Ultimately, it is the task of the researcher to be able to properly choose one or more means that will provide the best access to the required data (see Table 10-2). Having provided the foundation of the concept of surveys, the next step is to understand and develop the primary survey instrument, the questionnaire.

Summary

Data collection can take many forms. The most popular method tends to be the survey. Surveys can be either self-administered or interviews. Self-administered surveys can be accomplished through the mail or by

Table 10-2   Data Collection Methods—Advantages and Disadvantages

Survey	*Interview*	*Observation*	*Unobtrusive Means*
Advantages	**Advantages**	**Advantages**	**Advantages**
Wide variety of topics	Wide variety of topics	Actual observation of behaviors in natural setting	Wide variety of topics
Simple to administer	Can give complex answers		Cost-effective
Cost-effective	Clarifications	Better ability to link behavior to concept	Simple to administer
Anonymous	Increases response rate		Anonymous
			Comparable
Comparable	Can consider nonverbal cues		
Disadvantages	**Disadvantages**	**Disadvantages**	**Disadvantages**
Misinterpretation	Misinterpretation	Observer influence	Misinterpretation
Nonresponse to questions	Interviewer biases	Only current behaviors observable	Researcher biases
Low return rates	Costly		Limited by what has been done previously
Cannot clarify questions	Not all behavior is observable	Costly	Cannot clarify questions
Cannot expand answers			Cannot expand answers

direct distribution to respondents. Interviews can be conducted in person (face-to-face) or over the telephone. They may be structured, unstructured, or in-depth. Other means of collecting data include observation, archival, and through unobtrusive means.

Methodological Queries:

Previously you were asked to decide what type of research design you would use to study the following topics. Now, what form of data collection would you employ? Why?

    (1) Gang activity in prisons

    (2) Sentencing patterns of a particular court

    (3) The effect of a treatment program for drug users

    (4) Perceived job stress of police officers

    (5) Caseload of parole officers

    (6) The effect of a community policing program on crime

    (7) Recidivism and first-time DUI offenders

    (8) Race and sentencing of drug offenders

References

Adler, E. S. and Clark, R. (1999). *How It's Done: An Invitation to Social Research.* Belmont, CA: Wadsworth Publishing.

Babbie, E. (1998). *The Practice of Social Research, Eighth Edition.* Belmont, CA: Wadsworth Publishing.

Dantzker, M. L. (1994). Requirements for the position of municipal police chief: A content analysis. *Police Studies,* (17)3, 33-42.

Dantzker, M. L. and Waters, J. E. (1999). Examining students' perceptions of policing—A pre- and post-comparison between students in criminal justice and non-criminal justice courses. In M. L. Dantzker (Ed.), *Readings for Research Methods in Criminology and Criminal Justice,* pp. 27-36. Woburn, MA.: Butterworth-Heinemann.

Flanyak, C. M. (1999). Accessing data: Procedures, practices, and problems of academic researchers. In M. L. Dantzker (Ed.), *Readings for Research Methods in Criminology and Criminal Justice,* pp. 157-180. Woburn, MA: Butterworth-Heinemann.

Ford, M. and Williams, L. (1999). Human/cultural diversity training for justice personnel. In M.L. Dantzker (Ed.), *Readings for Research Methods in Criminology and Criminal Justice,* pp. 37-60. Woburn, MA.: Butterworth- Heinemann.

Gordon, J. (1999). Correctional officers' attitudes toward delinquents and delinquency: Does the type of institution make a difference? In M.L. Dantzker (Ed.), *Readings for Research Methods in Criminology and Criminal Justice,* pp.85-98. Woburn, MA: Butterworth-Heinemann.

Hunter, R. D. (1988). *The Effects of Environmental Factors upon Convenience Store Robbery in Florida.* Tallahassee, FL: Florida Department of Legal Affairs.

Liddick, Jr., D. R. (1999). Women as organized criminals: An examination of the numbers gambling industry in New York City. In M. L. Dantzker (Ed.), *Readings for Research Methods in Criminology and Criminal Justice*, pp. 123-138. Woburn, MA.: Butterworth-Heinemann.

Memory, J. M. (1999). Some impressions from a qualitative study of implementation of community policing in North Carolina. In M. L. Dantzker (Ed.), *Readings for Research Methods in Criminology and Criminal Justice,* pp. 1-14. Woburn, MA: Butterworth-Heinemann.

Moriarty, L. J., Pelfrey, W. V., and Vasu, M. L. (1999). Measuring violent crime in North Carolina. In M. L. Dantzker (Ed.), *Readings for Research Methods in Criminology and Criminal Justice*, pp. 75-84. Woburn, MA: Butterworth-Heinemann.

Senese, J. D. (1997). *Applied Research Methods in Criminal Justice.* Chicago, IL: Nelson-Hall Publishers.

Stevens, D. J. (1999). Women offenders, drug addiction, and crime. In M. L. Dantzker (Ed.), *Readings for Research Methods in Criminology and Criminal Justice*, pp. 61-74. Woburn, MA: Butterworth-Heinemann.

Talarico, S. M. (1980). *Criminal Justice Research: Approaches, Problems, and Policy.* Cincinnati, OH: Anderson Publishing Company.

Warchol, G. L. and Johnson, B. R. (1999). A cross-sectional quantitative analysis of federal asset forfeiture. In M. L. Dantzker (Ed.), *Readings for Research Methods in Criminology and Criminal Justice*, pp. 139-156. Woburn, MA: Butterworth-Heinemann.

PART V

Data Analysis

Data Processing and Analysis

■ **Vignette 11-1**
Now What Do I Do with All This Data?

Having just gotten out of your 11:00 a.m. class and needing to be at work by 1:00 p.m. you realize that you had better grab some lunch here at the University. So you head into the student union where you run into some friends and all decide to have lunch together. There is one person there whom you do not know other than by sight, since he is a year behind you in the program. You are introduced and he immediately begins to question you about the research methods class. He is currently in the statistics class and is debating taking the methods course next semester. You suggest that he do just that because you made the mistake of waiting a year after taking statistics, a prerequisite, to take the methods course. Now you are getting close to having to start analyzing data and you can barely recall what you learned in statistics. He suggests reviewing your statistics book, but you, in your infinite wisdom (or just the need for quick cash), sold the book back. He asks whether your methods text discusses statistics because he recalls his statistics teacher complaining about the lack of pure statistics books for criminal justice and criminology and that until recently she had to use a combined methods/statistics text. Although you do not have your book with you, you recall that there was something about statistics in the text. You make yourself a mental note to check your syllabus and your text on the off chance that something on statistics is in it. You also wonder if it has material in it on what you do once the data is analyzed and it is time to write up the research project.

■ **CHAPTER 11**
Learning Objectives:

After studying this chapter the student should be able to:

1. Identify and discuss the three stages of data processing.
2. Describe what occurs during the data coding process.
3. Describe the data-cleaning process.
4. Compare and contrast the different means of dealing with missing data.
5. Explain why data may need to be recoded. Provide an example of how recoding may be done.
6. Identify and describe the three types of data analysis.
7. Recognize and explain the three types of statistical analysis.
8. Present and discuss the four types of frequency distributions.
9. Describe the various means of presenting data in addition to frequency tables.
10. Identify and discuss the three measures of central tendency.
11. Present and discuss the three measures of variability.
12. Discuss what is meant by the terms skewness and kurtosis.

Data Processing and Analysis

To this point you have been indoctrinated with a wealth of information on how to go about conducting research. The time has finally come to address what to do with that data once they are collected: processing and analysis. (Note: In an earlier chapter we advised you that data is the plural of datum. We remind you here that whenever you refer to data in your research, use it as a plural.)

Be aware that this chapter is not intended to teach you how to do statistical analyses; that is for another book and a different class. Instead what this chapter provides is a general overview of the issues involved in processing and analyzing data as well as an introduction to the terminology needed to communicate with whomever might be analyzing the data for you.

Data Processing

Will the results support the hypothesis(es)? Has something new been discovered? Are these findings consistent with previous research? These are examples of questions one hopes to answer through the data analyses. Thus, the data is collected and ready to be analyzed, now what? The first task is to prepare the data for analysis, what is generally referred to as data processing. Data processing consists of data coding, data entry, and data cleaning.

Data Coding

Coding is simply assigning values to the data for statistical analyses. Not all data needs to be coded. Quantitative data that is already in a numerical format can be left as is, such as age, or numerical responses to scales. Nonnumerical variables such as gender, marital status, or race, however, need to be coded. How these are coded is up to the researcher, but it is common to use a standard numbering format.

It is usually easier for the researcher if the coding scheme is developed in advance. Precoding is when the coding scheme has been incorporated into the questionnaire or observational checklist design. Such a design may enable the researcher to input data directly from the survey form rather than having to translate it to a code sheet. If the survey form has provided for edge coding, it is very easy to input data directly into the computer. Figure 11-1 is the field research checklist previously displayed in Chapter 10. Note how the form allows for edge coding and how the data are run to have consistent responses (run in a logical format based upon knowledge of the subject so that during statistical analysis positive and negative influences will be consistent in their directionality).

During the coding process qualitative data may also be converted into quantitative data. For example, an open-ended question about prior arrests may later be converted into numerical groupings based upon the number of arrests, type of offense, seriousness of the charges, conviction versus acquittal, or other logical groupings created by the researcher. Remember our earlier warning about false precision when doing such a conversion. Be certain that there is an explainable logic to your numerical assignments.

Ultimately, it is the researcher's decision to code the data in a manner that will be best for analyses. While part of this depends upon the computer statistics package you use, the coding should be clear. To ensure clarity you should create codebooks or coding keys to show others (and remind yourself) exactly where the variables and attributes are located. The coding scheme for a survey document may be a one-page coding key as displayed in Figure 11-2 or it may be a lengthy codebook that details how and why every variable was scored and located.

Data Entry

Once the data are coded they can then be entered into a computer software program for analyses (see Figure 11-3).

Store: _____

Location: _____

City (if applicable):_____

County: _____

Law Enforcement Jurisdiction:_____

Variable Score: 1   2   3

	1	2	3	
1. Location of cashier:	Cent.	Side		____
2. Number of clerks:	Three	Two	One	____
3. Visibility within:	Good	Poor		____
4. Visibility from outside:	Good	Poor		____
5. Within two blocks of major street:	No	Yes		
6. Amount of vehicular traffic:	Heav.	Mod.	Light	____
7. Type of land use nearby:	Com.	Res.	Unused	____
8. Concealed access/escape:	No	Yes		____
9. Evening commercial activity nearby:	Yes	No		
10. Exterior well lighted:	Yes	No		____
11. Gas pumps:	Yes	No		____
12. Security devices in use:	Yes	No		____
13. Cash handling procedures:	Good	Poor		____
14. Hours of operation:	Day	6-12	24 hr	____

Figure 11-1 On-Site Evaluation Form

Coded Data Example, Computer Entries

At various points in the text, it has been suggested that a computer can assist in conducting differing aspects of the research process. The same is true for the analysis portion.

Today there are a number of statistical software packages available to researchers, such as Dbase, QuattroPro, Statistical Package for the Social Sciences (SPSS), and Statistical Analysis System (SAS). Each has its own quirks and specialties that require individuals to choose what best suits their needs and abilities.

Regardless of which is chosen, each allows for the entry, analyses, and storage of data. We recommend SPSS, which is now available for personal computers after years of only being accessible through mainframes. We find that it provides us with the ability to conduct almost every type of statistical technique we might require. It seems to be a

Gender	**1** 'Male' **2** 'Female'
Ethnicity	**1** 'White' **2** 'Black' **3** 'Hispanic' **4** 'Other'
Age	**1** '20-25' **2** '26-35' **3** '36-45' **4** 'Over 45'
Rank	**1** 'Officer' **2** 'Corporal' **3** 'Sergeant' **4** 'Lieutenant' **5** 'Other'
Years of Experience	**1** 'Less Than 2 Years' **2** '2-5' **3** '6-10' **4** '11-15' **5** 'Over 15'
Education	**1** 'Diploma' **2** 'Associate' **3** 'Bachelors' **4** 'Masters' **5** 'Doctoral'
No Degree	**1** 'Less Than 60 Hrs' **2** '60-90' **3** 'Over 90' **4** 'Not Applicable'
Shift	**1** 'Days' **2** 'Evenings' **3** 'Midnights' **4** 'Other'
Recruit Degree Requirement	**1** 'High School' **2** 'Some College' **3** 'Degree'
Dept. Size	**1** 'Less Than 250' **2** '251–999' **3** '1000–2499' **4** 'Over 2500'
Received Degree	**0** 'No Degree' **1** 'Prior' **2** 'After'

Figure 11-2 Data Coding Key

```
01001112141 14134444443421344411344334423
01002112133 14314433443333442412244334423
01003113132 25113333342342434542344444423
01004112343 44114133442443434432    23
01005132122 3 14344454432341444345444 4423
01006112123145555224343325553541355445423
01007114553 35233244525523344312554244423
01008132132 43343243331132432311334443423
01009113343 43422242432423444422444334423
01010114151212554221321223321321223233223
0101111315 314334323443334444334353444423
01012114154 14134 44533355444 2355443323
01013143353 13234142433333433341344244423
01014113453 15134135543445555231354444523
01015114142 13344322333243223331233233323
01016132132 44553112553454443521434243323
01017113353 14233124553444544531455344323
01018113353 12433244222344443431233334323
01019114353 43531144433555445314441 43323
01020111123 34453225554 44434541344233323
```

Figure 11-3 Coded Data Examples,
Computer Entries

common tool for many criminal justice and criminological researchers. Before choosing any of the packages, the researcher should test several to see which is most comfortable to him or her. Once the choice is made it is simply a matter of learning how to use it and being able to interpret the results. Most statistical packages not only have handbooks but excellent tutorials as well.

The key to data entry is accuracy. If possible, have a reliable person read the data to you as you enter it into the computer so that you do not have to continuously switch your viewing from the code sheet to the computer screen. This will help prevent mistakes. However, you should still review what you have inputted to make certain that it is accurate.

Of course the above assumes that you are entering the data yourself. With modern technology this may not be the case. You may have obtained the data from existing sources, in which case it probably was provided on a computer disk. If it is compatible with your statistical package, a great deal of time is saved. If you conducted a telephone survey, you may have been able to enter the data directly into the computer as you asked the questions. Another shortcut is to use optical scan sheets such as the scantrons that you have used in taking multiple-choice exams. This permits the data to be entered directly from the sheets marked by the respondents. Regardless of which technique is utilized, the data will need to be cleaned.

Data Cleaning

Data cleaning is the preliminary analysis of your data. Here you "clean" any mistakes that might have occurred during the initial recording of data or data entry. As mentioned above, the first step is reviewing what you have entered for accuracy.

If you have a computer program that is programmed to check for errors, it will either beep at you or refuse to accept data that does not meet the coding requirements for that variable. For example, assume that you have used a Likert Scale where 1 = Strongly Agree, 2 = Agree, 3 = Neither Agree or Disagree, 4 = Disagree, and 5 = Strongly Disagree. You entered a 6 as an answer. Most programs would not accept what is obviously an incorrect code. Babbie (1999, p. 345) refers to this as possible code cleaning. Cleaning takes place while you are entering the data in that only those codes that are possible are accepted.

If your computer program does not have possible-code-cleaning capability, you can easily find such errors during a visual review of the data. (This is time-consuming, however.) Even with such capability, if you type in a 3 when you meant to type a 2 the computer will not catch it. Your (or another's) review is necessary to correct such an error. Therefore, a visual review of the data is still necessary.

Another type of data cleaning is contingency cleaning. In this technique your review of the data is expedited by the knowledge that certain responses should only have been made by certain individuals. Not all females would indicate having given birth to a child. But no males should have indicated such.

As you are reviewing the data, there will be certain questions that will logically lead to similar responses on following questions. If they do not, you need to review that particular questionnaire or form to check the accuracy of what was entered. The next step is determining what to do with missing data.

Missing Data

Despite your best efforts if you have collected a great deal of data, you will find that you have "lost" some information. This may be due to an oversight in data entry (which can usually be easily corrected) or it may be because the respondents or recorders accidentally overlooked or deliberately chose not to answer a particular question. If missing data is the product of a data entry error, it may easily be corrected by obtaining the right information from the survey form or code sheet. If it is due to oversight or intentional omission, there are a number of ways to deal with this missing information.

If the data has been left out on a single question you may chose to input it as a non-response. If you are not using 0 as a response you may assign that as a value. Researchers frequently use 99 (assuming they are not using continuous variables in which 99 could be a response) to indicate missing data. This is, in our opinions, the preferred method of dealing with non-responses.

Another option for dealing with non-responses is to assume that the missing data is due to an oversight rather than an intentional omission. In this situation you might look at the other responses to try to determine what the response would most likely have been. For example if a respondent had indicated support for strict law enforcement on related questions, you might assume a similar answer on the unanswered question. We include this solution because some researchers use it, but we do not recommend it because it can lead to challenges about the objectivity and validity of your analysis.

Yet another option is to exclude the survey instrument containing the omission from your analysis. If there are several non-responses that may be appropriate. However, if only one or two questions in a survey are not answered, this solution can lead to the loss of worthwhile information.

If the instrument used is a Likert Scale, the solution is simple. Classify the response as a "neither agree nor disagree" or "don't know" (depending upon how your scale is worded). This solution allows the data to be used without the fear of skewing the results.

Recoding Data

Although some data may be received in a numerical format (for example, age), sometimes, for purposes of analysis, this data is recoded to fit into groups. If you have gathered data such as income or age you may find that you wish to use a simpler method of analysis such as crosstabulations to examine their relationships. If you run a frequencies table (discussed later in this chapter) you would note that these categories are quite extensive. A comparison of age by income could result in a table that is lengthy and confusing. Assuming that age was presented in rows and income in columns, if the people surveyed ranged from 20 years of age up to 70 years of age and their incomes ranged from $10,000 to $100,000 the resulting table would be enormous. Because each individual year of age would have to be represented, there would be 51 rows in our hypothetical table. Since there would likely be as many different incomes as there were respondents, we could end up with thousands of columns. Yet by collapsing the categories into logical groupings, the data can be presented clearly and concisely (see Table 11-1). The resulting table could easily be collapsed even further if necessary. In collapsing data please recall our earlier discussions of the different levels of measurement. Higher level data (such as ratio or interval data) can be collapsed down into lower level data (such as ordinal or nominal data) but you cannot do the opposite and convert lower level data to a higher level.

Data Analysis

Now that we have entered our data we may begin to analyze it. There are three types of data analysis: univariate, bivariate, and multivariate analysis. With univariate analysis, an examination of the case distribution is conducted one variable at a time (Babbie, 1999). The process by which this examination takes place is referred to as descriptive statistics. Descriptive statistics provide us with an understanding of the variable that we are investigating. Descriptive statistics will be discussed in detail later in this chapter.

Bivariate analysis is when the relationship between two variables is examined. This examination may be comparative or inferential depending upon the nature of the analysis. If we were exploring the relationship between the two variables, this would denote descriptive statistics, but since it also compares the two variables, it becomes comparative statistics. Comparative statistics usually involve analysis of the attributes of the variables being examined in order to better describe the relationship between the two variables. If our hypothetical Table 11-1 were real it would be an example of comparative statistics. Comparative statistics will be discussed further in bivariate techniques in Chapter 12. An example will also be provided near the end of this chapter.

If one of the variables is identified as being dependent and the other variable is identified as being independent, the analysis of their relationship becomes inferential. Inferential statistics simply mean that we are trying to not only describe the relationship but to use that knowledge

Table 11-1   Hypothetical Age by Income Comparison
(Ordinal Data)

Age	20-29	30-39	40-49	50-59	60-69	70+
Income						
$10,000 to $19,000	50	30	20	10	5	15
$20,000 to $29,000	100	80	50	30	50	80
$30,000 to $39,000	80	100	80	60	80	60
$40,000 to $49,000	50	100	160	120	100	80
$50,000 to $59,000	30	80	120	150	120	50
$60,000 to $69,000	20	50	100	120	100	40
$70,000 to $79,000	10	40	80	100	80	30
$80,000 to $89,000	5	30	60	80	60	20
$90,000 to $99,000	5	20	40	60	40	10
$100,000+	0	10	30	50	30	10

to make predictions or inferences about the dependent variable based upon the influence of the independent variable. You can see that bivariate analysis may be descriptive, comparative, or inferential in nature.

The final type of statistical analysis is multivariate analysis. Multivariate analysis is the examination of three or more variables. This technique is inferential in nature in that we have usually already conducted both descriptive and comparative statistical analyses (through univariate and bivariate analyses) of the data and are now seeking to examine the relationships among several variables. From this examination we try to develop explanations for the observed relationships. Inferential statistics will be covered in detail in Chapter 12.

Statistical Analysis

Statistics are viewed as "a set of problem-solving procedures" (Lurigio, Dantzker, Seng, & Sinacore, 1997, p. 4). Statistics are used in criminal justice and criminology to help describe a variety of associated aspects such as crime rates, number of police officers, or prison populations. In addition, statistics can be used to make inferences about a phenomenon. As discussed in the preceding section, there are three types of statistics:

1. Descriptive, whose function is describing the data
2. Comparative, whose function is to compare the attributes (or subgroups) of two variables
3. Inferential, whose function is to make an inference, estimation or prediction about the data

Note: We have categorized comparative statistics as a separate category as do Lurigio, Dantzker, Seng, and Sinacore (1997). Most methods texts include comparative in their discussion of descriptive statistics. Comparative statistics exist in a gray area between descriptive and inferential statistics. We do not really care how you classify them as long as you understand what is involved.

The remainder of this chapter focuses on providing an overview of the processes and terminology of descriptive statistics. We will not try to turn you into a statistician, but you should understand the basic principles so that you can comprehend the work of others and communicate with those who might be aiding you with statistical analysis of your own work.

Descriptive Statistics

When the researcher is interested in knowing selected characteristics about the sample, it requires some form of descriptive statistics. One of the most common descriptive statistics is the use of frequencies.

When data is first collected it is referred to as raw data; that is, it is not neatly organized. A first step to organizing the data, after coding and entry, is through a frequency distribution, which simply indicates the number of times a particular score or characteristic occurs in the sample. This can be reported in whole numbers and percentages. Frequencies are commonly used to describe sample characteristics.

Frequency Distributions

There are four types of frequency distributions: absolute, relative, cumulative, and cumulative relative (Lurigio, et al., 1997). Each offers a statistically sound indication of the sample's composition. None is recommended over the others. Instead we suggest that you select the one that appears to be the most desirable for reporting the data contained in your research.

Absolute frequency distributions simply display the data based upon the numbers assigned. Relative frequency distributions are the percentage equivalent of absolute frequency distributions. When dealing with large numbers, it is usually much easier for the reader to interpret percentages than raw numbers. Cumulative frequency distributions enable the reader to see what the products of the grouping are in the frequencies table by adding the absolute frequency of each previous variable. Cumulative relative frequency distributions do the same as cumulative frequency distributions but add relative frequencies rather than numbers. Table 11-2 demonstrates how the four types of frequencies are related.

Methodological Link

Several of the studies cited throughout this text make use of frequencies to either fully describe the samples or to describe a particular characteristic. Tables 11-3 through 11-5 are taken from three of the studies to demonstrate how the same method can be used differently.

Table 11-2   Absolute, Relative, Cumulative, and Cumulative Relative Frequency Distributions of Crime Types from Twenty Hypothetical Offense Reports

Type of Crime	Absolute Frequency	Relative Frequency (%)	Cumulative Frequency	Cumulative Relative Frequency (%)
Theft	6	30	6	30
Robbery	3	15	9	45
Auto Theft	4	20	13	65
Burglary	5	25	18	90
Assault	2	10	20	100
	n = 20	100		

(Source: Lurigio, et al., 1997, p. 23)

(continued on next page)

Table 11-3   Sample Frequencies: From Moriarty

Demographic	1994 Survey		Population Statistics	
Variable	f	%	f	%
Gender				
Male	315	39%	82,894	47.0%
Female	494	61%	91,927	53.0%
Race				
White	725	91%	159,005	91.0%
Black	46	6%	14,108	8.1%
Other	29	3%	1,708	.9%
Marital Status				
Single	154	19%	30,671	21.0%
Married	469	58%	82,773	58.0%
Divorced	83	10%	12,012	8.0%
Separated	29	4%	3,948	3.0%
Widowed	69	9%	13,333	9.0%
Education				
Less than high school	81	10%	30,551	25.0%
High school graduate	206	25%	35,723	29.0%
Some college	268	33%	30,632	26.0%
BA degree	155	19%	14,934	12.0%
Professional	97	12%	7,975	7.0%

Displaying Frequencies

Frequencies, by whole numbers and/or percentages in table form are just one means of describing the data. Other means include pie charts, bar graphs, histograms and polygons, line charts, and maps. As may be noted in Figure 11-4, in a pie chart the frequencies are presented as percentages. Such a display is clear and easily interpreted. Bar charts are also easily interpreted. They are used to display nominal and ordinal level data. Figure 11-5 demonstrates a bar chart. Histograms are bar graphs that are used to display interval and ratio data. They indicate the continuous nature of the variable by drawing the lines adjacent to each other (Lurigio, et al., 1997, p. 29). Figure 11-6 displays a histogram. Polygons display the same data as histograms but use dots instead of bars. Lines are then drawn between the dots to reveal the shape of the distribution. Figure 11-7 is an example of a frequency polygon.

In addition to the above frequency presentation techniques, criminological researchers may also use line charts and maps. Line charts are polygons that demonstrate scores across time. As such they are useful to reflect changes over time in the same dot and line format as frequency polygons. Figure 11-8 demonstrates a line chart.

Table 11-4   Sample Frequencies: From Ford and Williams

Characteristic	Percent [a]
	(n=260)
Race	
White	84.9
Non-white [b]	15.1
Gender	
Male	80.1
Female	19.9
Age of officer	
18-29	29.7
30-39	34.4
40-49	26.6
50 and older	
Years in policing or corrections	
1-4	31.8
5-9	32.6
10 or more years	35.7
(x=8.7; median=7; mode=1,3,7)	
Rank	
Line officer	70.7
Supervisor	29.3
Education	
High school/GED	56.1
2 year degree	25.5
4 year degree	13.3
Graduate school/degree	5.1

[a] Percents may not sum to 100 due to rounding.

[b] 2.8 percent Asian or Hispanic.

Table 11-5   A Sample Characteristic by Frequency: From Liddick

Male and Female Roles in Numbers Firms

Role	Male		Female		Total
Banker	138	(11.4%)	12	(6%)	150
Controller	239	(19.8%)	26	(13%)	265
Collector	398	(33%)	83	(41.7%)	481
Pickup	330	(27.4%)	59	(29.6%)	389
Clerk	100	(8.3%)	19	(9.5%)	119
Totals	**1205**		**199**		**1404**

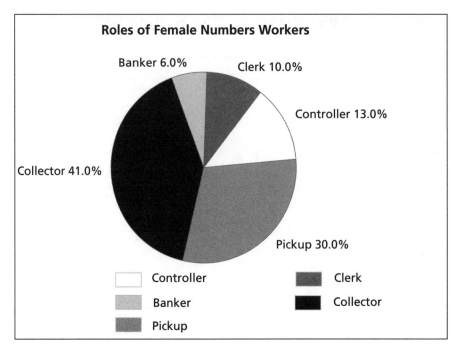

Figure 11-4 Frequencies via a Pie Chart

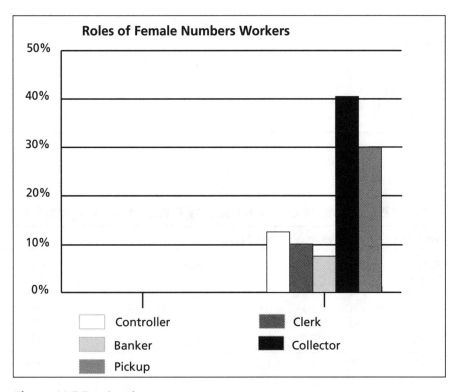

Figure 11-5 Bar Graph

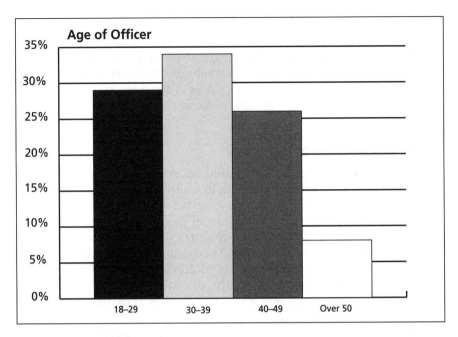

Figure 11-6 Histogram

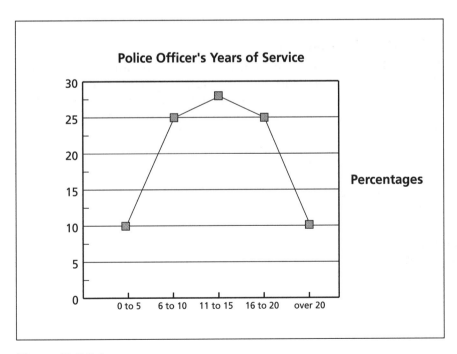

Figure 11-7 Polygon

Lastly, when studying geographical crime patterns, it may be useful to use mapping to show the geographic distribution. Figure 11-9 is an example of how a map might be utilized to display crime data.

In addition to the tables, graphs, and charts discussed above, there are four other ways to describe the properties of the data: measures of central tendency, measures of variability, skewness, and kurtosis.

Measures of Central Tendency

Because frequencies can be quite cumbersome, researchers sometimes require a way to summarize the data in a simpler manner. Measures of Central Tendency are one way to summarize data. The three most common measures are the mean, median, and mode. The mean is the arithmetic average. The median is the midpoint or the number that falls in the middle. The mode is the number that occurs most frequently. The mean is usually used as a measure of Central Tendency for interval or ratio level data. The median is used mostly for ordinal level data. The mode is generally used for nominal level data. Figure 11-10 shows how the three measures are obtained.

Using a measure of central tendency allows the researcher to simplify the numbers in a summary manner. Despite their more simplistic nature, researchers should be familiar with the characteristics of these measures before using them. In addition, these measures are often used in conjunction with measures of variability.

Measures of Variability

Despite their similarities, all statistics are not the same. The difference that occurs among statistics is called variability. The three main measures are range, variance, and standard deviation. The range is simply the difference between the highest and lowest scores. Variance is the difference between the scores and the mean. Standard deviation indicates how far from the mean the score actually is. To compute measures of dispersion, such as standard deviation, statisticians use z-scores. We will go no further into the use of this methodology in this text. If you need to calculate dispersion (variability) in your research, we recommend that you either take a course in statistics or consult with a statistician.

Methodological Link

As with frequencies, several of the studies cited made use of both measures of central tendency and variability to help describe the data. Tables 11-6 and 11-7 are examples.

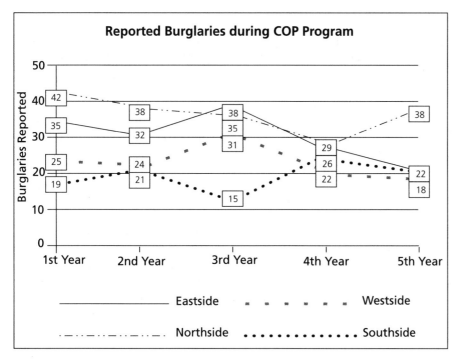

Figure 11-8 Line Charts

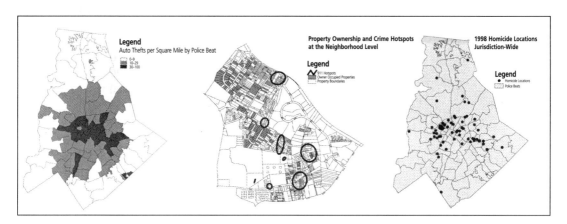

Figure 11-9 Maps
Courtesy of Charlotte-Mecklenburg Police Department

Skewness

In our discussion thus far we have alluded to the distribution of the data and have depicted it somewhat in the figures that were displayed. Many of the statistical techniques that we discussed in this chapter (and which will influence our discussions of inferential statistics in Chapter 12) are based on the assumption of a normal distribution. A normal distribution may also be referred to as a normal or bell curve. By using polygons or line charts (discussed earlier) or scatterplots (which will be discussed in Chapter 12) researchers are able to see the distribution of their data. If it is a normal distribution, the researcher is able to use a broader range of statistical techniques. If it is a non-normal (also known as nonparametric) distribution, the statistical techniques that may be used are more limited.

The measures that we have discussed previously (central tendency and variability) may be noted in the location of the center of the curve (central tendency) and in the spread of the curve (variability). They may also differ based upon the symmetry of the curve. If one side has more values so as to cause the slope of that side to tail further outward, the distribution is said to be skewed to that side. Skewness alerts the

---

Sample Data n = 100

Years of College Completed	Number of Responses	Responses x Years of College
1	10	10
2	20	40
3	30	90
4	20	80
5	10	50
6	8	48
7	2	14
	100	332

Mean = average
= 332/100
= 3.32 years of college

Mode = most frequent (30 responses) = 3 years of college
Median = midpoint = (30 responses are below 3 years, 40 responses above 3 years, 30 responses are within the 3 years grouping. The midpoint would be between the 20th and 21st respondents in the 3-year group.) = 3 years of college.

Figure 11-10 Measures of Central Tendency

researcher to the presence of outliers. Such knowledge aids the statistician in conducting analysis of the data.

Kurtosis

Kurtosis is another distribution consideration that warrants some discussion. Kurtosis refers to the amount of smoothness or pointedness of the curve. A high thin curve is described as being leptokurtic. A low flat curve is platykurtic. Frankly you will have little need of this knowledge except to recognize the terms if a statistician states that your data distribution exhibits such features.

These statistics, in tandem with measures of central tendency and variability, provide useful ways to describe the data. In general, descriptive statistics are primarily used to describe how the data is comprised. However, describing the data is usually just a small portion of what we truly want to do with the data, which is to make inferences from it.

Comparative Statistics

As we mentioned earlier, descriptive statistics usually consist of univariate statistics that describe the data. Inferential statistics consist of ether bivariate or multivariate analyses of the relationships among variables. Between the two lies comparative statistics. Comparative statistics are often classified as being part of descriptive statistics because they tend to provide more insight about the nature of the variables than their relationships with other variables. However comparison of variable attributes as indicated in Table 11-6 moves beyond simple description and begins the inferential process. Depiction of crime rates over time, noting the percentage of change in criminal activity, and trend analyses are all examples of comparative statistics. Depending upon the text that is utilized, such activities may be categorized as either descriptive or inferential statistics. In this text we have chosen to discuss comparison as being within both.

Summary

Once the data collection is accomplished, the next two phases in completing the research are data processing and data analysis. Since the data are often obtained in a raw manner, they must be coded for entry into a statistical software program. Once the data have been entered they must be cleaned to ensure accuracy and appropriateness for subsequent statistical analysis. At this point missing data are dealt with and recoding may also be required.

Univariate analysis is conducted to gain knowledge about the data prior to any bivariate and multivariate analyses. Descriptive statistics are then utilized. Description may involve the use of frequency distribution tables, as well as charts and graphs. The researcher will also exam-

Table 11-6　Measures of Central Tendency: From Stevens
Criminal Activities of Sample (N=68)

Criminal Activities	Percent*	Frequency**	Age	Range
Shoplifting	65%	very often	14	10–25
Prostitution	16%	sometimes	15	12–23
Assault	4%	seldom	15	13–21
Armed Robbery	3%	seldom	16	14–15
Property Crimes	3%	sometimes	13	12–15
Other	6%	seldom	12	12–14
Murder	3%	once	25	23–27

* Percents rounded

**NOTE: In discussing coding, it was intimated that all data is reported in numerical fashion. Obviously, this example shows how data can be reported non-numerically despite the numerical orientation to the variable.

Table 11-7　Combination of Descriptive Measures: From Gordon
Demographic Characteristics

Variable	Open-Security		Closed-Security	
Age				
Mean	34.08		37.35	
Standard Deviation	12.00		13.06	
Gender				
Male	18	(69%)	87	(69%)
Female	8	(31%)	40	(31%)
Race				
White	20	(77%)	68	(53%)
Non-White	6	(23%)	56	(44%)
Education				
Less than High School	0	(0%)	1	(1%)
High School Graduate	6	(23%)	19	(15%)
Some College	8	(31%)	49	(39%)
Bachelor Degree	12	(46%)	42	(33%)
Graduate Degree	0	(0%)	16	(12%)
Length at Current Position (in months)				
Mean	31.23		63.36	
Standard Deviation	29.98		80.26	

ine the data by using measures of central tendency and measures of variability. The data may be further assessed by reviewing the shape of the data distribution.

While the data are being examined the analysis may progress from description to comparison of variables. This process links description to inferential statistics, which are discussed in the following chapter.

Methodological Queries:

Based on the idea of the College Students' Criminality study:

(1) What type of data will be required? Descriptive or inferential? Explain.

(2) How will you report it? Describe the formats you might use to show the results.

(3) One variable collected is raw age. Describe the differing ways you could report this variable.

(4) What data will you simply describe? What data will you compare?

References

Babbie, E. (1999) *The Basics of Social Research*. Belmont, CA: Wadsworth Publishing.

Ford, M. and Williams, L. (1999). Human/cultural diversity training for justice personnel. In M. L. Dantzker (Ed.), *Readings for Research Methods in Criminology and Criminal Justice*, pp. 37-60. Woburn, MA: Butterworth-Heinemann.

Golden, M. P. (Ed.) (1976). *The Research Experience*. Itasca, IL: F.E. Peacock Publishers, Inc.

Hunter, R. D. (1988). The effects of environmental factors upon convenience store robbery in Florida. Tallahassee, FL: Florida Department of Legal Affairs.

Liddick, Jr., D. R. (1999). Women as organized criminals: An examination of the numbers gambling industry in New York City. In M. L. Dantzker (Ed.), *Readings for Research Methods in Criminology and Criminal Justice*, pp. 123-138. Woburn, MA: Butterworth-Heinemann.

Lurigio, A., Dantzker, M. L., Seng, M., and Sinacore, J. (1997). *Criminal Justice Statistics: A Practical Approach*. Woburn, MA: Butterworth-Heinemann.

Moriarty, L. J. (1999). The conceptualization and operationalization of the intervening dimensions of social disorganization. In M. L. Dantzker (Ed.), *Readings for Research Methods in Criminology and Criminal Justice*, pp. 15-26. Woburn, MA: Butterworth-Heinemann.

Stevens, D.J. (1999). Women offenders, drug addiction, and crime. In M. L. Dantzker (Ed.), *Readings for Research Methods in Criminology and Criminal Justice*, pp. 61-74. Woburn, MA: Butterworth-Heinemann.

Inferential Statistics

Vignette 12-1
Numerically Explaining Relationships

Consider that the College Students' Criminality study has been conducted. Let us assume we want to infer how much unreported or unfounded crime is actually happening on campus and who is most likely to commit what types of offenses. The descriptive data might tell us that among the sample there were 57 thefts, 14 burglaries, 2 sexual assaults, and a variety of drug-and-alcohol-related offenses. Essentially these numbers are telling us how much crime there was, however they do not allow us to infer who is more likely to commit these crimes. The task of inferential statistics is to allow us to explain relationships and to predict future events based upon that knowledge. A reminder: the type of inferential statistic used depends on the level of measurement used to gather the data.

■ **CHAPTER 12**
Learning Objectives

After studying this chapter the student should be able to:

1. Differentiate between descriptive, comparative, and inferential statistics.
2. Discuss measures of association and provide examples.
3. Explain what is meant by statistical significance and describe how tests of significance are used.
4. Present and describe the commonly used comparative statistics techniques.
5. Discuss bivariate analysis and provide examples.
6. Discuss multivariate statistics and provide an example of a multivariate technique for nominal and ordinal level data.

7. Describe the various multivariate techniques for interval level data.

8. Explain what is meant by nonparametric techniques.

Statistical Analysis

In the previous chapter we discussed the three types of statistics. Descriptive statistics describe the data being analyzed. A variety of descriptive statistics were presented in Chapter 11. Comparative statistics, whose function is to compare the attributes of two variables, were also introduced. As you recall, we stated that comparative statistics are within a "gray area" that moves from description to inference. As such, comparative statistics are often classified as either descriptive or inferential rather than as a separate category. An example of how comparative statistics might be used for description was provided.

Inferential statistics were also defined in Chapter 11. The purpose of inferential statistics are to make inferences, estimations, or predictions about the data. In this chapter we shall provide an overview of inferential statistics. How comparative statistics may be used to begin making inferences about the data will be demonstrated. We shall then present and discuss a variety of inferential techniques utilized by criminological researchers.

An Overview of Inferential Statistics

Inferential statistics allow the researcher to develop inferences (predictions) about the data. If the sample is representative, these predictions may be extended to the population from which the data were drawn. Inferential statistics allow criminological researchers to conduct research that can be generalized to larger populations within society. When making inferences about data sets, researchers rely upon measures of association to determine the strength of the relationship(s) between or among variables. Tests of significance are also used in order to discover whether the sample that was examined is representative of the population from which it was drawn.

Measures of Association

Measures of association are the means by which researchers determine the strengths of relationships among the variables that are being studied. The measure of association that is used is dependent upon the type of analysis that is being conducted, the distribution of the data, and the level of data under analysis. There are many measures of association that are utilized within criminological research. Individual researchers may prefer to use different measures. However, some measures are considered to be standards. Lambda is commonly used for nominal level data. Gamma is commonly used for ordinal level research. Pearson's r and R2 are commonly used for interval and ratio level data.

Typically, measures of association for nominal level data tell researchers how strong the relationship is but do not indicate directionality. A measure such as lambda runs from 0 (no relationship) to 1 (perfect relationship). A .00001 would indicate a very weak relationship. A .9999 would indicate an extremely strong relationship. Depending upon the measure used (some tend to be more powerful than others) the researcher would assess the relationship as being weak, moderate, or strong. For example, a lambda score of .5367 would indicate a moderate relationship whereas a lambda score of .8249 would be an indicator of a relatively strong relationship. The researcher would have to assess the contingency table (crosstabulation) to determine whether the relationship was positive or negative.

Measures of association for ordinal level data tell the researcher both the strength of the relationship and the direction of the relationship. The ordinal measures range from -1 to +1. A zero (0) indicates no relationship; a negative one (-1) indicates a perfect negative relationship (as one variable increases, the other variable decreases); and a positive one (+1) indicates a perfect positive relationship (as one variable increases, the other variable increases). A score of -.8790 for the commonly used gamma indicates a strong negative relationship. A score of +.2358 indicates a weak positive relationship. It should be noted that there are several other measures available for researchers to use (some of which have the advantage of being PRE-proportional reduction in error measures that are more attractive to statisticians). We are merely providing the more commonly used measures. To review the advantages of other choices we recommend that the reader consult with a statistician, take a statistics course, or consult a statistics text.

Measures of association for interval and ratio data are determined by the statistical technique that is used. For correlation, Pearson's r is the measure of association; for simple linear regression and multiple regression, R2 is used. Other techniques use different measures. However, they, like ordinal measures, range from -1 to +1. Different interval measures will be discussed within the various strategies presented.

Statistical Significance

Statistical significance is how researchers determine whether their sample findings are representative of the population they are studying. If you are using a complete enumeration (the entire population is studied rather than just a sample from that population) then statistical significance is a moot point in that we already know that the population is accurately represented. However, complete enumerations are rare because very small populations limit generalizabilty and large populations are too costly and time-consuming to study as a whole.

Statistical significance is based upon probability sampling. Nomothetic explanations of causality are based upon probabilities. It is this use of probability that enables us to make inferences based upon a relatively few observations. Generally, social science research desires a statistical significance of .05 or better. This means that we are 95 percent confident that our findings represent the population that was sampled. Before computers were readily accessible to researchers, the statistical significance of data was obtained by using calculators to laboriously figure mathematical equations. Today, thanks to statistical packages, this work is performed by the computers, which provide the significance in exacting detail.

Comparative Statistics

There are several comparative techniques available to criminal justice researchers. The ones that we shall briefly discuss are crime rates, crime-specific rates, percentage change, and trend analyses.

Crime Rates

Crime rates are perhaps the most frequently presented data within criminal justice and criminological research. These are nothing more than the number of crimes for an area (city, county, state, etc.) divided by the population for that area and then multiplied by 100,000. Crime rates for index crimes are commonly displayed in Uniform Crime Reports. An example of crime rates is displayed within Table 12-1. By viewing the rates presented in the following table, the reader may easily compare the rates among the various states.

Table 12-1 1997 Index Crime Rates (per 100,000) for Selected States

State	Crime Index Total	Violent Crime	Property Crime
Alabama	4,889.7	564.5	4,325.3
Arizona	7,195.0	623.7	6,571.3
California	4,865.3	798.3	4,067.1
Georgia	5,791.7	606.6	5,185.1
Idaho	3,925.2	256.8	3,668.4
Maryland	5,653.1	846.6	4,806.5
Montana	4,408.8	132.1	4,276.7
Nevada	6,064.5	798.7	5,265.8
New York	3,910.9	688.6	3,222.4
Texas	5,480.5	602.5	4,878.0

Source: Uniform Crime Report for the United States 1997 (1998). Washington, D.C.: Federal Bureau of Investigation (www.fbi.gov/ucr/Cius_97/97crime/97crime1.pdf)

Crime-Specific Rates

Crime-specific rates differ from crime rates in that they use a different base than population within the computations. For example, Lurigio, et al (1997) used auto thefts as an example. The number of registered automobiles in the United States in 1990 was shown as 143,026,907. The number of automobile thefts for that year was 1,635,907. Using the number of auto thefts divided by the number of autos multiplied by 100,000 provided an auto theft rate per 100,000 automobiles of 1,143.8 (Lurigio, et al, 1997, p. 98). This method can also be used to calculate victimization rates, arrest rates, and clearance rates.

Percentage Change

Percentage change statistics allow researchers to compare data over time and across jurisdictions. The computation for this is rather straightforward: Subtract the earlier number from the later number. Then divide the difference by the earlier number. For example, if your city had 200 murders in 1997 and 250 in 1998, you would divide the difference (50) by 200. Murders would have increased by 25 percent. If the numbers had been reversed (250 in 1997 and 200 in 1998) the results would show a decline of 20 percent.

Trend Analyses

Trend analyses are yet another way of comparing differences over time. We may examine on a histogram how rates have increased for a particular offense or we may use other means of determining how the data have changed. Trend analyses are quite useful in assessing the impact of crime prevention strategies. An example of the impacts on assault rates of increased sanctions for weaponless assaults on police officers in Minnesota and a comparison with neighboring states is shown in Figure 12-1. (For a more detailed explanation of trend analyses see Lurigio, et al., 1997, p. 100-105).

Inferential Statistics

Due to the nature of inferential statistics, to do justice in explaining them requires a text of its own. Because it is not a goal of this text to teach statistics, further explanations are left for statistics courses and only brief descriptions of selected statistics are offered.

Bivariate Analysis

Bivariate analysis is the examination of the relationship between two variables. Usually this involves attempting to determine how a dependent variable is influenced by an independent variable. The more

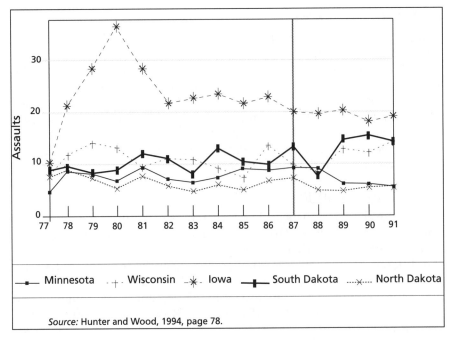

Source: Hunter and Wood, 1994, page 78.

Figure 12-1 Weaponless Assaults per 100 Officers,
Minnesota and Adjoining States

commonly used bivariate techniques are crosstabulation (contingency tables) and bivariate (simple linear) regression. In assessing the relationship between the two variables we examine the contingency table or regression scatterplot results, the measure of association (such as gamma or R2), and the level of statistical significance (hopefully .05 or lower).

Contingency Tables

With nominal level data, two popular statistical techniques are contingency tables (crosstabulations) and chi-square, which is a common statistic for a contingency table. A contingency table is a set of interrelated cells. Each cell can display a variety of data (see Table 12-2). From this data, a chi-square statistic is available. Chi-square is one test of statistical significance. These techniques offer a statistical relationship from which one might make an inference.

Bivariate Regression

Bivariate regression, also known as simple linear regression, is based on the principle that over time things tend to regress toward the mean. For example if you were to measure the heights of female students enrolled at your school you would find that they would range from well above average to well below average height for women. Assuming a normal population, most of the heights would tend to cluster around the mean (average) height. A scatterplot of these heights would most likely enable a line to be drawn showing most heights to be near the mean height.

Table 12-2   Contingency/Crosstabs Example
Overall Job Satisfaction by Level of Education/Degree

Count Exp Val Row Pct Col Pct Tot Pct		H.S. Diploma 1	Assoc. Deg. 2	Bach. Deg. 3	Master's Deg. 4	Row Total
OVERALL	2	1 .5 100.0% 4.5% 2.3%	0 .2 .0% .0% .0%	0 .3 .0% .0% .0%	0 .0 .0% .0% .0%	1 2.3%
Neutral	3	11 10.2 55.0% 50.0% 25.6%	4 4.2 20.0% 44.4% 9.3%	4 5.1 20.0% 36.4% 9.3%	1 .5 5.0% 100.0% 2.3%	20 46.5%
	4	9 9.2 50.0% 40.9% 20.9%	3 3.8 16.7% 33.3% 7.0%	6 4.6 33.3% 54.5% 14.0%	0 .4 .0% .0% .0%	18 41.9%
Extremely Satisfied	5	1 2.0 25.0% 4.5% 2.3%	2 .8 50.0% 22.2% 4.7%	1 1.0 25.0% 9.1% 2.3%	0 .1 .0% .0% .0%	4 9.3%
Column Total		22 51.2%	9 20.9%	11 25.6%	1 2.3%	43 100.0%

Chi-Square	Value	DF	Significance
Pearson	5.12525	9	.82326
Likelihood Ratio	5.53040	9	.78584
Linear-by-Linear Association	.61069	1	.43453

Minimum Expected Frequency – .023

Cells with Expected Frequency < 5 – 13 of 16 (81.3%)

Approximate Statistic	Value	ASE1	Val/ASE0	Significance
Phi	.34524			.82326
Cramer's V	.19933			.82326
Contingency Coefficient	.32634			.82326

If you are using interval level data, are dealing with a normal distribution (determined through earlier descriptive statistics), and have a linear relationship, this would be an appropriate procedure to see how an independent variable would predict the outcome of a dependent variable. We will not go into a description of the principles upon which simple linear regression is based. However, if you have a linear relationship, as X (the predictor variable) increases so should Y (the dependent variable). Conversely, if a negative relationship exists (such as a crime prevention strategy), as X (the strategy used) increases, Y (the specific crime targeted) will (hopefully) decrease. An example of bivariate regression is shown in Figure 12-2. Note that in addition to the scatterplot, we use the R^2 (discussed earlier) and the significance level to assess the relationship. In the example shown, the relationship is positive, has a high R^2 and is statistically significant. This indicates that the independent variable is a good predictor of the dependent variable.

Multivariate Analysis

Multivariate analysis is the examination of the relationship between three or more variables. Usually this involves attempting to determine how a dependent variable is influenced by several independent variables. This methodology offers more insights than bivariate analysis in that we are able to study the relationships among several variables at

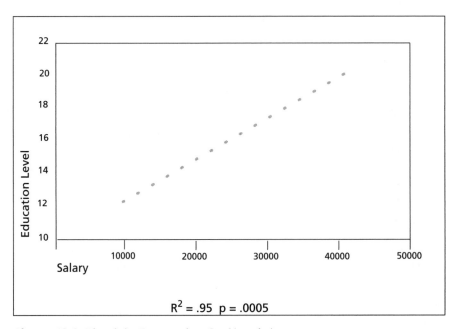

Figure 12-2 Bivariate Regression Scatterplot
Fictitious Relationship Between Education Level and Salary

one time. The more commonly used multivariate techniques are correlation, multiple regression, Student's t test, analysis of variance, discriminant analysis, probit regression, factor analysis, and path analysis. In assessing the relationship between the multiple variables we examine the correlation table, regression scatterplot results, or other indicators (depending on the technique used); the measure of association (such as Pearson's r, R2, Wilke's Lambda or other appropriate measure); as well as the level of statistical significance. We shall provide a number of multivariate examples in this chapter.

Student's T Test

The Student's t test is used to compare groups (which can be either nominal or ordinal measures) and hypothesis testing. Computing Student's t is a fairly complex process that contrasts expected outcomes with observed outcomes. The differences among the means of the variables are then assessed. The Student's t test provides means for each variable by group and then offers a statistic called the t-value, which indicates whether the relationship between the groups is statistically significant (see Table 12-3). As stressed earlier, we do not intend to teach you how to compute this measure but to inform you of what to look for in others' work and what to discuss with your statistician if you use this strategy. As seen in Table 12-3 the differences between the means are obvious. The t values will not mean anything to you at this point but indicate the values used by the computer to calculate the significance (which should mean something to you by now).

Table 12-3   Student's T
Student's Perceptions of Policing—Comparison of Selected Means Scores, by Time (Dantzker and Ali-Jackson, 1998)

Variable	Mean (T1)	Mean (T2)	T-value
Primary Role	.554	− .458	5.49*
Level of Competency	− .747	−1.289	4.29*
Serve and Protect	−1.000	− .800	−1.27
Corrupt Act	− .598	− .390	−1.33
Strike a Minority	− .171	− .500	2.37*
Ignore Needs	−1.000	−1.060	.55
Preventing Crime	− .476	− .951	2.97*
Harass or Help	−1.374	−1.470	.96
Unknown Reaction	.482	.716	−1.65
Professionalism	.183	.598	−3.38*
Help Society	.627	.928	−1.84
Benefit of Doubt	.256	.646	−2.39*

*=p≤.05

NOTE: T1 and T2 represent the distribution of the questionnaire. T1 was at the beginning of the semester and T2 was the end of the semester.

Correlation

Correlation is a commonly used technique for evaluating interval and ratio level data. In our earlier discussion of bivariate regression we talked about how relationships between two variables were examined based upon the assumption of a linear relationship. In correlation relationships are assessed based upon covariation. Covariation simply means that as changes occur in one variable X they will also change in another variable Y. A positive correlation would reveal that as X values increase, Y values would also increase. Assessing correlations is based upon how the variation in one value corresponds to variation in the other value.

The means of assessing the correlation of interval level data is Pearson's Product-Moment Correlation. Pearson's r is used to determine the strength of the association among variables by dividing the covariance of X and Y by the product of the standard deviation of X and Y. You do not have to calculate these numbers; the computer does it for you. What you are interested in is the direction of r (recall we are looking at a number between negative 1 and positive 1), the strength of r, and the significance of r. Table 12-4 is an example of correlation in analyzing interval data.

Table 12-4   Correlation

		Incomp	*Motto*	*Corrupt*	*Gender*	*Age*	*Year in College*
Role	Pearson's r	.119*	.133**	.058	.074	−.112*	−.145*
	Sig. (2-tailed)	.013	.006	.230	.125	.021	.003
	N	439	435	437	433	424	413
Incomp	Pearson's r	1.000	.346**	.308**	.048	−.163**	−.054
	Sig. (2-tailed)		.000	.000	.314	.001	.277
	N	440	436	438	434	425	414
Motto	Pearson's r	.346**	1.000	.349**	.015	−.152**	−.085
	Sig. (2-tailed)	.000		.000	.763	.002	.086
	N	436	436	434	430	421	410
Corruption	Pearson's r	.308**	.349**	1.000	.012	−.176**	−.106*
	Sig. (2-tailed)	.000	.000		.809	.000	.032
	N	438	434	438	432	424	412
Gender	Pearson's r	.048	.015	.012	1.000	−.205**	.037
	Sig. (2-tailed)	.314	.763	.809		.000	.451
	N	434	430	432	434	425	414
Age	Pearson's r	−.163**	−.152**	−.176**	−.205**	1.000	.121*
	Sig. (2-tailed)	.001	.002	.000	.000		.015
	N	425	421	424	425	425	405
College Yr	Pearson's r	−.054	−.085	−.106*	.037	.121*	1.000
	Sig. (2-tailed)	.277	.086	.032	.451	.015	
	N	414	410	412	414	405	414

* Correlation is significant at the 0.05 level (2-tailed).
** Correlation is significant at the 0.01 level (2-tailed).

Analysis of Variance

Analysis of Variance, commonly referred to as ANOVA, is another means of examining interval level data. Where correlation uses Pearson's r to determine the nature of relationships among variables, ANOVA uses something known as an F ratio to compare the means of groups. This technique helps avoid committing errors that might occur when using multiple t tests (Iverson and Norpoth, 1976). ANOVA allows statisticians to determine significance by assessing the variability of group means. Therefore this is a useful method for evaluating grouped data (such as the outcomes of correctional treatments on inmate groups). Table 12-5 is an example of Analysis of Variance findings.

Multiple Regression

Multiple regression (sometimes referred to as Ordinary Least Squares Regression by statisticians) is yet another means of evaluating interval level data. It is based upon the same assumptions as bivariate regression. However, instead of assessing the relationship between only two variables it usually examines several variables at once. This popular technique enables researchers to look not only at how the independent variables predict the outcome of the dependent variable but the

Table 12-5   Selected ANOVA Results from a Perceptions Study

Value Label

	Mean	*Std Dev*	*Sum of Sq*	*d.f.*	*F*
AVOID					
Springfield Acad	-1.3750	.5310	13.2500		
MA Regional Acad	-1.7500	.4935	9.5000	1	11.60*
CORRUPT					
Springfield Acad	-1.4375	.7693	27.8125		
MA Regional Acad	-1.4000	.9282	33.6000	1	.04
DRUGS					
Springfield Acad	.0625	1.4790	102.8125		
MA Regional Acad	.4500	1.4313	79.9000	1	1.54
EXPECTATIONS					
Springfield Acad	.1702	1.2036	66.6383		
MA Regional Acad	-.2500	1.0801	45.5000	1	2.89
HELP SOCIETY					
Springfield Acad	1.3750	.7889	29.2500		
MA Regional Acad	1.4000	.8412	27.6000	1	.02
IGNORE					
Springfield Acad	-1.3958	.8440	33.4792		
MA Regional Acad	-1.6500	.6222	15.1000	1	2.50

*p≤.01

relationships among the independent variables. Regression builds upon bivariate regression and correlation by examining partial correlations. In other words it uses variance to assess the ability of an independent variable to predict the dependent variable. But it goes beyond this analysis by assessing variance among the independent variables (Lewis-Beck, 1980). The influence on total variation that additional variables cause on the prior variables is known as partial correlation. We are able to see how the variables interact and use this knowledge to add or remove independent variables from the regression equation. Computers will do this for you in a process known as step-wise regression.

As in previous sections, you do not have to understand the process to be able to interpret multiple regression. You look for the same criteria as in bivariate regression. The direction of R2, the strength of R2 and the significance are important. Additionally, the relationships between the independent variables must be examined by reviewing their correlation coefficients. However, to determine whether to use multiple regression and how to deal with problems that may arise, you should consult with a statistician or someone experienced in using regression. An example of multiple regression results is shown in Table 12-6.

Other Multivariate Techniques

In addition to the previous multivariate techniques there are several others that are popular among criminologists. All of them require a solid understanding of the statistical procedures involved. Probit Analysis (also referred to as Probit Regression or just Probit) is similar to, yet different, from Multiple Regression. It is in effect a cumulative distribution regression model that helps straighten out an s-shaped distribution (Montgomery and Peck, 1982). It is also appropriate when you have interval independent variables but an ordinal level dependent variable (Aldrich and Cnudde, 1975).

Logit Analysis is also known as Logit and Logistic Regression. Like Probit Analysis it is a type of regression that may be used to deal with

Table 12-6   Multiple Regression
Regressions of County Population against Crime and Arrests in Montgomery County, 1970-1990 (Guynes and McEwen, 1998)

Variable	b0	b1	R2	F	Sig F
Part I Crimes	1,810.7	38.3	.50	18.7	.000
Part II Crimes	3,029.4	56.4	.29	7.8	.012
Total Crimes	4,840.1	94.7	.50	18.6	.000
Part I Arrests	3,177.5	2.6	.40	12.6	.002
Part II Arrests	-1,059.8	11.9	.47	16.9	.001
Total Arrests	2,117.7	14.6	.60	28.0	.000

s-shaped distributions. Logistic analysis is a sophisticated technique used by statisticians when the cumulative distribution is logistic rather than normal as in Probit Analysis. Like regression, both Logit and Probit results are assessed using R^2 as the measure of association.

Discriminant Analysis is a favorite technique of the authors. It is appropriate when you have interval independent variables and a nominal level dependent variable. Where regression is based upon the ability of the independent variables to predict the dependent variable, discriminant analysis focuses upon the ability to classify observations to the nominal categories of the dependent variable based upon their values on a set of independent variables. The measure of association for discriminant analysis is Wilkes' Lambda.

Factor Analysis also categorizes data. It is used to determine patterns among the variation of values of the variables being studied. Variables that are highly correlated are clustered together based upon computer-generated "factors" (Kim and Mueller, 1978). This is an extremely complex procedure that must later be interpreted by the researcher to determine whether the factor loadings have logical meaning.

Path Analysis seeks to provide a graphic depiction of the causal relationships among the independent variables in order to explain their influences upon the dependent variable. Like factor analysis, it is a complex procedure that is best left to statisticians.

Nonparametric Techniques

When the distribution of the data is not normal, standard statistical techniques are usually not appropriate. In those cases, other procedures that are used include chi-square (based upon the statistic discussed earlier), nonparametric correlation, and nonlinear regression. The strategies used in nonparametric analysis are complex. The reader is advised to consult with a statistician in these circumstances. We mention them here so that you will know that there are techniques that are available should you have data that are not in a normal distribution.

Summary

In this chapter we have provided an overview of several statistical techniques that should aid the reader in understanding other's research as well as preparing their own. We do not claim to give you the knowledge needed for in-depth data interpretation (that is provided in statistics texts) but you should be able to grasp the principles involved in conducting inferential statistics. Today's reality is that researchers do not really need to be expert statisticians. Many statistical analyses can be completed through a variety of user-friendly software. Often all the researcher needs to do is be able to code and enter data, choose what statistical techniques should be run, interpret the results, and report their findings.

To attain a better understanding of statistical analyses without a statistics course, we suggest that you read almost any criminal justice or criminological study focusing particularly on the statistics portion. If the companion reader for this text is being used, examining Chapters 2 through 10 provides the opportunity to view a wide range of statistical techniques "in action." In addition, to reinforce this aspect of the research, reviewing Dantzker, Lurigio, Seng, and Sinacore (1998), *Practical Applications for Criminal Justice Statistics* (Butterworth- Heinemann), would be helpful.

Methodological Queries:

Based on the idea of the College Students' Criminality study:

(1) Which statistical techniques would you use? Identify at least one descriptive, comparative, and inferential statistics technique.

(2) Which variables would you use for measures of association?

(3) What might be the most statistically significant relationship you would want to find?

(4) What tests of significance would you use?

References

Aldrich, J. and Cnudde, C. F. (1975) "Probing the bounds of conventional wisdom: A comparison of regression, Probit, and discriminant analysis." *American Journal of Political Science*, XIX, 3: 571-608.

Dantzker, M. L. and Ali-Jackson, N. (1998). Examining students' perceptions of policing and the effect of completing a police-related course. In M. L. Dantzker, A. J. Lurigio, M. J. Seng, and J. M. Sinacore, *Practical Applications for Criminal Justice Statistics*, pp. 195-210. Boston, MA: Butterworth-Heinemann.

Dantzker, M. L., A. J. Lurigio, M. J. Seng, and J. M. Sinacore (1998*). Practical Applications for Criminal Justice Statistics*. Boston, MA: Butterworth-Heinemann.

Guynes, R. and McEwen, T. (1998). Regression analysis applied to local correctional systems. In M. L. Dantzker, A .J. Lurigio, M. J. Seng, and J. M. Sinacore, *Practical Applications for Criminal Justice Statistics*, pp. 149-168. Boston, MA: Butterworth-Heinemann.

Hunter, R. D. and Wood, R. L. (1994) Impact of felony sanctions: An analysis of weaponless assaults upon American police. *American Journal of Police*, XII!, 1: 65-89.

Iverson, G. R. and Norpoth, H. (1976) Analysis of Variance. Sage University Paper Series on Quantitative Applications in the Social Sciences, 07-001. Beverly Hills and London: Sage Publications.

Kim, J. and Mueller, C. W. (1978) Introduction to Factor Analysis: What It Is and How to Do It. Sage University Paper Series on Quantitative Applications in the Social Sciences, 07-013. Beverly Hills and London: Sage Publications.

Lewis-Beck, M. S. (1980) Applied Regression: An Introduction. Sage University Paper Series on Quantitative Applications in the Social Sciences, 07-022. Beverly Hills and London: Sage Publications

Lurigio, A. J., Dantzker, M. L., Seng, M. J., and Sinacore, J. M. (1997) *Criminal Justice Statistics: A Practical Approach.* Boston: Butterworth-Heinemann.

Montgomery, D. C. and Peck, E. A. (1982) *Introduction to Linear Regression Analysis.* New York: John Wiley and Sons.

Uniform Crime Report for the United States 1997 (1998).Washington, D.C.: Federal Bureau of Investigation.

Writing the Research

■ Vignette 13-1
The End Is Near!!

The semester is winding down. Next semester will be here too soon and it will be time to write your final project. Your research class has been quite helpful in preparing you to conduct your research, but you are still not quite sure how to write up the findings. Yes, you have read many articles; but how they were put together still eludes you. Hopefully, during the last few weeks of your course, how research is put on paper will become clearer.

■ CHAPTER 13
Learning Objectives

After studying this chapter the student should be able to:

1. Explain the purpose of the title page and describe its structure.
2. Explain the purpose of the abstract and describe its contents.
3. Explain the purpose of the introduction and describe its contents.
4. Explain the purpose of the literature review and describe its contents.
5. Explain the purpose of the methodology section and describe its contents.
6. Explain the purpose of the results section and describe its contents.
7. Explain the purpose of the conclusions section and describe its contents.

8. Explain the purpose of the references and describe their structure.

9. Explain the purpose of tables and figures and describe their contents.

10. Explain the purpose of appendices and describe their contents.

The Research Paper

The topic is chosen, the design implemented, the questionnaire constructed, the data collected and analyzed, and now you think, here comes the hard part. For many people, students and scholars alike, conducting the research is seen as the easy or fun part and would be great to do if it did not have to be written up. Our experiences suggest that students, in particular, really can "get into" the designing and collecting of the data, fear the analyses, and loathe having to provide a written explanation. However, since the written project is generally the required final goal, whether for fulfilling a course requirement or attempting to get published, it must be taken as seriously as the research itself.

Because each of us has our own writing style, we will not begin to try to tell you how to go about writing. We will, however, suggest an order for your paper and what should be included. The basic order should be title page, abstract, introduction, methodology, results, conclusions, references, and appendices. Within this chapter we shall provide you not only with an overview of what should be included within each of the above but an APA (American Psychological Association writing style) example from a previously unpublished paper.

The Title Page

The title of your research paper (article, or thesis) should tell the reader in clear and concise terms what your research is about. Often individuals who are perusing journals or article abstracts do not have (or will not take) the time to read the abstracts. The title is what draws their attention to your paper as possibly being of interest to them. The author's (or authors') identity and affiliation then follow. If the research has been funded by an external organization, that is also indicated on the title page. The journal, organization, or instructor to whom the completed research is being submitted may have specific requirements as to how this page is structured.

EXAMPLE

Educational Level and Perceptions of Job Satisfaction among Police Officers with the Rank of Sergeant or Above
by
M.L. Dantzker
University of Texas-Pan American

Abstract

The abstract is the summary or synopsis of the information being presented in the paper and starts with the research title. The abstract presents the paper's major argument and describes the methods that were used. Note that this abstract is limited to one paragraph. Generally the abstract is between 100 and 150 words in length.

EXAMPLE

Abstract

Job satisfaction is important to organizations—including the police organization. Yet, job satisfaction in policing has received minimal attention from administrators and researchers. On the other hand, educational requirements for police officers have received, and continue to receive, attention from practitioners and academics. Despite the amount of attention this subject has received, the focus has been rather narrow with emphasis usually on educational requirements for the police recruit and their effect. As part of an in-depth study of job satisfaction that began in 1992, this article examines what effect education may have on the perception of job satisfaction among ranking officers (sergeant and above).

The Introduction

This section will vary in length, depending on whether there is a page limit or on how much information is really available. Regardless of length, this section needs to establish the research problem and the literature that supports its existence and the reason to research it. Furthermore, this section must report the research question(s) and hypothesis(es) and will usually briefly describe what was done and how.

The introduction and literature review may be contained within one section or broken into two sections. If separated, the researcher introduces the reader to the topic and research question within the introduction. Whether separated or not, this introductory paragraph should alert the reader as to what to expect from the paper. This is followed by the main portion or the literature review where the writer offers a body of support for the research.

In some cases there may be very little support, which must be acknowledged; while for others the writer will have to decide how to limit the extensive amount of evidence that is available. Finally, the literature review section should end with a summary paragraph that indicates what the research is that is being reported and how it was accomplished.

EXAMPLE

Introduction and Literature Review

Job satisfaction is an important concept to organizations (see Baron and Byrne, 1991; Bullock, 1986; Landy, 1989; Robbins, 1993). Its importance relates to the relationship job satisfaction has with critical organizational factors, such as employee turnover, absenteeism, productivity, and stress (see Baron and Byrne, 1991; Burke, 1989; Carroll, 1973; Culver, Wolfe, and Cross, 1990; Landy, 1989; Quinn and Staines, 1979; Steers, 1981). These factors are also relevant to the police organization; therefore, it would appear that study of job satisfaction among police officers would be relatively important. However, the concept of job satisfaction in policing has received a minimal amount of attention (see Buzawa, 1984; Dantzker, 1994; Griffin, Dunbar, and McGill, 1978; Hunt and McCadden, 1985; Love and Singer, 1988).

The formal study of job satisfaction is about sixty years old, and numerous studies have been conducted (Locke, 1983). Yet, the number of job satisfaction studies related to the police organization have been limited. These studies have looked at various correlates for job satisfaction such as stress (Jayaratne and Chess, 1984; Martelli, Waters, and Martelli, 1989; Wolpin, Burke, and Greenglass, 1991), tension (Bateman and Strasser, 1983; Klenke-Hamel and Mathieu, 1990), communication (Hochstedler and Dunning, 1983), cynicism (Lester, 1987; Regoli, Crank, and Culbertson, 1989), skill utilization (Grant, Garrison, and McCormick, 1990) and career stage (Burke, 1989). Although not limited to police organizations, elements of particular interest in policing because of their association with recruitment and promotion, such as age, gender, ethnicity or race, rank, years of experience, and education, have received little attention (Burke, 1989; Dantzker, 1993a, 1993b; Dhillon, 1990).

The apparent lack of study of this concept with respect to police organizations allows for a variety of studies to be undertaken to examine job satisfaction in the police organization. This article examines one of those directions: the influence or effects education has on job satisfaction among police officers with the rank of sergeant and above.

Requiring police officers to possess a college education has been debated and studied since the early 1900s when Vollmer first began hiring police officers with some college education (see Carter and Sapp, 1992; Hoover, 1975; Hudzik, 1978; Sherman, 1978; Shernock, 1992; Worden, 1990). National commissions, scholars, and practitioners have all offered a variety of recommendations and perspectives on whether a police officer should possess a college education. Despite the continuously growing literature on this subject, little of the research appears to extend past discussions of entry-level requirements. Therefore, there appears to be a need to extend the literature base examining education and promotion in policing.

According to Carter and Sapp (1992), the level of education among police officers has slowly risen over the past thirty years and will continue to rise. As police agencies hire college-educated recruits, it is inevitable that the educational level of ranking officers will also rise. Yet, we have paid limited attention to this growing trend and, since ranking officers can have as much of an impact (in some circumstances a greater impact) on the police organization as line officers, it seems natural that consideration needs to be given to what effect education has on these ranking officials. One such consideration is job satisfaction, which has been found to be somewhat affected by education (see Quinn and Baldi de Mandilovitch,

1975; Glenn and Weaver, 1982; Martin and Shehan, 1989; Mottaz, 1984; Ross and Reskin, 1992). This paper explores the possible relationship between education and job satisfaction among ranking police officers.

Methodology

Despite the relevance and importance of the introductory section, the methodology section is really the mainstay of the paper. The writer should discuss the hypothesis(es), the research design, and the data-gathering technique. This includes explaining the research population, the sampling frame, and the questionnaire or other method used to gather the data.

It is within this section that the researcher can fully explain where, when, how, and why the data was attained and analyzed. It may be written up in one complete section or subdivided. In the example provided Dantzker chose to divide this section into two parts, the sample and the questionnaire. The reason for this was that the reported research resulted from a larger research effort, which had been reported elsewhere.

Example

Sample

The data reported here was taken from a purposive sample of police officers representing eleven municipal police agencies from seven states (Alabama, California, Georgia, Illinois, Massachusetts, Nebraska, and Texas). Department sizes ranged from 26 to 1156 sworn officers. All sworn officers were eligible to participate in the study.

(A purposive sample was used in this research because of the size of the population, which was all police officers, and the easier accessibility to individual departments than a randomly selected national sample. For purposive sampling refer back to Chapter 9.)

The questionnaire was distributed to the sample (n=4566) through each agency's "standard chain of document dispersal." Completed questionnaires were collected by an agency representative and then returned to the researcher. From the 4566 questionnaires distributed, 2611 (57%) were returned. Among the 2611 respondents, 530 (20.3%) identified themselves at a rank of sergeant or above. Among these 530 ranking officers, 473 (89.2%) were male, 418 (78.9%) were White, 252 (47.5%) were between the ages of 36 and 45, 368 (69.4%) were sergeants, 366 (69.1%) had over 15 years of police experience, and 216 (40.8%) possessed bachelor's degrees (see Table 13-1).

Questionnaire

A review of the literature on job satisfaction found that a variety of validated job satisfaction measures exist (see Hackman & Oldham, 1975; Locke, 1983; Reiss, 1967; Robbins, 1993; Smith, Kendall, and Hulin, 1975).

However, the majority of these instruments were believed to have very limited utility for application to the police organization. This is primarily because of the differences between the police work environment and the environments of organizations for which these measures were originally designed, such as factories, where the environment is relatively stable and productivity is more easily measured.

Others, recognizing the shortcomings of these measures and their relation to policing, created measures that had a more direct relationship to policing, but appeared too specific to each study's target sample in that their content was directed toward the agency being studied, to allow them to be generally used (see Burke, 1989; Buzawa, 1984; Lester, Benkovich, Brady, et al, 1981; Regoli, et al, 1989). Therefore, to study job satisfaction among police officers as a group, a general-purpose police job satisfaction measure was created and validated (see Dantzker, 1993a).

It has been suggested that job satisfaction can be studied as facet-specific, facet-free (global), or a combined satisfaction (see Locke, 1983; Muchinsky, 1990; Nord, 1977; Seashore and Taber, 1975; Wanous and Lawler, 1972). This study's questionnaire combined all three.

For the facet-free or global measures, three statements were offered. The first statement required respondents to indicate, on a Likert scale where 5 was "extremely satisfied," how satisfied they were with their jobs (Overall). The second and third global statements inquired as to whether the respondent would change police departments without losing seniority (Change) and if offered a position not in policing would the respondent immediately accept it. Both of these statements were also measured using a Likert scale. However, these scales were based on a strongly agree to strongly disagree continuum, 5 being "strongly agree."

The remaining statements, 23 facet-specific, dealt with job items often cited in the job satisfaction literature as relevant indicators for satisfaction. These items were written in a Likert-style format (one to five, extremely dissatisfied to extremely satisfied) in which respondents were asked to identify their level of satisfaction with each item. The questionnaire also included several demographic indicators such as age, gender, ethnicity, years of experience, and education. The demographic variable of interest in this article is education which was divided into five levels: High School diploma/GED only, Associate's degree, Bachelor's degree, Other (includes graduate and professional degrees), and No Degree (some amount of college hours but no college degree).

The validity of the questionnaire was established through traditionally accepted methods of face validity, criterion-related validity, and construct validity. Reliability has been established based on pre-test and post-test comparisons, item-to-item and item-to-scale analyses, and the use of Cronbach's alpha. (Please note how the questionnaire's validity and reliability are discussed and accepted, as per Chapters 4 and 8.)

Results

Whether this is a separate section or part of the methodology is actually a matter of preference. Either way, in this section the writer describes the sample's characteristics, the statistical techniques used, the results, and whether they supported the hypothesis(es). It is in this section that various tables, graphs, and charts are commonly used to describe the data.

EXAMPLE

Results

To examine the effect of education on perceived satisfaction among ranking officers two types of analyses were used, analysis of variance and multiple regression. The data represented responses to the three facet-free items and the 23 facet-specific items. In addition, the 23 items were examined as elements of a total Job Satisfaction scale and four subscales. These scales are General Administration (interdepartment transfers, community relations, in-service training, current administrators, educational requirements for recruits, off-duty job policy, grading/evaluation, appeal/grievance process, and promotional system); Extras (insurance, educational incentives, retirement program, salary, benefits, and overtime compensation); Job (current assignment, general duties, report-making system, and the three supervisor items—consultation, availability, willingness); and Equipment (availability and quality). (The Cronbach's alphas for the scales were .90, .82, .74, .90, and .69, respectively.)

Using the technique ANOVA the levels of education were examined by mean scores and the F ratio (strength of relationship between mean scores). The probability of a significant relationship existing by level of education and rank was also provided.

(ANOVA was selected because it provides one of the best ways to examine the relationship between groups using a very simple statistic, the mean. Refer to Chapter 12.)

Beginning with the facet-specific items as a complete scale, respondents with a bachelor's degree had the highest mean (3.05), suggesting they were the most satisfied. With respect to the subscales, for General Administration respondents with an associate's degree were most satisfied (2.98); respondents with an associate's degree were the most satisfied (2.98) with the items in the scale Extras; the scale Equipment has respondents with graduate or professional degrees as the most satisfied (2.97); and for the Job scale, respondents with an associate's degree had the highest mean score (3.57). None of the findings for the scales were statistically significant (see Table 13-2).

Examining the facet-free variables, respondents with a bachelor's degree had the highest mean (3.57) for overall job satisfaction, indicating the most satisfaction. Respondents with a bachelor's degree also had the lowest mean (2.66) for the variable Change, suggesting that they would not agree to leave their agency for another agency even without losing seniority. Finally, for the variable Offer (leaving policing for a better-paying job), respondents with graduate or professional degrees had the lowest mean scores (2.98) indicating that they would not leave policing for a better-paying job outside policing. However, using the F ratio for each set of means educational level was statistically significant for any of the three (see Table 13-2).

The analyses of the facet-specific items found that educational level was significantly related (p=≤.01 for all except recruit educational requirements which was p=≤.05) to seven items: retirement program, community relations, salary, insurance, educational incentives, in-service training, and recruit educational requirements. For retirement program, respondents with a bachelor's degree were the most satisfied (3.11). Respondents with a bachelor's degree were also the most satisfied with community relations (2.94), salary (2.66), and insurance (3.21). The group with only a high school diploma were the most satisfied with educational incentives (3.28), in-service training (2.91), and recruit educational incentives (3.00) (see Table13-2).

The results noted above only consider the relationship of the educational levels to job satisfaction for rank. Further ANOVA analyses (ONEWAY) allowed for recognition of whether there were significant differences between the means for each educational level.

Although for the scales and the facet-free variables no significant differences existed between the means of the educational levels, seven facet-specific variables were found to have a significant relationship, all at the .05 level of significance. Beginning with retirement program, significant differences occur between the means for educational levels Other (3.05) and High School (3.11) and between Bachelor's degree (2.94) and High School (3.11) and No Degree (2.64). For community relations the significant relationship was between respondents with a Bachelor's degree (2.94) and with No Degree (2.40). With the item salary, respondents with a Bachelor's degree (2.66) are significantly more satisfied than those with only a High School Diploma (1.85) and those with No Degree (2.25). The insurance variable finds three significant relationships: Other (3.17) and No Degree (2.70), Bachelor's Degree (3.21) and No Degree (2.70), and Associate's Degree (2.84) and No Degree (2.70). Means for educational incentives were significantly different in three pairings, too: Associate's Degree (3.09) and Other (2.41), No Degree (3.11) and Other (2.41), and High School (3.28) and Other (2.41). For the last two significant variables, in-service training and recruit educational requirements, one significant pairing each was found: High School (2.91) and Bachelor's Degree (2.18) and High School (3.00) and Other (2.38), respectively (see Figure 13-1).

To better understand the relationship of educational levels to job satisfaction by ranks, an additional ANOVA technique was used. A total of fifteen groups were established consisting of the three ranks (sergeant, lieutenant, and other) at each of the five educational levels (high school, associate's degree, bachelor's degree, other, and no degree but some college). This analysis produced several statistically significant (.05) differences between means.

For the complete job satisfaction scale, two sets of relationships were found. Lieutenants and Others with Bachelor's degrees were statistically more satisfied than Sergeants with No Degree but some college (3.19, 3.44 to 2.78, respectively). All four subscales had at least one set of significantly different means: General Administration had four sets where Extras, Equipment, and Job all had one set. While the educational level differed, either the Lieutenants or the Others were the most satisfied (see Table 13-3 and Figure 13-2).

For the facet-specific items, 13 of the variables had at least one set of statistically, significantly different means. In fourteen sets, ranks with a Bachelor's degree were the most satisfied. Out of the 37 sets of means' comparisons found among the 13 variables only four sets were found where Lieutenants or above with only a High School education were the most satisfied (educational incentives, in-service training, equipment quality, and equipment availability) (see Figure 13-3).

Finally, a correlation technique was used to see if education would remain significant for any of the facet specific variables when other dependent variables (ethnicity, age, rank, years experience, department size) were not excluded. In this correlation mix, educational level is significantly related to two of the facet-specific variables, retirement system and overtime compensation, both at .001 level of significance. Rank, itself, is the most significant variable with respect to job satisfaction (see Table 13-4).

Conclusions

Usually the last section of the research paper is the conclusion(s). Generally this section is used to offer insights about the research, whether it did what was expected and possible problems. This section can also be used to discuss implications of the research and to provide a forum for suggestions for future related research. Some authors choose to divide this information into two sections: discussion and conclusions. There is no wrong or right here, it is simply a matter of preference.

EXAMPLE

Conclusions

As noted by Kalleberg (1977), "The concept of job satisfaction traditionally has been of great interest to social scientists concerned with the problems of work in an industrial society" (p. 124). These problems include turnover, absenteeism, and lower productivity; problems also experienced by police organizations. If job satisfaction is related to these problems, both police organizations and police administrators who relish the positive outcomes of managing a satisfied work force should be interested in job satisfaction and its attributes.

Requiring police officers to possess a college education continues to be the subject of debate among practitioners and scholars. To date, the research on the utility of such a requirement is ambiguous at best. However, the same is true for research examining education and its effect on job satisfaction. For example, Quinn and Baldi de Mandilovitch (1975) noted that,

> The relationship between education and job satisfaction has not been sufficiently well demonstrated, however, to qualify as an unquestionable assumption. The magnitude of the relationship, as well as its form and its generality have yet to be established conclusively. Moreover, the social and psychological processes that may link education and job satisfaction are scarcely understood (p. 1).

Yet, Quinn and Baldi de Mandilovitch (1975) did find that individuals who had a college degree were consistently more satisfied with their job than those without a degree. Others have noted similar findings (see Glenn and Weaver, 1982; Mottaz, 1984; Ross and Reskin, 1992). However, other reports indicate that education has little influence on job satisfaction (see Martin and Shehan, 1989).

The result of this research appears to support the research findings of Quinn, et al. It seems that, overall, education does have a significant, positive effect on job satisfaction among ranking police officers. Officers with a Bachelor's degree tend to be more satisfied than those without a degree, and in some instances, were more satisfied than those with more education than a Bachelor's degree.

With the number of college-educated officers on the rise, better-educated ranking officers are sure to follow. Since management is a key element to the success of a police organization, factors that affect a police manager's activities and satisfaction with the job are important. Considering the findings reported here, it appears that a Bachelor's degree is one of those factors that can positively affect a police manager. This seems especially true with respect to perceptions of job satisfaction. Although further study is required, these findings are important to the future of police educational requirements. They certainly tend to support requiring college degrees for promotion to the rank of sergeant or above.

Despite the findings, caution should be taken as to their application. While there were a number of high mean scores for officers with a Bachelor's degree, the number of statistically significant relationships, both for education as a variable and between means by rank and educational level, was limited. Although there may be several reasons for this, the best interpretation might best be derived from Glenn and Weaver (1982) who stated that,

> A probable reason for the lack of a strong positive relationship is that education can have important negative as well as positive effects on job satisfaction; to the extent that education increases job expectations and aspirations more than it increases ability to attain, it is likely to contribute to dissatisfaction with work. For instance, it would seem that college-educated persons who must take jobs that do not require a college education should tend to be less satisfied with these jobs than they would have been if they had not gone to college (p. 47).

This may be quite a practical observation with respect to ranking police officers who find themselves in positions requiring little effort or knowledge and who find that their formal education is little used. This should be a managerial concern for the future: College-educated officers will require positions that will make use of their education or they could experience lower levels of satisfaction with the job.

Obviously, for this particular paper Dantzker chose to incorporate everything into the conclusions section rather than separating it into two components. Ultimately, the choice is left to the writer unless under specific instruction to do otherwise.

References and/or Bibliography

Unless the topic has never been addressed in research prior to your project (a very unlikely event), there are always some sources that help to support the research. These sources are what help establish the literature review. When using other sources—whether quoting, paraphrasing, or simply as an outlet for affirming what is already known—the source should be recognized. Not only can this be done throughout the paper by various citation methods but must be done at the end in the form of a reference list or a bibliography. The format depends upon the source the paper is being submitted to. Failing to cite sources can lead to charges of plagiarism, something every writer should strive to avoid.

The majority of the papers written for criminal justice and criminology follow the APA style for reference citing in the text and at the end of the paper. Reviewing the introduction section you will observe how two different formats are used, one is for paraphrasing or using some else's ideas and giving credit (author(s)' name(s) and publication date) and the other for direct quotes (author(s)' names, publication date, and page numbers). For the reference list, only those sources cited in the body of the text should be listed and the information listed should include the author(s) names, year of publication, name of publication (if it is an article, the article title comes first followed by the publication title), and if a book, the city, state, and name of publisher; or if a journal, the volume and issue number and the page numbers.

EXAMPLE

References from Example used throughout this chapter.

Baron, R. A. and Byrne, D. (1991). Social psychology (6th ed.). Boston, MA: Allyn and Bacon.

Bateman, T. S. and Strasser, S. (1983). A cross-lagged regression test of the relationship between job tension and employee satisfaction. Journal of Applied Psychology, 68(3), 439-445.

Bullock, R. J. (1986). Improving job satisfaction. NY: Pergamon Press.

Burke, R. J. (1989). Career stages, satisfaction, and well-being among police officers. Psychological Reports, 65 (1), 3-12.

Buzawa, E. S. (1984). Determining officer job satisfaction: The role of selected demographic and job specific attitudes. Criminology, 22 (1), 61-81.

Carroll, B. (1973). Job satisfaction. Ithaca, NY: Publications Division, Cornell University.

Carter, D. L. and Sapp, A. D. (1992). College education and policing: Coming of age. FBI Law Enforcement Bulletin,(Jan), 8-14.

Culver, S. M., Wolfe, L. M., and Cross, L. H. (1990). Testing a model of teacher satisfaction for Blacks and Whites. American Educational Research Journal, 27(2), 323-349.

Dantzker, M. L. (1993a). Designing a measure of job satisfaction for policing: A research note. Journal of Crime and Justice, XVI(2), 171-181.

—————————— (1993b). An issue for policing—Educational level and job satisfaction: A research note. American Journal of Police, 12(2), 101-118.

—————————— (1994). Identifying determinants of job satisfaction among police officers. Journal of Police and Criminal Psychology, 10(1), 47-56.

Dhillon, P. K. (1990). Some correlates of job satisfaction: A study of police personnel. Psychological Studies, 35(3), 197-204.

Glenn, N. D. and Weaver, C. N. (1982). Education and job satisfaction. Social Forces, 61(1), 46-55.

Grant, N. K., Garrison, C. G., and McCormick, K. (1990). Perceived utilization, job satisfaction and advancement of police women. Public Personnel Management, 19(2), 147-154.

Griffin, G. R., Dunbar, R.L.M., and McGill, M. E. (1978). Factors associated with job satisfaction among police personnel. Journal of Police Science and Administration, 6(1), 77-85.

Hackman, J. R. and Oldham, G. R. (1975). Development of the job diagnostic survey. Journal of Applied Psychology, 60,159-170.

Hochstedler, E. and Dunning, C. M. (1983). Communication and motivation in a police department. Criminal Justice and Behavior, 10(1), 47-69.

Hoover, L. T. (1975). Police educational characteristics and curricula. Washington, DC: U.S. Department of Justice.

Hudzik, J. K. (1978). College education for police: Problems in measuring component and extraneous variables. Journal of Criminal Justice, 6(1), 69-81.

Hunt, R. G. and McCadden, K. S. (1985). A survey of work attitudes of police officers: Commitment and satisfaction. Police-Studies, 8(1), 17-25.

Jayaratne, S. and Chess, W. A. (1984). Job satisfaction, burnout, and turnover: A national study. Social Work, 29, 448-53.

Kalleberg, A. L. (1977). Work values and job rewards: A theory of job satisfaction. American Sociological Review, 42(Feb), 124-143.

Klenke-Hamel, K. E. and Mathieu, J. E. (1990). Role strains, tension, and job satisfaction influences on employees' propensity to leave: A multi-sample replication and extension. Human Relations, 43(8), 791-807.

Landy, F .J. (1989). Psychology of work behavior (4th ed.), Pacific Grove, CA: Brooks-Cole Publishing Company.

Lester, D., Benkovich, C., Brady, J., Dietrich, M., and Solis, A. (1981). Stress and job satisfaction in police officers. Police Studies, 4(1), 34-42.

———————— (1987). Correlates of job satisfaction in police officers. Psychological Reports, 60(2), 550.

Locke, E. A. (1983). The nature and causes of job satisfaction. In Seashore, S. E., Lawler, E. E. III, Mirvis, P. H., and Cammann, C. (Eds.), Assessing organizational change: A guide to methods, measures and practices (pp. 1297-1349). NY: John Wiley and Sons.

Love, K. and Singer, M. (1988). Self-efficacy, psychological well-being, job satisfaction and job involvement: A comparison of male and female police officers. Police Studies, 11(2), 98-102.

Martelli, T.A., Waters, L.K., and Martelli, J. (1989). The police stress survey: Reliability and relation to job satisfaction and organizational commitment. Psychological Reports, 64(1), 267-273.

Martin, J. K. and Shehan, C. L. (1989). Education and job satisfaction: The influences of gender, wage-earning status, and job values. Work and Occupations, 16(2), 184-199.

Mottaz, C. (1984). Education and work satisfaction. Human Relations, 37(11), 985-1004.

Muchinsky, P. M. (1990). Psychology applied to work (3rd ed.). Pacific Grove, CA: Brooks/Cole Publishing Co.

Nord, W. R. (1977). Job satisfaction reconsidered. American Psychologist, (Dec), 1026-1035.

Quinn, R. P. and Baldi de Mandilovitch, M. S. (1975). Education and job satisfaction: A questionable payoff. MI: University of Michigan Survey Research Center.

———————— and Staines, G. L. (1979). The 1977 quality of employment survey. Ann Arbor, MI: University of Michigan.

Regoli, R. M., Crank, J. P., and Culbertson, R. (1989). Police cynicism, job satisfaction, and work relations of police chiefs: An assessment of the influence of department size. Sociological Focus, 22(3), 161-171.

Reiss, A. (1967). Career orientations, job satisfaction, and the assessment of law enforcement problems by police officers. In Studies in crime and law enforcement in major metropolitan area, V2, Field surveys III. Washington, DC: U.S. Government Printing Office.

Robbins, S. P. (1993). Organizational Behavior (6th ed). Englewood Cliffs, NJ: Prentice-Hall.

Ross, C. E. and Reskin, B. F. (1992). Education, control at work, and job satisfaction. Social Science Research, 21, 134-148.

Seashore, S. E. and Taber, T. D. (1975). Job satisfaction indicators and their correlates. American Behavioral Scientist, 18(3), 333-368.

Sherman, L. W. (1978). The Quality of Police Education. San Francisco, CA: Jossey-Bass Publishers.

Shernock, S. K. (1992). The effects of the college education on professional attitudes among police. Journal of Criminal Justice Education, 3(1), 71-92.

Smith, P., Kendall, L., and Hulin, C. (1975). The Job Development Index. Bowling Green, OH: Bowling Green State University Press.

Steers, R. M. (1981). Introduction to Organizational Behavior. Glenview, IL: Scott, Foreman and Company.

Wanous, J. P. and Lawler, E. E. (1972). Measurement and meaning of job satisfaction. Journal of Applied Psychology, 56(2), 95-105.

Wolpin, J., Burke, R. J., and Greenglass, E. R. (1991). Is job satisfaction an antecedent or a consequence of psychological burnout. Human Relations, 44(2), 193-209.

Worden, R.E. (1990). A badge and a baccalaureate: Policies, hypotheses, and further evidence. Justice Quarterly, 7(3), 565-592.

Tables and Figures

Most likely your research paper will include at least one table or figure. As previously noted these items can be placed within the text, kept separate and noted where they should be inserted, or placed at the end of the paper. Regardless of their location, tables and figures need to be clear as to their content and readily understandable. (see all Examples used throughout.)

Appendices

This last section is not a requirement of every paper. However, it is often useful to include a copy of the questionnaire or other tools that should be shared but do not belong in the body of the paper. There are no limitations to the number of appendices a paper can have except for those established by the instructor or the journal.

Summary

Regardless of the fear or loathing one feels about writing up the research, it is important. It may also be required. By formatting the paper in the manner suggested, it can make the process easier. It should also be acknowledged that grammar and spelling are extremely important along with using language that the intended audience can understand. Today, with the availability of various word-processing software, which often includes spelling and grammar checkers, this aspect of the writing should not be as difficult as in years past. Ultimately, the goal should be to submit the most efficiently written paper possible.

The objective of this chapter was to better demonstrate the research process through a completed paper, divided into sections to better explain each. Consequently, you should have a much better understanding of research methods. We trust you have found by this point that conducting and reporting research is not as intimidating as you perhaps perceived it at the beginning of this text.

Table 13-1   Respondent Demographics (n=530)

Variable	n	Percent		n	Percent
Gender			**Ethnicity**		
Male	473	(89.2)	White	418	(78.9)
Female	54	(10.2)	Black	61	(11.5)
Missing	3	(.6)	Hispanic	24	(4.5)
			Other	7	(1.3)
			Missing	20	(3.8)
Age			**Rank**		
20–25	1	(.2)	Officers	N/A	
26–35	84	(15.8)	Sergeant	368	(69.4)
36–45	252	(47.5)	Lieutenant	96	(18.1)
Over 45	181	(34.2)	Other	64	(12.1)
Missing	12	(2.3)	Missing	2	(.4)
Education			**Yrs Experience**		
High School	33	(6.2)	Under 2	5	(.9)
Associates	68	(12.8)	2–5	9	(1.7)
Bachelors	216	(40.8)	6–10	42	(7.9)
Other	88	(16.6)	11–15	100	(18.9)
No Degree	122	(23.0)	Over 15	366	(69.1)
Missing	3	(.6)	Missing	8	(1.5)

Table 13-2   Means by Education

Variable		All	HS	Assoc	Bach	Other	No Degree	f
Job Satisfaction	m	2.99	2.97	3.00	**3.05**	2.94	2.92	
	sd	(.63)	(.70)	(.62)	(.60)	(.67)	(.63)	.88
Subscales								
General		2.95	2.93	2.95	**3.02**	2.94	2.86	
Administration		(.69)	(.75)	(.71)	(.67)	(.72)	(.69)	1.08
Extras		2.90	2.96	**2.98**	2.95	2.77	2.85	
		(.68)	(.74)	(.66)	(.66)	(.74)	(.66)	1.39
Equipment		2.76	2.88	2.66	2.70	**2.96**	2.75	
		(1.19)	(1.34)	(1.09)	(1.15)	(1.17)	(1.27)	1.00
Job		3.47	3.40	**3.57**	3.53	3.44	3.36	
		(.78)	(.92)	(.71)	(.78)	(.72)	(.81)	1.34
Facet Free								
Overall	m	3.51	3.41	3.47	**3.57**	3.56	3.39	
Satisfaction	sd	(1.03)	(1.24)	(.96)	(.95)	(1.02)	(1.12)	.74
Change		2.78	2.82	2.78	2.66	2.76	**2.98**	
Departments		(1.47)	(1.45)	(1.55)	(1.45)	(1.46)	(1.49)	.96
Offer Outside		3.17	3.21	**3.49**	3.09	2.98	3.28	
Policing		(1.35)	(1.54)	(1.32)	(1.34)	(1.35)	(1.33)	1.76
Facet Specific								
Retirement		2.93	2.39	2.99	**3.11**	3.05	2.64	
Program		(1.15)	(1.06)	(1.22)	(1.11)	(1.15)	(1.14)	5.33[c]
Promotional		2.54	2.68	**2.71**	2.47	2.42	2.62	
Procedures		(1.18)	(.94)	(1.26)	(1.19)	(1.19)	(1.16)	1.01
Interdepartment		2.36	2.37	**2.45**	2.43	2.33	2.20	
Transfers		(1.12)	(1.10)	(1.08)	(1.13)	(1.15)	(1.11)	.96
Supervisor		3.08	3.06	3.06	**3.12**	3.06	3.06	
Support		(1.22)	(1.22)	(1.17)	(1.19)	(1.24)	(1.32)	.09
Supervisor		3.85	3.85	3.88	3.85	3.76	**3.91**	
Willingness		(1.07)	(1.20)	(1.07)	(1.08)	(1.05)	(1.06)	.26
Supervisor		3.83	3.79	3.76	**3.88**	3.80	3.80	
Assistance		(1.11)	(1.11)	(1.23)	(1.10)	(1.12)	(1.08)	.24
Evaluations/		2.45	**2.94**	2.46	2.46	2.31	2.41	
Grading		(1.07)	(1.15)	(1.16)	(1.02)	(1.14)	(.99)	2.00
Grievance/		3.08	3.03	3.07	**3.20**	3.10	2.84	
Appeal Procedure		(1.02)	(1.17)	(.97)	(1.05)	(.99)	(.97)	2.36[a]
Community Relations		2.74	2.72	2.67	**2.94**	2.76	2.40	
		(1.18)	(1.28)	(1.13)	(1.17)	(1.13)	(1.15)	4.36[c]
Salary		2.45	1.85	2.47	**2.66**	2.41	2.25	
		(1.17)	(1.09)	(1.10)	(1.20)	(1.13)	(1.12)	5.09[c]

Table 13-2   **Means by Education** *(continued)*

Variable	All	HS	Assoc	Bach	Other	No Degree	f
Benefits	3.34	3.15	3.25	**3.40**	3.39	3.30	
	(1.12)	(1.18)	(1.16)	(1.17)	(1.06)	(1.05)	.60
Insurance	3.06	2.70	**3.26**	3.21	3.17	2.70	
	(1.19)	(1.33)	(1.07)	(1.20)	(1.12)	(1.19)	5.22[c]
Overtime	3.14	3.21	3.04	3.21	2.83	**3.25**	
Compensation	(1.32)	(1.41)	(1.24)	(1.33)	(1.30)	(1.33)	1.70
Off-duty	3.25	3.44	3.22	**3.33**	3.05	3.21	
Job Policy	(1.13)	(.98)	(1.20)	(1.09)	(1.21)	(1.14)	1.29
Educational	2.86	3.28	**3.09**	2.76	2.41	3.11	
Incentives	(1.25)	(1.33)	(1.15)	(1.21)	(1.28)	(1.25)	5.94[c]
In-service	2.38	2.91	2.40	2.18	2.44	**2.55**	
Training	(1.27)	(1.33)	(1.19)	(1.16)	(1.35)	(1.39)	3.27[b]
Reporting	2.90	3.15	2.93	2.87	**2.98**	2.80	
System	(1.02)	(1.00)	(.94)	(1.01)	(.93)	(1.14)	.97
Current	3.90	3.58	3.99	**4.00**	3.82	3.82	
Assignment	(.99)	(1.32)	(.93)	(.96)	(.94)	(.96)	1.94
General Duties	3.63	3.48	**3.81**	3.71	3.56	3.48	
	(1.05)	(1.09)	(.93)	(1.03)	(1.08)	(1.10)	1.71
Current	2.94	**3.09**	3.04	2.96	3.06	2.71	
Administrators	(1.34)	(1.18)	(1.33)	(1.36)	(1.31)	(1.37)	1.28
Educational	2.65	**3.00**	2.64	2.64	2.38	2.76	
Requirements	(1.09)	(1.05)	(1.16)	(1.03)	(1.14)	(1.11)	2.50[a]
Equipment	2.82	2.97	2.69	2.76	**2.98**	2.84	
Quality	(1.25)	(1.40)	(1.17)	(1.23)	(1.19)	(1.33)	.79
Equipment	2.71	2.79	2.63	2.64	**2.95**	2.66	
Availability	(1.22)	(1.41)	(1.14)	(1.18)	(1.24)	(1.28)	1.20

a=$p \leq .05$ b=$p \leq .01$ c=$p \leq .001$

Table 13-3: MEANS By Education by Rank (ALL)

Variable		Sergeants					Lieutenants				
		HS	Assoc	Bach	Other	NoDeg	HS	Assoc	Bach	Other	NoDeg
Job Satisfaction	m	2.84	2.99	2.95	2.95	2.78	3.12	2.87	3.19	2.79	3.26
	sd	(.63)	(.62)	(.62)	(.57)	(.58)	(.71)	(.79)	(.53)	(.85)	(.66)
Scales											
General		2.74	2.90	2.92	2.92	2.71	3.00	2.87	3.14	2.83	3.25
Administration		(.61)	(.70)	(.67)	(.64)	(.66)	(.88)	(.76)	(.62)	(.91)	(.60)
Extras		2.83	2.97	2.87	2.81	2.74	3.14	3.10	3.02	2.65	3.09
		(.68)	(.66)	(.67)	(.65)	(.60)	(.85)	(.85)	(.53)	(.91)	(.71)
Equipment		2.40	2.61	2.61	3.07	2.54	3.75	2.50	2.82	2.72	3.21
		(1.20)	(.99)	(1.12)	(1.14)	(1.18)	(.50)	(1.54)	(1.20)	(1.29)	(1.35)
Job		3.39	3.63	3.42	3.44	3.25	3.08	2.96	3.79	3.25	3.76
		(.98)	(.69)	(.78)	(.62)	(.79)	(.57)	(.90)	(.77)	(.84)	(.85)
Facet Free											
Overall	m	3.38	3.43	3.44	3.60	3.22	3.50	3.44	3.69	3.50	3.85
Satisfaction	sd	(1.32)	(.94)	(.95)	(1.05)	(1.15)	(1.00)	(1.33)	(.89)	(1.10)	(1.09)
Change		3.12	2.83	2.76	2.73	**3.17**	2.00	3.11	2.48	2.90	2.19
Departments		(1.39)	(1.46)	(1.45)	(1.50)	(1.46)	(.82)	(2.03)	(1.47)	(1.41)	(1.40)
Offer Outside		3.37	3.48	3.11	3.12	3.47	3.25	**3.67**	3.10	3.05	2.52
Policing		(1.50)	(1.28)	(1.33)	(1.30)	(1.28)	(1.71)	(1.58)	(1.34)	(1.50)	(1.33)
Facet Specific											
Retirement		2.25	3.04	3.08	3.22	2.54	2.75	2.67	3.00	2.90	3.05
Program		(1.03)	(1.19)	(1.10)	(1.07)	(1.12)	(1.50)	(1.41)	(1.19)	(1.12)	(1.28)
Promotional		2.50	2.82	2.38	2.31	2.44	3.00	2.00	2.45	2.40	3.14
Procedures		(.88)	(1.26)	(1.18)	(1.19)	(1.14)	(1.15)	(1.50)	(1.11)	(1.23)	(1.20)
Interdepartment		2.12	2.43	2.29	2.31	2.07	2.75	1.78	2.43	2.30	2.38
Transfers		(.99)	(1.04)	(1.12)	(1.08)	(1.01)	(1.25)	(.97)	(1.02)	(1.34)	(1.20)
Supervisor		2.83	2.98	2.94	2.96	2.77	3.00	3.22	3.45	2.90	3.67
Support		(1.05)	(1.16)	(1.20)	(1.27)	(1.29)	(1.63)	(1.48)	(1.13)	(1.41)	(.97)
Supervisor		3.83	3.81	3.69	3.78	3.81	3.00	4.55	4.19	3.40	4.14
Availability		(1.20)	(1.10)	(1.08)	(1.09)	(1.02)	(1.41)	(.73)	(.99)	(1.14)	(1.11)
Supervisor		3.79	3.71	3.76	3.65	3.73	3.50	4.11	4.10	3.75	3.95
Assistance		(1.14)	(1.25)	(1.10)	(1.22)	(1.07)	(1.00)	(1.27)	(1.05)	(1.07)	(1.07)
Evaluations/		2.78	2.38	2.47	2.42	2.36	3.00	2.56	2.28	2.17	2.30
Grading		(1.12)	(1.11)	(1.02)	(1.10)	(.97)	(1.41)	(1.51)	(1.03)	(1.20)	(.98)
Grievance/		2.83	3.04	3.06	3.00	2.72	3.00	3.11	3.32	3.15	3.10
Appeal Procedure		(1.12)	(.88)	(1.03)	(.87)	(.87)	(1.15)	(1.54)	(1.06)	(1.31)	(1.09)

| | | *Other* | | | |
HS	Assoc	Bach	Other	NoDeg	*f*
3.83 (.78)	3.19 (.56)	3.44 (.46)	3.07 (.78)	3.35 (.57)	2.93[b]
3.95 (.65)	3.39 (.68)	3.53 (.50)	3.14 (.74)	3.30 (.68)	3.82[b]
3.76 (.79)	2.86 (.43)	3.36 (.64)	2.77 (.84)	3.30 (.74)	2.30[b]
4.50 (.71)	3.08 (1.28)	3.14 (1.18)	2.94 (1.20)	3.38 (1.45)	2.66[b]
3.73 (.86)	3.83 (.28)	**3.86** (.66)	3.64 (.80)	3.42 (.78)	2.50[b]
3.50 (1.29)	3.80 (.45)	**4.24** (.83)	3.47 (.94)	3.77 (.72)	1.70[a]
2.00 (1.73)	2.00 (1.41)	2.24 (1.34)	2.56 (1.42)	3.00 (1.48)	1.51
2.40 (1.67)	3.50 (1.52)	3.00 (1.45)	2.55 (1.29)	3.23 (1.30)	1.47
2.80 (.84)	3.17 (1.33)	**3.48** (.98)	2.71 (1.40)	2.69 (.95)	2.36[b]
3.67 (.58)	2.80 (.45)	3.14 (1.20)	2.72 (1.18)	3.00 (.85)	2.01[a]
3.50 (1.00)	**3.50** (.84)	3.48 (.87)	2.39 (1.18)	2.83 (1.40)	3.38[b]
4.20 (1.30)	3.50 (.84)	3.75 (.91)	3.56 (.78)	4.00 (1.29)	2.95[b]
4.60 (.55)	3.67 (1.03)	4.33 (.91)	4.17 (.71)	4.23 (1.17)	2.18[b]
4.00 (1.22)	3.83 (1.17)	4.33 (1.02)	**4.33** (.76)	4.00 (1.22)	1.09
3.75 (.96)	2.83 (1.17)	2.65 (.99)	2.19 (1.28)	2.92 (1.08)	1.26
4.25 (.96)	3.17 (.75)	3.95 (.80)	3.29 (.92)	3.33 (1.23)	2.79[b]

continued on next page

Table 13-3: MEANS By Education by Rank (ALL) *(continued)*

Variable	Sergeants					Lieutenants				
	HS	Assoc	Bach	Other	NoDeg	HS	Assoc	Bach	Other	NoDeg
Community Relations	2.46 (1.28)	2.57 (1.14)	2.75 (1.19)	2.69 (1.10)	2.24 (1.09)	3.25 (.96)	2.67 (1.12)	3.26 (1.13)	2.58 (1.35)	2.62 (1.20)
Salary	1.62 (1.06)	2.46 (1.11)	2.65 (1.17)	2.53 (1.12)	2.11 (1.10)	2.25 (1.25)	2.33 (1.32)	2.45 (1.27)	2.37 (1.12)	2.67 (1.15)
Benefits	2.92 (1.10)	3.25 (1.12)	3.36 (1.14)	3.45 (.91)	3.15 (1.05)	3.25 (1.50)	3.22 (1.56)	3.41 (1.25)	3.40 (1.19)	3.71 (.85)
Insurance	2.54 (1.17)	3.17 (1.06)	3.22 (1.18)	3.31 (1.08)	2.63 (1.19)	3.00 (1.41)	**4.00** (1.12)	3.10 (1.28)	2.95 (1.28)	2.71 (1.19)
Overtime Compensation	2.92 (1.41)	3.04 (1.24)	3.12 (1.32)	3.02 (1.25)	3.11 (1.27)	3.25 (.96)	3.33 (1.22)	3.36 (1.36)	2.55 (1.36)	3.57 (1.36)
Off-duty Job Policy	3.29 (.91)	3.27 (1.19)	3.27 (1.07)	3.20 (1.15)	3.05 (1.08)	3.25 (.95)	3.22 (1.39)	3.40 (1.15)	2.85 (1.39)	3.71 (1.10)
Educational Incentives	3.04 (1.33)	2.96 (1.13)	2.62 (1.15)	2.39 (1.27)	2.93 (1.20)	3.50 (1.00)	3.44 (1.42)	2.93 (1.30)	2.11 (1.24)	3.33 (1.32)
In-service Training	2.62 (1.21)	2.29 (1.05)	2.07 (1.14)	2.24 (1.27)	2.25 (1.27)	3.00 (1.41)	2.56 (1.74)	2.38 (1.21)	2.35 (1.39)	3.14 (1.53)
Reporting System	3.08 (1.10)	2.98 (.96)	2.76 (1.02)	3.02 (.91)	2.67 (1.13)	3.00 (.00)	2.38 (1.06)	3.21 (.81)	2.75 (.97)	3.14 (1.20)
Current Assignment	3.67 (1.31)	4.06 (.92)	3.88 (.97)	3.80 (.96)	3.70 (.97)	3.00 (1.41)	3.37 (1.19)	4.24 (.98)	3.75 (1.02)	4.14 (.79)
General Duties	3.42 (1.21)	3.87 (.93)	3.58 (1.02)	3.55 (1.04)	3.39 (1.09)	3.25 (.50)	3.12 (.99)	3.90 (1.08)	3.25 (1.33)	4.00 (.89)
Current Administrators	2.83 (1.09)	2.92 (1.36)	2.72 (1.32)	2.90 (1.31)	2.46 (1.28)	3.00 (1.41)	3.12 (1.36)	3.31 (1.37)	2.95 (1.43)	3.24 (1.51)
Educational Requirements	2.87 (1.12)	2.54 (1.18)	2.67 (1.01)	2.35 (1.19)	2.61 (1.06)	3.25 (.50)	2.62 (1.06)	2.55 (1.13)	2.50 (1.28)	3.14 (1.31)
Equipment Quality	2.50 (1.32)	2.62 (1.09)	2.65 (1.20)	3.10 (1.18)	2.65 (1.25)	**3.75** (.50)	2.62 (1.60)	2.93 (1.31)	2.70 (1.34)	3.29 (1.38)
Equipment Availability	2.29 (1.27)	2.60 (1.07)	2.56 (1.15)	3.04 (1.19)	2.43 (1.18)	3.75 (.50)	2.37 (1.51)	2.71 (1.24)	2.75 (1.33)	3.14 (1.35)

a=p≤.05   b=p≤.01

HS	Assoc	Other Bach	Other	NoDeg	f
3.75 (.96)	3.33 (1.03)	3.71 (.56)	3.11 (.96)	3.17 (1.19)	3.86[b]
2.66 (.89)	2.67 (.82)	**3.14** (1.20)	2.17 (1.20)	2.46 (1.05)	2.52[b]
4.20 (.84)	3.33 (1.21)	3.71 (1.19)	3.28 (1.27)	3.62 (1.19)	1.12
3.20 (2.05)	3.17 (.75)	3.43 (1.16)	3.11 (1.02)	3.15 (1.14)	2.26b
4.60 (.89)	2.67 (1.51)	**3.62** (1.36)	2.56 (1.41)	3.62 (1.56)	1.69
4.50 (1.00)	2.83 (1.17)	3.67 (1.11)	2.89 (1.18)	3.50 (1.38)	1.50
4.50 (1.00)	3.67 (.82)	3.43 (1.21)	2.78 (1.35)	3.92 (1.19)	3.79[b]
4.50 (1.00)	3.00 (1.41)	2.62 (1.12)	2.78 (1.52)	3.62 (1.26)	3.65[b]
3.60 (.89)	3.17 (.41)	2.95 (1.20)	3.11 (.96)	3.17 (.94)	1.53
3.60 (1.52)	4.17 (.41)	4.38 (.67)	3.94 (.87)	4.08 (1.04)	1.85[a]
4.00 (.71)	4.17 (.41)	**4.24** (.83)	3.89 (.83)	3.23 (1.30)	2.32[b]
4.40 (.55)	3.83 (.98)	4.00 (1.00)	3.61 (1.09)	3.58 (1.24)	3.72[b]
3.50 (1.00)	3.50 (1.05)	2.62 (.92)	2.28 (.89)	3.17 (.94)	1.62
4.60 (.55)	3.17 (1.33)	3.19 (1.21)	2.94 (1.11)	3.38 (1.50)	2.29[b]
4.40 (.89)	3.00 (1.26)	3.10 (1.18)	2.94 (1.35)	3.38 (1.45)	2.70[b]

Table 13-4: Correlations (p≤.01)

Variable	Gender	Ethnicity	Age	Rank	Yrs Exp	Education
Job Satisfaction	.0315	.0856	−.0336	.1763*	−.1259*	.0856
Scales						
General Administration	.0110	.0528	−.0146	.1964*	−.1028	.0660
Extras	.0771	.0945	−.0834	.1248*	−.1859*	.0808
Equipment	.0270	.1454*	.0112	.1447*	−.0027	.0587
Job	−.0373	.0248	.0159	.0800	−.0392	.0901
Facet Free						
Overall Satisfaction	.0360	.0758	−.0611	.1666*	−.1409*	.0583
Change Departments	−.0880	.0210	−.0286	−.1645*	−.0087	−.0217
Offer Outside Policing	−.0570	.0650	.0392	−.1025	.1094	−.1065
Facet Specific						
Retirement Program	.0019	−.0905	.0592	.1073	−.0053	.1243*
Promotional Procedures	.0452	.1194*	−.0722	.0879	−.1601*	−.0252
Interdepartment transfers	.0027	.0564	.0465	.1438*	−.0827	.0675
Supervisor support	−.0326	−.0068	−.0629	.1512*	−.0985	−.0068
Supervisor availability	−.0326	−.0944	−.0098	.0925	−.0436	.0481
Supervisor assistance	−.0426	−.0525	−.0638	.1219*	−.0566	.0280
Evaluations/grading	.0100	.1359*	−.1450*	−.0577	−.2255*	.0448
Grievance/appeal proc	.0082	.0011	−.0012	.2329*	−.0678	.0340
Community Relations	.0431	.0966	.0291	.2405*	−.0578	.0622
Salary	.0423	−.0667	−.0226	.1320*	−.1083	.0902
Benefits	.0365	.0659	−.0501	.0608	−.0517	.0584
Insurance	.1133*	.0951	−.1249*	.0621	−.1379*	.0521
Overtime compensation	.0783	.0168	−.0542	.0788	−.1650*	.1226*
Off-duty job policy	.0361	−.0264	−.0281	.0674	−.1292*	.1036
Educational incentives	.0562	.1014	.0357	.1229*	.0191	.0310
In-service training	.0780	.1504*	−.0333	.1367*	−.0755	.0430
Reporting system	.0296	.0931	−.0206	.0550	−.0695	.0543
Current assignment	−.0687	−.0208	.0729	.0720	.0321	.0800
General Duties	−.0418	−.0044	−.0209	.0617	−.0627	.0776
Current administrators	−.0201	.0699	.0800	.1666*	.0247	−.0167
Educational requirements	−.0056	.2227*	−.0838	−.1222	−.1240*	−.0734
Equipment quality	.0175	.1447*	.0250	.1638*	.0114	.0565
Equipment availability	.0338	.1309*	−.0040	.1100	−.0168	.0548

FACET-SPECIFIC	
Variable	**Educational Level**
Retirement Program	Other (3.05) and High School (2.39)
	Bachelor's (3.11) and High School (2.39) No Degree (2.64)
Community Relations	Bachelor's (2.94) and No Degree (2.40)
Salary	Bachelor's (2.66) and High School (1.85) No Degree (2.25)
Insurance	Other (3.17) and No Degree (2.70)
	Bachelor's (3.21) and No Degree (2.70)
	Associate's (2.84) and No Degree (2.70)
Educational Incentives	Associate's (3.09) and Other (2.41)
	No Degree (3.11) and Other (2.41)
	High School (3.28) and Other (2.41)
In-Service Training	High School (2.91) and Bachelor's (2.18)
Recruit Educ Requirements	High School (3.00) and Other (2.38)

Figure 13-1 Relationship Between the Means (Significant Variables Only; p=.05)
by Education and Rank (Sgt. and Above)

Figure 13-2 Relationship Between the Means (Significant Variables Only; p=.05)
by Education and Rank (Sgt. and Above), *continued on next page*

JOB SATISFACTION	Lt/Bach (3.19) and Sgt/No Degree (2.78) Other/Bach (3.44) and Sgt/No Degree (2.78)
SCALES **General Administration**	Lt/Bach (3.14) and Sgt/No Degree (2.71) Lt/No Degree (3.25) and Sgt/No Degree (2.71) Other/Bach (3.53) and Sgt/No Degree (2.71) Sgt/HS (2.71) Sgt/Assoc (2.90) Sgt/Bach (2.92) Sgt/Oth (2.92) Lt/Assoc (3.95) and Sgt/No Degree (2.71)
Extras	Other/Bach (3.36) and Sgt/No Degree (2.74)
Equipment	Other/Assoc (4.50) and Sgt/HS (2.40) Sgt/No Degree (2.54) Sgt/Assoc (2.61) Sgt/Bach (2.61)
Job	Lt/Bach (3.79) and Sgt/No Degree (3.25)
FACET-FREE **Overall**	Other/Bach (4.24) and Sgt/No Deg (3.22) Other/Bach (4.24) and Sgt/Bach (3.45)
FACET-SPECIFIC **Retirement Program**	Sgt/Bach (3.08) and Sgt/HS (2.25) Sgt/No Degree (2.54) Sgt/Oth (3.22) and Sgt/HS (2.25) Sgt/No Degree (2.54) Other/Bach (3.48) and Sgt/HS (2.25) Sgt/No Degree (2.54)
In-House Transfers	Other/Bach (3.48) and Lt/Assoc (1.78) Sgt/No Degree (2.07) Sgt/HS (2.12) Sgt/Bach (2.29) Lt/Other (2.30) Sgt/Other (2.31) Lt/No Degree (2.38) Lt/Bach (2.43) Sgt/Assoc (2.43)
Supervisor Support	Other/No Degree (4.00) and Sgt/No Degree (2.77)
Grievance Procedures	Other/Bach (3.95) and Sgt/No Degree (2.72) Sgt/HS (2.83) Sgt/Other (3.00) Sgt/Assoc (3.04) Sgt/Bach (3.06)
Community Relations	Sgt/Bach (2.75) and Sgt/No Degree (2.24) Lt/Bach (3.26) and Sgt/No Degree (2.24) Other/Bach (3.71) and Sgt/No Degree (2.24) Sgt/HS (2.46) Sgt/Assoc (2.57) Sgt/Other (2.69) Sgt/Bach (2.75)
Salary	Sgt/Bach (2.65) and Sgt/HS (1.62) Sgt/No Degree (2.11) Other/Bach (3.14) and Sgt/HS (1.62) Sgt/No Degree (2.11)
Insurance	Sgt/Bach (3.22) and Sgt/No Degree (2.63)

Figure 13-2, *continued from previous page*

FACET-SPECIFIC *(continued)*

Educational Incentives	Oth/Bach (3.43) and Lt/Other (2.11) Sgt/Other (2.39) Other/No Degree (3.92) and Lt/Other (2.11) Sgt/Other (2.39) Sgt/Bach (2.62) Other/HS (4.50) and Lt/Other (2.11)
In-Service Training	Lt/No Degree (3.14) and Sgt/Bach (2.07) Other/No Degree (3.62) and Sgt/Bach (2.07) Sgt/Other (2.24) Sgt/No Degree (2.25) Sgt/Assoc (2.29) Lt/HS (4.50) and Sgt/Bach (2.07) Sgt/Other (2.24) Sgt/No Degree (2.25) Sgt/Assoc (2.29)
General Duties	Lt/Bach (4.24) and Sgt/No Degree (3.39)
Current Administration	Lt/Bach (3.31) and Sgt/No Degree (2.46) Other/Other (3.61) and Sgt/No Degree (2.46) Other/Bach (4.00) and Sgt/No Degree (2.46) Sgt/Bach (2.72)
Equipment Quality	Other/HS (4.60) and Sgt/HS (2.50) Sgt/Assoc (2.62) Sgt/No Degree (2.65) Sgt/Bach (2.65)
Equipment Availability	Other/HS (4.40) and Sgt/HS (2.29) Sgt/No Degree (2.43) Sgt/Bach (2.56)

Methodological Queries:

Based on the idea of the College Students' Criminality study:

(1) Describe the elements you would include in the introduction, methodology, and conclusions? Would you need an appendix? If so, what would be in it?

(2) Why do you think students fear writing research papers?

PART VI

Closure

Summing Up

■ Vignette 14-1
In a Nutshell!

Next week is finals. It has been an interesting semester, especially in your research methods class. The information you have received will definitely assist you in the completion of your senior project. However, the more pressing matter is the final for the research course. You understand that it is comprehensive and therefore, anything goes, but you obviously do not have the time or inclination to reread every chapter. Your notes are good, but you are not completely confidant that you have everything you need to know. Suddenly you realize that thirteen chapters of your book were covered during the course, but not the last one. So, you decide to check out the last chapter with a hope that maybe it will be the study guide you were looking for. Here it is!!!

■ CHAPTER 14
Learning Objectives

After studying this chapter the student should be able to:

1. Present and discuss the issues involved in *Research: What, Why, and How*.

2. Recognize and explain the issues involved in *Research Ethics*.

3. Present and discuss the issues involved in *Getting Started*.

4. Identify and describe the issues involved in *The Language of Research*.

5. Present and discuss the issues involved in *Qualitative Research*.

6. Recognize and explain the issues involved in *Quantitative Research*.

7. Present and discuss the issues involved in *Research Designs.*
8. Identify and describe the issues involved in *Questionnaire Construction.*
9. Present and discuss the issues involved in *Sampling.*
10. Explain the issues involved in *Data Collection.*
11. Recognize and explain the issues involved in *Data Processing and Analysis.*
12. Present and discuss the issues involved in *Inferential Statistics.*
13. Present and discuss the issues involved in *Writing the Research.*

Summing Up

The purpose of this chapter is to provide an overview of the key elements of research discussed in the previous chapters of this text. Our intent is to help you see how all of the information provided earlier enables you to progress from the development of a possible research topic to the completion of a methodologically sound research paper. This should refresh your memory in preparation for a possible final examination in this course. In addition, it will aid as a reference for dealing with future research assignments.

Doing Criminological Research

Ordinary human inquiry may be flawed due to inaccurate observation, overgeneralization, selective observation, and illogical reasoning. The scientific method seeks to prevent the errors of casual inquiry by utilizing procedures that specify objectivity, logic, theoretical understanding, and knowledge of prior research in the development and use of a precise measurement instrument designed to accurately record observations.

Types of Research

Research creates questions, but ultimately, regardless of the subject or topic under study, it is the goal of research to provide answers. Research may occur in one of four formats or types, as descriptive, explanatory, predictive, and intervening knowledge. Knowledge that is descriptive allows us to understand what something is. Explanatory research tries to tell us why something occurs, the causes behind it. Predictive research gives some foresight as to what may happen if something is implemented or tried. Intervening knowledge allows one to intercede before a problem or issue gets too difficult to address.

Steps in Research

Whether the research is applied or basic, qualitative or quantitative, the basic steps are applicable to each. There are five primary steps in conducting research:

1. Identifying the Problem

   Identifying or determining the problem, issue, or policy to be studied is what sets the groundwork for the rest of the research.

2. Research Design

   The research design is the "blueprint," which outlines how the research is conducted.

3. Data Collection

   Regardless of the research design, data collection is a key component. A variety of methods exist. They include surveys, interviews, observations, and previously existing data.

4. Data Analysis

   Proper analysis and interpretation of the data is integral to the research process.

5. Reporting

   The last phase of any research project is the reporting of the findings. Regardless of the audience or the medium used, the findings must be coherent and understandable.

Research Ethics

Ethics were defined as doing what is morally and legally right in the conducting of research. This requires the researcher to be knowledgeable about what is being done; use reasoning when making decisions; be both intellectual and truthful in approach and reporting; and consider the consequences, in particular, to be sure that the outcome of the research outweighs any negatives that might occur.

Ethical neutrality requires that the researchers' moral or ethical beliefs are not allowed to influence the gathering of data or the conclusions that are made from analyzing the data. Objectivity is striving to prevent personal ideology or prejudices from influencing the process. In addition to these concerns, the researcher must also ensure that their research concerns do not negatively impact upon the safety of others.

Ethical Concerns

Ethical concerns include:

1. Harm to Others

   Physical harm most often can occur during experimental or applied types of research. Psychological harm might result through the type of information being gathered. Social harm may be inflicted if certain information gathered is released that should not have been.

2. Privacy Concerns

   Individuals in America have a basic right to privacy. In many cases, research efforts may violate that right. Ethically speaking, if a person does not want his or her life examined, then that right should be granted.

3. Informed Consent

   Normally, this requires having the individual sign an "Informed Consent" form or for the instructions to indicate that the survey is completely anonymous, voluntary, and that the information is only being used for the purpose of research.

4. Voluntary Participation

   Participation should be voluntary. If not, there must be valid reasons that can be given showing that the knowledge could not otherwise be reasonably obtained and that no harm will come to the participants from their compulsory involvement. To ensure that informed consent is provided, and to judge the value and ethical nature of the research, many universities have Institutional Review Boards (IRBs).

5. Deception

   Some types of research (particularly field research that requires the researcher to in essence "go undercover" in order to gain the knowledge that he/she is seeking) cannot be conducted if the subjects are aware that they are being studied. Such research is controversial and must be carefully thought out before it is undertaken.

Ethical Research Criteria

The following criteria should be followed to produce ethical research:

1. Avoid harmful research.
2. Be objective in designing, conducting, and evaluating your research.
3. Use integrity in the performance and reporting of the research.
4. Protect confidentiality.

Getting Started

As with so many issues in life, often the hardest aspect of research is getting started. There are a number of issues involved in beginning criminological research. Proper preparation is vital to the successful completion of a research project.

Picking a Topic

Before the topic is chosen, one should consider:

1. What currently exists in the literature
2. Any gaps in theory or the current state of art
3. The feasibility of conducting the research
4. Whether there are any policy implications
5. Possible funding availability

Reviewing the Literature

Ultimately, the best way to begin a research effort is to focus on a particular issue, phenomenon, or problem that most interests the individual. In doing so, one must be sure to determine what the problem, issue, or phenomenon is, and organize what is known about it. Once a literature search is completed, the research question(s) can be formulated.

The Research Question

A well-worded research question should give a clear indication of the outcomes one might expect at the conclusion of the research. After establishing the research question(s), the researcher must next offer what specifically is going to be studied and the expected results. This is usually accomplished through statements or propositions referred to as hypotheses.

Hypotheses

A hypothesis is *a specific statement describing the expected result or relationship between the independent and dependent variables.*
   The three most common types are:

1. The research hypothesis, which is a statement of the expected relationship between variables offered in a positive manner
2. The null hypothesis, which is a statement that the relationship or difference being tested does not exist
3. The rival hypothesis, which is a statement offering an alternate explanation for the research findings

Variables

Variables are factors that can change or influence change. They result from the Operationalization of a concept. The two types of variables are:

1. The *dependent* variable(s), which is/are the factor(s) being influenced to change over which the researcher has no controls. Basically, the dependent variable(s) is/are the outcome item(s) or what is being predicted.
2. The *independent* variable(s), which is/are the factor(s) that will influence or predict the outcome of the dependent variable. This variable is something the researcher can control.

The Language of Research Theory

All criminal justice practice is grounded in criminological theory. A theory is a statement that attempts to make sense of reality. Proving that a theory is valid is a common goal of criminological and criminal justice researchers.

Conceptualization

Concepts are viewed as the beginning point for all research endeavors and are often very broad in nature. They are the bases of theories and serve as a means to communicate, introduce, classify, and build thoughts and ideas. To conduct research, the concept must first be taken from its conceptual or theoretical level to an observational level. This process is known as conceptualization.

Operationalization

Operationalization is describing how a concept is measured. This process is best described as *the conversion of the abstract idea or notion into a measurable item*. The primary focus of the operationalization process is the creation of variables and subsequently developing a measurement instrument to assess those variables. Variables are concepts that may be divided into two or more categories or groupings known as attributes.

Variables

A dependent variable is a factor that requires other factors to cause or influence change. Basically the dependent variable is the outcome factor or that which is being predicted. The independent variable is the influential or the predictor factor. These are the variables believed to cause the change or outcome of the dependent variable and are something the researcher can control.

Hypotheses

Once the concept has been operationalized into variables fitting the theory in question, most research focuses on testing the validity of statement(s) called hypothesis(es). The hypothesis is *a specific statement describing the expected relationship between the independent and dependent variables.* There are three common types of hypotheses: research, null, and rival.

Sampling

A sample is *a group chosen from within a target population to provide information sought.* There are a number of sampling strategies that are available in criminological research. These include: random sampling; stratified random sampling; cluster sampling; snowball sampling; and, purposive sampling.

Validity

Validity is a term describing whether the measure used accurately represents the concept it is meant to measure. There are four types of validity *face, content, construct,* and *criterion.*

Face Validity

This is the simplest form of validity and basically refers to whether the measuring device appears, on its face, to measure what the researcher wants to measure. This is primarily a judgmental decision.

Content Validity

Each item of the measuring device is examined to determine whether each element is measuring the concept in question.

Construct Validity

This validity inquires as to whether the measuring device does indeed measure what it has been designed to measure. It refers to the fit between theoretical and operational definitions of the concept.

Criterion (or Pragmatic) Validity

This type of validity represents the degree to which the measure relates to external criterion. It can either be *concurrent*, does the measure enhance the ability to assess the current characteristics of the concept under study?; or *predictive*, the ability to accurately foretell future events or conditions.

Reliability

Reliability refers to how consistent the measuring device would be over time. In other words, if the study is replicated the measuring device provides consistent results. The two key components of reliability are stability and consistency. Stability means the ability to retain accuracy and resist change. Consistency is the ability to yield similar results when replicated.

Data

Data are simply pieces of information gathered from the sample that describe events, beliefs, characteristics, people, or other phenomena. This data may exist at one of four levels, nominal, ordinal, interval, and ratio.

Nominal Data

This level data are categorical based on some defined characteristic. The categories are exclusive and have no logical order. For example, gender is a nominal level data form.

Ordinal Data

Ordinal data are categorical, too, but whose characteristics may be rank-ordered. These data categories are also exclusive but are scaled in a manner representative of the amount of characteristic in question, along some dimension. For example, types of prisons composed as minimum, medium, and maximum.

Interval Data

Categorical data for which there is a distinctive, yet equal, difference among the characteristics measured are interval data. The categories have order and represent equal units on a scale with no set zero starting point (e.g., the IQ of prisoners).

Ratio Data

This type of data is ordered, has equal units of distance, and a true zero starting point (for example, age, weight, income).

Qualitative Research

Qualitative research is defined as the nonnumerical examination and interpretation of observations for the purpose of discovering underlying meanings and patterns of relationships. Such analysis enables researchers to verbalize insights that quantifying of data would not permit. It also allows us to avoid the trap of "false precision" which frequently occurs when subjective numerical assignments are made.

Types of Qualitative Research

Field Interviewing

Field interviewing consists of structured interviews, semi-structured interviews, unstructured interviews, and focus groups. A structured interview entails the asking of preestablished open-ended questions of every respondent. A semi-structured interview goes beyond the responses given to the actual questions for a broader understanding of the answer. Unstructured interviews seldom keep to a schedule nor are there usually any predetermined possible answers. Focus groups interview several individuals in one setting.

Field Observation (or Participant-Observer)

Field observation consists of observing individuals in their natural setting. The method of observation is determined by the role of the researcher. The *full participant* method allows the researcher to carry out observational research, but does so in a "covert" manner. The *participant researcher* participates in the activities of the research environment but is known to the research subjects to be a researcher. The *researcher who participates* method requires nothing more than observation by the researcher whose status as a researcher is known to the research subjects. The *complete researcher* avoids all possible interaction with the research subjects.

Ethnographical Study

Ethnographical study or field research overlaps with field observation in that the researcher actually enters the environment under study, but does not necessarily take part in any activities.

Sociometry

Sociometry is a technique by which the researcher can measure social dynamics or relational structures such as who-likes-whom. Information can be gathered through interviews or by observation and will indicate who is chosen and the characteristics about those who do the choosing.

Historiography

Historiography (also known as historical/comparative research) is basically the study of actions, events, phenomena, etc., that have already occurred. This type of research often involves the study of documents and records with information about the topic under study. Historiography can be either qualitative or quantitative in nature depending on the materials being utilized and the focus of the research.

Content Analysis

Like historical research, content analysis is the study of social artifacts to gain insights about an event or phenomenon. It differs in that the focus is upon the coverage of the event by the particular medium being evaluated rather than the event. Depending upon how the research is conducted, this may be either qualitative or quantitative in nature.

Quantitative Research

Quantitative research was defined as the numerical representation and manipulation of observations for the purpose of describing and explaining the phenomena that those observations represent. It is based upon empiricism. The use of the scientific method with its focus on causation rather than casual observation is what makes empiricism important. It is this emphasis upon empiricism rather than idealism that is the basis upon which positive criminology is founded.

Causality

In applying empirical observation to criminal justice research we focus upon causal relationships. When we try to examine numerous explanations for why an event occurred this is known as *idiographic* explanation. When researchers focus upon a relatively few observations in order to provide a partial explanation for an event this is known as *nomothetic* causation. Nomothetic explanations of causality are based upon probabilities. It is this use of probability that enable us to make inferences based upon a relatively few observations.

The Criteria for Causality

The first criterion is that the independent variable (the variable that is providing the influence) must occur before the dependent variable (the variable that is being acted upon). The second criterion is that a relationship between the independent and dependent variable must be observed. The third criterion is that the apparent relationship is not explained by a third variable.

Necessary and Sufficient Cause

In investigating causality we must meet the above criteria but we do not have to demonstrate a perfect correlation. If a condition or event must occur in order for another event to take place, that is known as a *necessary cause*. The cause must be present for the effect to occur.

When the presence of a condition will ordinarily cause the effect to occur this is known as a *sufficient cause*. The cause will usually create the effect but will not always do so.

False Precision

When quantifying data it is imperative that the numerical assignments are valid. If you arbitrarily assign numbers to variables without a logical reason for doing so, the numbers have no true meaning. This assignment is known as *false precision*. We have quantified a concept but that assignment is subjective rather than objective. The precision that we claim really does not exist.

Types of Quantitative Research

Survey Research

One of the most popular research methods in criminal justice is the survey. The survey design is used when researchers are interested in the experiences, attitudes, perceptions, or beliefs of individuals, or when trying to determine the extent of a policy, procedure, or action among a specific group. Surveys may consist of *personal interviews, mail questionnaires,* or *telephone surveys.*

Field Research

If *field observations* were made (such as observing how many vehicles ran a certain stop sign in a given time period or how many times members of the group being observed exhibited specific behaviors) that allowed for numerical assignments then this would be quantified field research.

Unobtrusive Research

Unobtrusive research is research that does not disturb or intrude into the lives of human subjects to obtain research information. Examples of quantitative unobtrusive research include analysis of existing data, historical research and content analysis. In the *analysis of existing data* the researcher obtains the existing data and reanalyzes it. *Historical research* and *content analysis* are conducted as discussed previously but emphasize statistical rather than verbal analysis.

Evaluation Research

The evaluation research is a quantified comparative research design that assists in the development of new skills or approaches. It aids in the solving of problems with direct implications to the "real world." This type of research usually has a quasi-experimental perspective to it. Evaluation research that studies existing programs is frequently referred to as *program evaluation.*

Combination Research

Combinations of different quantitative methods are commonly used. They may include the use of survey research and field observation, survey research and unobtrusive research, unobtrusive research and field observation, or a combination of all three.

Research Designs

There are a number of issues to consider in selecting a research design. These include:

1. Purpose of Research
   The purpose of the research project. It should be clearly indicative of what will be studied.

2. Prior Research
   Review similar or relevant research. This will promote knowledge of the literature.

3. Theoretical Orientation
   Describe the theoretical framework upon which the research is based.

4. Concept Definition
   List the various concepts that have been developed and clarify their meanings.

5. Research Hypotheses
   Develop the various hypotheses that will be evaluated in the research.

6. Unit of Analysis
   Describe the particular objects, individuals, or entities that are being studied as elements of the population.

7. Data Collection Techniques
   Determine how the data are to be collected. Who will collect it, who will be studied, and how will it be done.

8. Sampling Procedures
   Sample type, sample size, as well as the specific procedures to be utilized.

9. Instrument(s) Used
   The nature of the measurement instrument or data collection device that is used.

10. Analytic Techniques
    How the data will be processed and examined. What specific statistical procedures will be used.

11. Time Frame
    The period of time covered by the study. This will include the time period examined by research questions as well as the amount of time spent in preparation, data collection, data analysis, and presentation.

12. Ethical Issues
    Will address any concerns as to the potential harm that could occur to participants. Will also deal with any potential biases or conflicts of interest that could impact upon the study.

Types of Design

There are a number of designs used by criminological researchers.

Historical

Historical designs allow the researcher to systematically and objectively reconstruct the past. This is accomplished through the collection, evaluation, verification, and synthesis of information, usually secondary data already existing in previously gathered records, to establish facts.

Descriptive

Descriptive research design focuses on the describing of facts and characteristics of a given population, issue, policy, or any given area of interest in a systematic and accurate manner. Like the historical design, a descriptive study can also rely on secondary or records data.

Developmental or Time Series

This type of research design allows for the investigation of specifically identified patterns and events, growth, and/or change over a specific amount of time. There are several time-series designs that are available: cross-sectional studies, longitudinal studies, trend studies, cohort studies, and panel studies.

Cross-sectional Studies

The primary concept of the cross-sectional design is that it allows for a complete description of a single entity during a specific time frame.

Longitudinal Studies

Where cross-sectional studies view events or phenomena at one time, longitudinal studies examine events over an extended period. For this reason, longitudinal studies are useful for explanation as well as exploration and description.

Trend Studies

Trend studies examine changes in a general population over time. For example, one might compare results from several census studies to determine what demographic changes have occurred within that population.

Cohort Studies

Cohort studies are trend studies that focus upon the changes that occur in specific subpopulations over time. Usually cohort studies employ age groupings.

Panel Studies

Panel studies are similar to trend and cohort studies except that they study the same set of people each time. By utilizing the same individuals, couples, groups, etc., researchers are able to more precisely examine the extent of changes and the events that influenced them.

Case Studies

The case (sometimes referred to as case and field) research design allows for the intensive study of a given issue, policy, or group in its social context at one point in time even though that period may span months or years. It includes close scrutiny of the background, current status, and relationships or interactions of the topic under study.

Correlational

One of the more popular research designs is one that allows researchers to investigate how one factor may affect or influence another factor, or how the one factor correlates with another. In particular, this type of design focuses on how variations of one variable correspond with variations of other variables.

Causal-Comparative

This design allows the researcher to examine relationships from a cause-and-effect perspective. This is done through the observation of an existing outcome or consequence and searching back through the data for plausible causal factors.

True or Classic Experimental

This type of design allows for the investigation of possible cause-and-effect relationships where one or more experimental units will be exposed to one or more treatment conditions. The outcomes are then compared to the outcomes of one or more control groups that did not receive the treatment. This design includes three major components: (1) independent and dependent variables, (2) experimental and control groups, and (3) pre- and post-testing.

Quasi-Experimental

Unlike the true experimental design where the researcher has almost complete control over relevant variables, the *quasi-experimental* design allows for the approximation of conditions similar to the true experiment. However, the setting does not allow for control and/or manipulation of the relevant variables.

Questionnaire Construction

Whenever possible use a questionnaire that has previously been developed and tested. The primary reason for this is because it eliminates the worries of validity and reliability, two major concerns of questionnaire development. In creating a new survey instrument there are several aspects for consideration including reliability and validity and the level of measurement to use.

Rules for Questionnaire Construction

1. Start with a list of all the items you are interested in knowing about the group, concept, or phenomenon.
2. Be prepared to establish validity and reliability.
3. The wording in the questionnaire must be appropriate for the target audience.
4. Be sure that it is clearly identifiable as to who should answer the questions.
5. Avoid asking any questions that are biased, leading, threatening, or double-barreled in nature.
6. Prior to construction, a decision must be made whether to use open- or closed-ended questions, or a combination.
7. Consider that the respondents may not have all the general information needed to complete the questionnaire.
8. Whenever possible pretest the questionnaire before it is officially used.
9. Set up questions so that the responses are easily recognizable whether it is self-administered or interview.
10. The questionnaire should be organized in a concise manner that will keep the interest of the respondent, encouraging him or her to complete the entire questionnaire.

Scales

A common element of survey research is the construction of scales. A scale can either be the measurement device for a question or statement or a compilation of statements or questions used to represent or acknowledge change. The items making up the scale need to represent one dimension befitting a continuum that is supposed to be reflective of only one concept. The representativeness of any scale will rely greatly on the level of measurement used.

Arbitrary Scales

This type of scale is designed to measure what the researcher believes it is measuring and is based on face validity (discussed earlier) and professional judgment. While this allows for the creation of many different scales, it is easily criticized for its lack of substantive support.

Attitudinal Scales

More commonly found in criminal justice and criminological research are the attitudinal scales. There are three primary types available: Thurstone, Likert, and Guttman.

Thurstone Scales

The construction of a Thurstone scale relies on the use of others (sometimes referred to as "judges") to indicate what items they think best fit the concept. There are two methods for completing this task. The first method is the "paired comparisons." Here the judges are provided several pairs of questions or statements and asked to choose which most favorably fits the concept under study. The questions or statements picked most often by the judges become part of or comprise the complete questionnaire.

Likert Scales

Probably the most commonly used method in attitudinal research is the Likert scale. This method generally makes use of a bipolar, five point response range (i.e., strongly agree to strongly disagree). Questions that all respondents provide similar responses to are usually eliminated. The remaining questions are used to comprise the scale.

Guttman Scales

The last scale, the Guttman scale, requires that an attitudinal scale measure only one dimension or concept. The questions or statements must be progressive so that if the respondent answers positively to a question, he or she must respond the same to the following one.

Sampling

A population is the complete group or class from which information is to be gathered. A sample is a group chosen from within a target population to provide information sought.

Probability Theory

Probability theory is based on the concept that over time there is a statistical order in which things occur. The knowledge that over time things tend to adhere to a statistical order allows us to chose samples that are representative of a population in general.

Probability Sampling

The general goal when choosing a sample is to obtain one that is representative of the target population. Representation requires that every member in the population or the sampling frame have an equal chance of being selected for the sample. This is a probability sample. Four types of probability samples exist: simple random, stratified random, systematic, and cluster.

Simple Random Samples

A simple random sample is one in which all members of a given population have the same chances of being selected. Furthermore, the selection of each member must be independent from the selection of any other members.

Stratified Random Samples

These strata are selected based upon specified characteristics that the researcher wishes to ensure for inclusion within the study. This type of sample requires the researcher to have knowledge of the sampling frame's demographic characteristics. These characteristics (selected variables) are then used to create the strata from which the sample is chosen.

Systematic Samples

There seems to be some debate over this type of sampling. It includes random selection and initially allows inclusion of every member of the sampling frame. With a systematic sample, every nth item in the sampling frame is included in the sample.

Cluster Samples

The last of the probability sampling methods is the cluster sample (also know as area probability sample). This sample consists of randomly selected groups, rather than individuals. Basically, the population to be surveyed is divided into clusters. Subsequent sub-samples of the clusters are then selected.

Nonprobability Sampling

The major difference between probability and nonprobability sampling is that one provides the opportunity for all members of the sampling frame to be selected while the other does not.

Purposive Samples

Among the nonprobability samples, the purposive sample appears to be the most popular. Based on the researcher's skill, judgment, and needs, an appropriate sample is selected. When the subjects are selected in advance based upon the researcher's view that they reflect normal or average scores this is sometimes referred to as *typical-case sampling*. If subgroups are sampled to permit comparisons among them, this technique is known as *stratified purposeful sampling*.

Quota Samples

These types of research efforts often rely on quota sampling. For this type of sample, the proportions are based on the researcher's judgment for inclusion. Selection continues until enough individuals have been chosen to fill out the sample.

Snowball Samples

Although not a highly promoted form of quantitative sampling, snowball sampling is commonly used as a qualitative technique. The snowball sample begins with a person or persons who provides names of other persons for the sample.

Convenience Sample

Undoubtedly the last choice for a sample is the convenience sample or *available subjects sample.* Here there is no attempt to ensure any type of representativeness. Usually this sample is a very abstract representation of the population or target frame. Units or individuals are chosen simply because they were "in the right place at the right time." Convenience samples are often useful as explorations upon which future research may be based.

Sample Size

Usually, the sample size is the result of several elements:

1. How accurate must the sample be
2. Economic feasibility (how much do you have to spend)
3. The availability of requisite variables (including any subcategories)
4. Accessibility to the target population

Confidence Levels

Addressing how large the sample should be requires an understanding of *confidence intervals.* The smaller the confidence interval the more accurate the estimated sample. The estimated probability that a population parameter will fall within a given confidence interval is known as the *confidence level.* Thus to reduce *sampling error* the researcher would desire a smaller confidence interval. To do so, he or she would select a smaller confidence level.

Generally, in social science research, we seek a sample size that would vary 95 times out of 100 by 5 percent or less from the population. A sampling formula and sample size selection chart was provided in Chapter 9.

To ensure that the necessary numbers are obtained, we recommend that you always oversample by twenty percent. If this isn't enough, you can always add more observations as long as they are randomly selected from the same population and any time differences would not impact upon responses.

Data Collection

There are four primary data collection techniques available: survey, interview (often classified in surveys), observation, and unobtrusive means.

Survey Research

Probably the most frequently used method for data collection is the survey. There are two primary means for collecting data through surveys: mail surveys and self-completing questionnaires. A common means of distributing questionnaires is through the mail or by direct distribution.

Mail Surveys

This method allows for use of fairly large samples, broader area coverage, and the cost in terms of time and money can be kept to a minimum. Additional advantages include that no field staff is required, it eliminates the bias effect possible in interviews, allows the respondents greater privacy, places fewer time constraints on the respondents so that more consideration can be given to the answers, and finally, offers the chance of a high percentage of returns improving the representativeness of the sample. The most frustrating disadvantage of mail surveys is the lack of responses.

Ways to increase responses rates include offering some type of remuneration or "reward" for completing the survey; appealing to the respondent's altruistic side; using an attractive and shortened format; being able to indicate that the survey is sponsored or endorsed by a recognizable entity; personalizing the survey; and enhancing the timing of the survey.

Self-Administered Surveys

The self-administered survey is generally a written questionnaire that is distributed to the selected sample in a structured environment. Respondents are allowed to complete the survey in a given time period and then return it to the researcher, often through an emissary of the sample.

Interviews

There are several types of interviews that may be utilized in criminological research.

Structured Interviews

Probably the most used type of interview in criminal justice research is the structured interview. This requires the use of close-ended questions that every individual interviewed must be asked in the same order. Responses are set and can be checked off by the interviewer. It is in reality a questionnaire that is being administered orally with the interviewer completing the form for the respondent.

Unstructured Interviews

The unstructured interview offers respondents open-ended questions where no set response is provided. While this allows for more in-depth responses, it is much more difficult to quantify the responses.

In-depth Interviews

The in-depth interview can make use of both fixed and open-ended questions. The difference from the others is that the interviewer can further explore why the response was given and could ask additional qualifying questions.

Face-to-Face Interviews

Face-to-face interviews provide contact between the researcher and the respondent. This contact can be positive reinforcement for participating in the research. Oftentimes simply receiving a questionnaire in the mail can be very sterile and because of that lack of personal touch might cause would-be respondents to simply ignore the survey.

Telephone Surveys

The advantages of telephone surveying begin with being able to eliminate a field staff and can allow for the creation of a very small in-house staff. It is also easier to monitor interviewer bias; specifically, it eliminates being able to send any nonverbal cues. In addition, the telephone interview is less expensive and very quick.

Observation/Field Research

Like survey research, observational research has its advantages and disadvantages. One of the best advantages is the direct collection of the data. Rather than having to rely on what others have seen, here the researcher relies only on his or her observations.

Unobtrusive Data Collection

The last means for collecting data is through what is referred to as unobtrusive measures. These are any methods of data collection where the subjects of the research are completely unaware of being studied and that study is not observational. Two of the more commonly used types of unobtrusive data collection have been discussed previously in this chapter. They are: the use of archival data (analyzing existing statistics and/or documents) and content analysis.

Data Processing and Analysis

Data processing consists of data coding, data entry, and data cleaning. Coding is simply assigning values to the data for statistical analyses.

Once the data are coded they can then be entered into a computer software program for analyses. The key to data entry is accuracy. Data cleaning is the preliminary analysis of your data. Here you "clean" any mistakes that might have occurred during the initial recording of data or data entry.

Dealing with Missing Data

There are a number of ways to deal with missing information. If the data has been left out on a single question you may chose to input it as a non-response. Another option is to assume that the missing data is due to an oversight rather than an intentional omission. Yet another option is to exclude the survey instrument containing the omission from your analysis. If the instrument used is a Likert Scale the response may be classified as "neither agree nor disagree" or "don't know" (depending upon how your scale is worded).

Recoding Data

By collapsing the categories into logical groupings, the data can be presented clearly and concisely. The resulting table could easily be collapsed even farther if necessary. In collapsing data please recall our earlier discussions of the different levels of measurement. Higher level data (such as ratio or interval data) can be collapsed down into lower level data (such as ordinal or nominal data) but you cannot do the opposite and convert lower level data to a higher level.

Data Analysis

There are three types of data analysis: *univariate analysis, bivariate analysis,* and *multivariate analysis.* Univariate analysis is the examination of the distribution of cases on only one variable at a time. *Bivariate analysis* is when the relationship between two variables is examined. *Multivariate analysis* is the examination of three or more variables. This technique is inferential in nature in that we have usually already conducted both descriptive and comparative statistical analyses (through univariate and bivariate analyses) of the data and are now seeking to examine the relationships among several variables.

Statistical Analysis

There are three types of statistics:

1. Descriptive, whose function is describing the data
2. Comparative, whose function is to compare the attributes (or subgroups) of two variables
3. Inferential, whose function is to make an inference, estimation or prediction about the data

Frequency Distributions

There are four types of frequency distributions to be familiar with: absolute, relative, cumulative, and cumulative relative. The most common are absolute frequency distributions that display the raw numbers and relative frequency distributions that convert the numbers into percentages for easier interpretation by readers.

Displaying Frequencies

Frequencies, by whole numbers and/or percentages in table form are just one means of describing the data. Other means include pie charts, bar graphs, histograms and polygons, line charts, and maps.

Other Ways to Describe the Data

In addition to frequency distributions the researcher may describe the properties of the data through measures of central tendency, measures of variability, skewness, and kurtosis.

Measures of Central Tendency

The three most common measures of central tendency are the mean, median, and mode. The mean is the arithmetic average. The median is the midpoint. The mode is the most frequently occurring number. The uses of measures of central tendency and how to compute them were discussed in detail in Chapter 11.

Measures of Variability

The three main measures of variability are range, variance, and standard deviation. The range is simply the difference between the highest and lowest scores. Variance is the difference between the scores and the mean. Standard deviation indicates how far from the mean the score actually is.

Skewness and Kurtosis

By using polygons, line charts, or scatterplots researchers are able to see the distribution of their data. If it is a normal distribution, the researcher is able to use a broader range of statistical techniques. If it is a non-normal (also known as nonparametric) distribution, the statistical techniques that may be used are more limited. Skewness alerts the researcher to the presence of outliers. Kurtosis refers to the amount of smoothness or pointedness of the curve. Such knowledge aids statisticians in conducting their analyses of the data.

Inferential Statistics

Inferential statistics allow the researcher to develop inferences (predictions) about the data. By using statistical analyses researchers are able to make estimations or predictions about the data. If the sample is representative, these predictions may be extended to the population from which the data were drawn. Inferential statistics allow criminological researchers to conduct research that can be generalized to larger populations within society.

Measures of Association

Measures of association are the means by which researchers are able to determine the strengths of relationships among the variables that are being studied. The measure of association that is used is dependent upon the type of analysis that is being conducted, the distribution of the data, and the level of data that is used. There are many measures of association that are utilized in criminological research. Individual researchers may prefer to use different measures. However, there are some measures that are considered to be standards. Lambda is commonly used for nominal level data. Gamma is commonly used for ordinal level research. Pearson's r and R2 are commonly used for interval and ratio level data.

Statistical Significance

Statistical significance is how researchers determine whether their sample findings are representative of the population that they are studying. If you are using a complete enumeration (the entire population is studied rather than just a sample from that population) then statistical significance is a moot point in that we already know that the population is accurately represented. However, complete enumerations are rare in that very small populations limit generalizabilty and large populations are too costly and time-consuming to study as a whole.

Statistical significance is based upon probability sampling. Generally social science research desires a statistical significance of .05 or better. This means that we are 95 percent confident that our findings represent the population that was sampled. As seen in Chapter 12, determining statistical significance varies depending upon the statistical procedures that are used.

Bivariate Analysis

Bivariate analysis is the examination of the relationship between two variables. Usually this involves attempting to determine how a dependent variable is influenced by an independent variable. The more commonly used bivariate techniques are crosstabulation (contingency tables), chi-square, and bivariate (simple linear) regression. In assessing the relationship between the two variables we examine the contingency table or regression scatterplot results, the measure of association (such as gamma or R^2), and the level of statistical significance (hopefully .05 or lower).

Multivariate Analysis

Multivariate analysis is the examination of the relationship between three or more variables. Usually this involves attempting to determine how a dependent variable is influenced by several independent variables. This methodology offers more insights than bivariate analysis in that we are able to study the relationships among several variables at one time. The more commonly used multivariate techniques are correlation, multiple regression, Student's t test, Analysis of Variance, discriminant analysis, probit regression, factor analysis, and path analysis. In assessing the relationship between the multiple variables we examine the correlation table, regression scatterplot results, or other indicators (depending on the technique used); the measure of association (such as Pearson's r, R^2, Wilke's Lambda or other appropriate measure); as well as the level of statistical significance.

Nonparametric Techniques

When the distribution of the data is not normal, standard statistical techniques are usually not appropriate. In those cases, other procedures that are used include: chi-square, nonparametric correlation, and nonlinear regression. As noted in Chapter 12, the reader is advised to consult with a statistician in these circumstances.

Writing the Research

In Chapter 13 a research paper example was provided. The outline recommended in that chapter is as follows.

The Title Page

The title of your research paper (article, or thesis) should tell the reader in clear and concise terms what your research is about.

Abstract

The abstract is the summary or synopsis of the information being presented in the paper and starts with the research title. The abstract presents the paper's major argument and describes the methods that were used.

The Introduction

This section establishes the research problem and the literature that supports its existence and the reason to research it. In addition, this section reports the research question(s) and hypothesis(es) and briefly describes what was done.

Methodology

The methodology section is the mainstay of the paper. The writer should discuss the hypothesis(es), the research design, and the data gathering technique. This includes explaining the research population, the sampling frame, and the questionnaire or other method used to gather the data. It is in this section that the researcher can fully explain where, when, how, and why the data was attained and analyzed.

Results

In this section the writer describes the sample's characteristics, the statistical techniques used, the results, and whether they supported the hypothesis(es). It is within this section that various tables, graphs, and charts are commonly used to describe the data.

Conclusions

Usually the last section of the research paper is the conclusion(s). Generally this section is used to offer insights about the research, whether it did what was expected and possible problems. This section can also be used to discuss implications of the research and to provide a forum for suggestions for future related research.

References

When using other sources, whether quoting, paraphrasing, or simply as an outlet for affirming what is already known, the source should be recognized. This is done throughout the paper by various citation methods. The complete list of references or bibliography is provided at the end of the paper. The format depends upon the source the paper is being submitted to. The majority of the papers written for criminal justice and criminology will follow the APA style for reference citing in the text and at the end of the paper.

Tables and Figures

Tables and figures are included in research papers to aid the author in presenting and explaining information. Regardless of their location, tables and figures need to be clear as to their content and readily understandable.

Appendices

It is often useful to include a copy of the questionnaire or other tools that need to be shared but just do not belong in the body of the paper. There are no limitations to the number of appendices a paper could have except for those established by the instructor or the journal.

Summary Statement

In this chapter we have summarized those issues from throughout the text that we thought important enough to warrant repetition. It is our hope that this text has provided you with the knowledge and insights necessary for successfully understanding and conducting research in criminal justice and/or criminology. We wish you the very best in your future research endeavors.

Index

A

Abstract, 211
Accuracy, 8
Analysis of variance, 203
Anonymity for subjects, 27
ANOVA (analysis of variance), 203
Applied research, 11-12
Archival research. *See* Historical research
Assumptions, 66
Authority, 6

B

Bar charts, 182, 184, 185
Basic research, 12
Bell curve, 186
Bibliographies, 219-222
Bivariate regression, 198, 200

C

Case studies, 18, 109-110
Causal-comparative design studies, 110-111
Causality, 90-91, 246
Central tendency, 186-189, 191, 258
Chi square, 198
Cluster samples, 67, 140, 253
Codes of ethics, 29-31
Cohort studies, 109
Concepts, 60, 242
Conceptualization, 60
Confidence levels, 144-147, 254
Confidentiality, 31-33
Content analysis, 18, 83, 98, 164
Convenience samples, 143-144
    See also Purposive samples
Correlation, 202
Correlational design studies, 110
Covariation, 202
Crime rates, 196-197, 198

Criminal justice, 8
Criminology, 8
Cross-sectional studies, 108

D

Data
    defined, 68, 244
    interval, 68, 244
    missing, 177, 257
    nominal, 68, 244
    ordinal, 68, 244
    ratio, 68, 244
Data analysis
    bivariate, 178-179
    multivariate, 179-180
    univariate, 178
Data cleaning, 176-177
Data coding, 173, 256
Data collection
    by field research, 160-163, 256
    by surveys, 152-160, 255-256
    method summary, 165
Data entry, 173-176
Data recoding, 177-178, 257
Deception in research, 29
Deductive logic, 9
Descriptive research, 13-14, 45, 106-108
Designing research
    common types, 17-19
    design types, 104-112, 249-250
    issues in, 105, 248
Discriminant analysis, 205
Doyle, Sir Arthur Conan, 8-9

E

Empiricism, 7, 89-90
Equal appearing interval method, 132
Ethical neutrality, 7, 25, 239

Ethics
    areas of concern, 30-31, 240
    codes of, 29-31
    defined, 24, 239
    problem characteristics, 25
Ethnographic studies, 82
Evaluative research, 11, 98-99
Experimental research, 18, 111-112
Explanatory research, 14, 45
Exploratory research, 44

F

Factor analysis, 205
False precision, 75, 91, 247
Feasibility, 43
Field interviewing. *See* Interviews
Field observation, 80-81
Field research
    data collection in, 160-163
    defined, 18
    quantified, 96-97
    researcher's roles in, 80-82
Focus groups, 79
Frequency distributions
    defined, 180, 258
    displaying, 181-189, 258
    leptokurtic, 189
    normal, 188
    platykurtic, 189
    types, 181
Frequency polygon, 182, 185

G

Gamma, 195, 259
Guttman scale, 132, 252

H

Harm, 26-27, 30
Histogram, 182, 185
Historical research
    data used in, 163-164
    defined, 98
    limitations of, 107
    nature and uses of, 104-106
Historiography, 83
Hypotheses
    defined, 51, 64, 66, 241, 243
    types of, 51-52, 241

I

Inductive logic, 8-9
Informed consent, 27-29
Inquiry modes
    casual, 6-7
    scientific, 7-8
Institutional review board submission, 35-37
Institutional review boards, 28-29
Integrity, 31
Internet searches, 48
Intersubjectivity, 7
Intervening research, 15
Interviews
    as quantitative research, 95
    defined, 76
    face-to-face, 158-159
    in-depth, 158
    semi-structured, 78
    structured, 77-78, 157-158
    telephone, 95-96, 159
    unstructured, 78-79, 158

J

Judgmental samples. *See* Purposive samples

K

Knowledge secondhand, 5-6
Kurtosis, 189, 258

L

Lambda, 195
Leptokurtic distribution, 189
Life histories, 18
Likert scale, 132, 252
Line charts, 182, 187
Literature review
    critiquing, 49-50
    reviewing, 46-48
    sources and resources, 47-48
Logit analysis, 204-205
Longitudinal studies, 108-109, 110
Lynch, Dr. Gerald, 55

M

Mail surveys, 153-156
Mean, 186

Measurement
  See also Scales
  defined, 91
  interval level, 93-94
  nominal level, 92
  ordinal level, 92-93
  ratio level, 94
Measures of association, 194-195, 259
Median, 186
Missing data, 177
Mode, 188
Multiple regression, 203-204
Multipurpose research, 13
Multivariate analysis, 200-205, 259-260

N

National Institute of Justice, 30, 33
Null hypotheses, 51, 64-65

O

Objectivity, 7, 25, 30, 237
Observations
  approaches to, 80-81, 160
  inaccurate, 6
  overview of, 160-163
  selective, 7
  theory and, 58
Operationalization, 60-62, 242
Over-generalization, 6

P

Paired comparisons method, 132
Panel studies, 109
Parsimony, 7-8
Partial correlation, 204
Path analysis, 205
Pearson's r, 195, 202
Percentage change, 197
Pie charts, 182, 184
Platykurtic distribution, 190
Police, 5
Populations, 66, 136
Precision, 8
Predictive research, 14-15
Privacy, 27, 31-32
Probability, 137-138, 252
Probit analysis, 204
Professionalism, 29

Pure research, 12
Purposive samples
  defined, 67, 253
  nature of, 141-142

Q

Qualitative research
  challenges of, 75
  defined, 74, 75, 244-245
  literature review vs., 75-76
  quantitative vs., 74-75, 88-89
  types of, 76-84, 245-246
Quantitative research
  defined, 74, 88, 246
  qualitative vs., 74-75, 88-89
  types of, 94-100, 247
Quasi-experimental design studies, 112
Questionnaires
  as survey research, 95-96
  construction rules, 119-130, 251
  escape responses in, 126
  examples of, 120, 121
  'golden rule' of, 118, 250
  instructions in, 128-129
  open/closed-ended questions in, 126, 127-128
  organization of, 130
  pre-testing of, 124, 128
  reliability of, 124
  split-half technique, 124
  use of existing, 118
  validity issues, 122-124
  wording of, 124-125
Quota samples, 142, 253-254

R

Random samples, 67, 138-139, 253
Range, 186
Reasoning, illogical, 7
Recoding data, 177-178, 257
Record studies, 18
References, 219-222
Reliability
  defined, 68, 244
  measuring device, 68
  questionnaire, 124
Reports
  abstract, 211
  appendices, 222

Reports *(continued)*
    bibliography, 219-222
    conclusions, 217-219
    figures, 222
    forms of, 19
    integrity of, 31
    introduction, 211-213
    methodology, 213-214
    references, 219-222
    results, 215-217
    tables, 222
    title page, 210
Research
    appropriateness of, 19
    defined, 8, 10, 19
    influences on, 16-17
    purposes of, 15-16
    steps outlined, 17-19, 69-70, 237
    types of, 11-15, 17-18, 97, 104-112
Research hypotheses, 51, 64
Research questions, 50-51
Researchers
    role of, 25-26
Rival hypotheses, 51, 65

S

Samples
    cluster samples, 67, 140, 253
    defined, 67, 243, 252
    purposive
        defined, 67, 253
        nature of, 141-142
    quota, 144, 253-254
    random, 67, 138-139, 253
    size of, 144, 254
    size selection chart, 147
    snowball, 67, 142-143, 254
    stratified random, 139, 253
    systematic samples, 139-140, 253
Sampling
    confidence levels, 144-147, 254
    formulas for, 145-147
    frames, 136-137
    nonprobability, 140-144, 253-254
    probability, 67, 138-140, 252-253
Scales
    advantages of, 133
    arbitrary, 131, 251
    attitudinal, 131-132, 251
    defined, 130-131, 251
Scientific method, 5, 7-8, 9

Secondhand knowledge, 5-6
Self-administered surveys, 156-157
Skepticism, 7
Skewness, 188, 258
Snowball samples, 67, 142-143, 254
Social science research, 5
Sociometry, 82-83
Sources of information, 47-48
Split-half technique, 124
Standard deviation, 186
Standardized field sobriety tests, 97
Statistical software, 174, 176
Statistics
    bivariate analysis, 197-200, 259
    comparative, 178, 180, 189, 196-197
    contingency tables, 198, 199
    defined, 180
    descriptive, 178, 180-189
    inferential, 178-179, 180, 194-197
    measures of association, 194-195, 259
    multivariate analysis, 200-205, 259-260
    nonparametric techniques, 205, 260
    percentage change, 197
    significance in, 195-196, 259
    trend analyses, 197
    variability measures, 186, 258
Step-wise regression, 204
Student's t test, 201
Subjects
    anonymity for, 27
    identity security for, 33
Survey research
    See also Interviews; Questionnaires
    by mail, 153-156
    defined, 17, 94
    methods compared, 160
    pros and cons, 96
    scales in, 130-133
    self-administered surveys, 156-157
    telephone surveys, 95-96, 159
Systematic samples, 139-140, 253

T

Telephone surveys, 95-96, 159
Theories
    defined, 8, 58
    examples of, 59
    observation and, 58
Thurstone scale, 131-132, 252
Time series studies, 108-109
Topic selection, 42-43, 45-46, 241

Tradition, 5-6
Trend analyses, 197
Trend studies, 109

U

Uniform Crime Reports, 163
Unit of analysis, 65
Unobtrusive research, 80, 97-99, 163-164

V

Validity, 67-68, 243

Variability measures, 186, 258
Variables
   defined, 52
   dependent, 52-53, 62-63, 242
   independent, 52-53, 62-63, 242
Variance, 189
Voluntary participation, 28

W

Women, 14
Writing styles, 49